Public Opinion, The Press, and Public Policy

Edited by J. DAVID KENNAMER

Westport, Connecticut
London

Library of Congress Cataloging-in-Publication Data

Public opinion, the press, and public policy / edited by J. David
  Kennamer.
      p. cm.
    Includes bibliographical references and index.
    ISBN 0–275–93743–7 (alk. paper) — ISBN 0–275–95097–2 (pbk. : alk.
paper)
    1. Public opinion—United States.   2. Mass media—Political
aspects—United States.   3. Mass media—United States—Influence.
4. United States—Politics and government.   I. Kennamer, J. David.
HN90.P8P85   1992
303.3'8—dc20   92–8400

British Library Cataloguing in Publication data is available.

Library of Congress Catalog Card Number: 92–8400
ISBN:0–275–93743–7
    0–275–95097–2 (pbk.)

First published in 1992
Paperback edition 1994

Praeger Publishers, 88 Post Road West, Westport, CT 06881
An imprint of Greenwood Publishing Group, Inc.

Printed in the United States of America

The paper used in this book complies with the
Permanent Paper Standard issued by the National
Information Standards Organization (Z39.48–1984).

10 9 8 7 6 5 4

Contents

Figures and Tables

1

Public Opinion, the Press, and Public Policy: An Introduction

J. David Kennamer

As the techniques of scientific assessment of public opinion have become better understood and more readily available, the measurement of, discussion about, and interest in public opinion in American life have become incessant. Because public opinion has become a category of news and a focus of journalistic competition, the news-consuming public is constantly informed of everything from its opinions on foreign trade policy to its preference for dogs or cats.

Much of this interest could be described as a sort of collective narcissism, and this may explain at least some of the journalistic interest in public opinion, or at least in the results of polls. But normative democratic theory calls for a much more serious role for public opinion—it is supposed to have something to do with the formation of public policy. Luttbeg (1974) notes, "Most persons would only be satisfied with a democracy which at least gave some expression to public wants in the policies enacted" (p. 1). Bernard Cohen (1973) has noted that this extraordinarily powerful normative view of the role of public opinion in governance leads to "a mechanical assumption that the public rules or at least participates in policy making, and to a readiness to assert the assumption as unquestioned fact" (p. 20). When one assumes something, one sees no reason to study it, and this of course does not lead to an explication of how such influence works and certainly allows no possibility for the discovery that perhaps it doesn't work. In this particular instance, Cohen (1973) notes that "one is left with the impression that opinion is absorbed, by osmosis, into the political bloodstream" (p. 11).

However, even osmosis is not a mystical process; in a biological sense, it involves the transfer of substances across a boundary. And likewise, if public opinion is to affect public policy, somehow the governed must communicate their preferences to those who govern. But most of us most of the time don't bother to write or call our city council representative when property tax assessments rise, let alone the president or Congress when armies are sent to the Persian Gulf. And if we did, it is unclear what we would expect the outcome of such involvement to be. Voting is the most visible and concrete sign of public opinion, but most of us vote with only the haziest notion of candidate positions on issues, if indeed we vote at all. At any rate, most campaigns are notably devoid of issue and policy information (Joslyn, 1990).

If we are dissatisfied with the biological analogy of osmosis, which would seem to require widespread involvement on the part of the public, then we must ask through what processes is public opinion, or some form or fashion of it, transmitted to policymakers. A consistent response from a variety of sources over the years is that the news media serve as sources of information about public opinion and even serve as surrogates for it. The news media have long been seen as serving a coordinating or organizing role in democratic society. Again quoting Bernard Cohen (1963), "The media . . . are one of the devices that keep the separate parts of the political system in touch with each other, and able to act in response to a more or less common set of political stimuli" (p. 16). It seems that this is very much what Harold Lasswell (1948) meant when he listed the "correlation of the parts of society in responding to the environment" (p. 38) as one of the functions of media in society.

More recently, Dominick (1990) has incorporated much of this meaning in the media function he has called "linkage." While this is a very complex concept, it means the ability of the media to link together individuals, groups, and institutions who otherwise would perhaps not know of each other's existence. Political scientists use the term "linkage" in a more specific, although consistent, way. Luttbeg (1974), for example, defines it as "any means by which political leaders act in accordance with the wants, needs, and demands of the public in making government policy" (p. 3).

The assumption of this book is that the news media are a major way by which the public is linked with the institutions and individuals concerned with governing. This process breaks down into two subprocesses: (1) the various ways in which information about the state of public opinion flows into policymaking structures and affects decision-makers' perceptions about the state of public opinion, and (2) the various ways in which public opinion is actually integrated into policymaking. The first, then, concerns the sources and techniques used by policymakers to obtain their readings of public opinion. The second is the difference this makes in terms of actual policy choice. The chapters and authors in this volume were chosen to illustrate aspects of the news media role in both subprocesses.

THE PROBLEM OF LINKAGE

In a series of studies, Brooks (1985, 1987, 1990) has presented evidence indicating that there is little if any direct relationship between "mass public opinion" and governmental policy in Western democracies. This illustrates a key problem in studying linkage: If the preferences of "mass publics" don't seem to register in policy, then *whose* "wants, needs, and demands" are transmitted to policymakers and incorporated in policymaking? The issue breaks down into three separate questions: "What public? What kind of opinion? What policy?" (Coughlin, 1980, p. 160). Who are the publics whose opinions are to be linked to policymaking? Lippmann (1922/1943) made the enduring point that the difficulties and activities of everyday life command attention in ways that politics rarely, if ever, does. It is therefore unwarranted to expect most people most of the time to be absorbed in the minutiae of politics and public policy unless these intrude in a very direct way on their everyday lives. Indeed, it seems that studies of the public's knowledge of such topics turn out to be studies of their lack of knowledge (see Delli Carpini and Keeter, this volume). So in no real sense does a general public opinion even exist, at least one that is focused on specific policies. The result may be, as Key (1961) pointed out, that public opinion may set the outside limits beyond which policymakers cannot go, but within those limits it is quite uninvolved, allowing "a wide latitude for the exercise of creative leadership" (p. 555). For example, Coughlin (1980) found in his comparative study of welfare policy in industrialized countries "an overall congruence between mass ideological climate and indicators of social policy development. . . . [I]t is clear that the mass ideological climate at minimum defines an outside perimeter within which policy debate takes place" (p. 160). Thus most of the time and on most issues "the real problem is finding more than a handful of people who even know what the issues are—much less what they are about" (B. Cohen, 1973, p. 186).

Within these broad perimeters, then, one must look to this "handful of people," often called the "attentive public," to find evidence of specific linkages. Strouse (1975), paraphrasing Key, defines this group as "the one with the most information on the issues and the knowledge about how one can influence and change public policy" (p. 29). Attentive publics overlap to a great degree with "effective" publics. These are made up of people who are most likely to contact public officials or cast a vote based on a single issue (Wilhoit & Weaver, 1980, p. 12). However defined, such attentive or effective publics are likely also to be organized publics, with the purpose of bringing their version of public opinion to the attention of policymakers. Herring, writing in 1929, noted, "The voice harkened to by legislators is not the lone voice of a citizen crying in a wilderness of individual opinions, but the chorus of a cause organized for a purpose and directed by a press agent" (1929/1967, p. 7).

The issue this discussion raises has been addressed by Dreyer and Rosenbaum: "If opinion is to affect policy, it must make its way through the political system to decision makers, and the system does not give equal weight to all opinion" (1966, pp. 382–383). This inequality of opinions has been called "biased pluralism" by Nachmias and Henry (1980, p. 472), meaning that society's segments are not equally "effective." Some are much more able to inject their versions of public opinion into the process. In fact, Schattschneider (1960) has referred to all forms of political organization as "the mobilization of bias" (p. 71). Brooks (1985) notes that "democratic frustration" might be the reason that there is little relationship between mass public opinion and public policy; majoritarian democracy is frustrated by an "elite-dominated political system" (p. 251).

A MODIFIED PRESSURE GROUPS MODEL OF LINKAGE

The importance placed on attentive, effective, and organized publics of varying degrees of access and success in the policymaking arena assumes a model of political decision-making referred to by Luttbeg (1974) as the pressure groups model of political linkage and by Hennessy as the group theory of politics. According to Luttbeg, in its purest form the model "conceives of society as composed of very few individuals unassociated with at least one group and government policy as the product of competition among groups each fighting for its preferences" (1974, p. 187). Such groups "either originate opinion or summarize it" and "are the source of all opinion or they express all opinion of importance" (Luttbeg, 1974, p. 5).

Hennessy (1985) gives groups a major role in his model of the "opinion-policy" process. It is through groups that individual "private ideas" are articulated and aggregated into policy proposals, which are then pressed upon policymakers (pp. 347–354). The presence of such groups vastly reduces the number of relevant actors from perhaps millions to a handful for any given issue. Herring (1929/1967) gave them a very central role: "These associations have taken to themselves two of the most important functions in a democracy; namely, the creation of public opinion and the use of this opinion in the promotion of specific legislative measures" (p. 240).

This book is organized around the pressure group model, with one major modification in the way it has been presented by both Luttbeg and Hennessy—the addition of the news media as a major player. While communication processes are implicit in both presentations of the model, neither lays them out specifically. Such an addition seems defensible given "the continuous and intimate interaction that takes place between the press and other institutions of government, as distinguished from the intermittent and politically limited or segmented contacts that characterize interest group or individual participation in policy-making" (B. Cohen, 1963, p. 31). Since Cohen, and certainly Herring, made their observations, the role of interest groups, particularly political action committee (PACs), has exploded (Sabato, 1984), but so has the role of the news media, which have largely replaced the political parties as "the principle intermediary between the public and its leaders" (Orren, 1986, p. 12).

To leave communications channels unexplicated seems to imply that they merely serve as conduits or conveyor belts for the information, persuasion, and influence that is promulgated by the policymakers and the groups acting on behalf of various segments of the public. And that is simply not the case. Cobb and Elder (1981) have called communication "the essence of policy" and said that "public policy is part of an ongoing process of communication and feedback, the dynamics of which are structured and constrained by communication capability" (p. 393). They present three ways in which the news media provide "linkage functions" and "structure the policy process." In the first, they say that by "selectively directing attention" to aspects of the policy environment, the media help establish "the basic inputs of the policy process" (p. 392). Here, they refer specifically to the agenda-setting function of the media. The second linkage occurs within policymaking processes and involves communication channels among policymakers. "They (the news media) allow the formal and often more restrictive channels of intragovernmental channels to be short-circuited or bypassed; and reduce the often overwhelming information-processing tasks confronting policymakers" (p. 392). An example of this is when one policymaker finds out what another is doing, not through interoffice memos, but by reading about it in the newspaper (Kingdon, 1984, p. 63). The third linkage Cobb and Elder mention "arises from the media's role as purveyors and interpreters of the public record" (p. 392). They point out that theoretically most of what goes on in public agencies is a matter of public record. However, "owing to the costs of accessing and digesting this information, that which is truly public tends to be limited to what is distilled by the media. Popular reactions to policy actions and actors are thus likely to hinge on what media choose to report and how. This may, in turn, affect the prospects of a policy being adopted or successfully implemented" (p. 392).

A large body of literature has clearly demonstrated the many ways in which journalistic norms, organizational structures, technologies, traditions, and ideologies make the news—much of which centers on public policy and policymakers—very much a "manufactured" product (Tuchman, 1978; Cohen & Young, 1981; Nimmo & Combs, 1983; Shoemaker & Mayfield, 1987). The news thus becomes only one of many possible versions of "reality," and, since news organizations are at heart businesses, news also becomes a commodity packaged for sale in the "marketplace of ideas." An explicit place for the news media in the center of the model allows for the influence on policymaking processes and outcomes of a unique journalistic perspective on events, issues, and persons.

This impact is noted by Linsky (1986) in his study of policymakers and their relationship to the media. He detected, for example, five impacts of television on policymaking: "Television diminishes the quality of communication among officials in public settings such as Congressional hearings; forces oversimplification of the issues; nationalizes a story and puts it on the policymakers' agenda; creates a supportive environment for certain options; and accelerates the policymaking process" (p. 66).

The roles for the media in the policy process specified by Cobb and Elder (1981) and by Linsky (1986) seem remarkably potent and demonstrate why the media deserve an explicit place in the pressure groups model. The reconstituted model is presented in Figure 1.1. The solid lines indicate the pathways of influence to be illustrated by the chapters in this book. Dotted lines indicate other pathways that may be important in and of themselves, but are not dealt with directly in this book.

INFLUENCE AS AGENDA-SETTING: STATUS CONFERRAL, FRAMING, AND LEGITIMACY

Many of the media influences on the policy process specified previously seem to involve the selection and definition of issues and a narrowing of the range of policy options relatively early in the policymaking process. Therefore, the approach that may be most useful is the study of the media role in establishing or changing policymakers' agendas. The agenda-setting hypothesis, as originally articulated by Bernard Cohen (1963) and elaborated by many others (McCombs & Shaw, 1972; Shaw & McCombs, 1977; Weaver, Graber, McCombs, &

Figure 1.1
Media-Centered Pressure Groups Model of Political Linkage

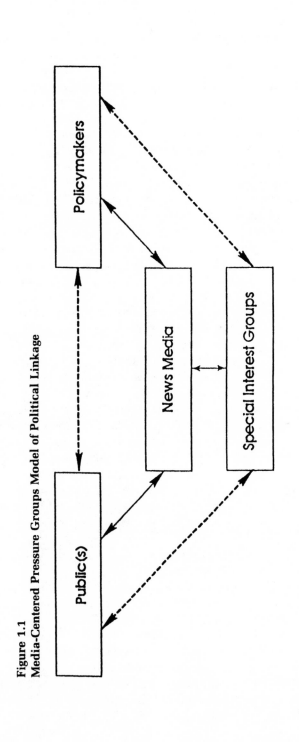

Eyal, 1981), simply states that one of the most important effects of the media is to establish the topics of concern and conversation for the public. Issues that attract media attention attract the attention of the public. If one accepts that public opinion must have some sort of effect on public policy, then this agenda-setting hypothesis also implies an impact on policymaking. This volume is not directly concerned with the public at large, but with agenda-setting among policymakers, the news media, and interest groups. It is not that the public is irrelevant, but that other actors seek to represent it, to shape it, to characterize it, or to use it as justification for policies.

The news media are at the center of the model because it is assumed here that they do serve coordinating functions among the various components of the system. The agenda-setting concept also illustrates the media's role in constructing the news rather than simply reporting it. Agenda-setting is the outcome of gatekeeping processes—those sets of decisions about what is news and how it is to be presented. The important point about gatekeeping for this volume is that gatekeeping decisions don't just involve the headline size, column inches, and placement devoted to a story, but also the themes used and the images evoked by the coverage. This has sometimes been called "framing."

Linsky (1986) provides a relevant example in the massive coverage during the Carter administration of the neutron bomb, described initially in a *Washington Post* article as one that "killed people but left buildings intact." This initial framing haunted all discussion of the bomb from that point on as "a singularly perverse weapon" (p. 220). The bomb could also have been described as one that would kill enemy soldiers in their tanks while reducing blast damage in civilian areas (Linsky, p. 220). The latter approach would have resulted, quite possibly, in an entirely different public and political discussion of the issue. Linsky writes, "The way the press frames the issue is as important as whether or not it is covered at all. If the press characterizes a policy option one way early on in the decision-making process, it is very difficult for officials to turn that image around to their preferred perspective. Policymakers are often faced with the nearly impossible task of catching up with the first story" (p. 94).

Journalists don't operate in social or cultural vacuums. They very much reflect the societies and cultures in which they operate. Thus they apply the standards and expectations of that dominant culture to everyday news stories, to provide the "framing" consistent with the standards and expectations of the dominant culture. In fact, these are the standards by which journalists and others judge their stories to be "objective." Hackett (1985) has written, "Far from being in some absolute sense neutral, news balance generally leads the media to reproduce the definitions of social reality which have achieved dominance in the electoral political arena" (p. 256). Therefore, people or groups that challenge the political consensus may be either ignored or ridiculed. In a study on media treatment of deviance, Shoemaker, Chang and Brendlinger (1987) summarize this impact as follows: "Critics of the U.S. mass media have suggested that the media act as agents of social control, not by preventing the publication of new and different ideas, but rather by varying their coverage of political groups according to how different the groups are from the status quo" (p. 362).

One of the earliest effects of the news media to be detected and discussed was its "status conferral" function (Lazarsfeld & Merton, 1948/1960). If an issue, person, or group attracts media attention, that issue, person, or group must be important. But the media are also able to define the status as they confer it. Therefore, the news media are able to confer status and legitimacy (or its opposite) on people, issues, and groups through normal gatekeeping processes, the judgments of which are driven by culturally dominant assumptions. One only needs to look at the evolution of news coverage of the movements for equal rights for blacks, women, and homosexuals to see this in action.

The impact of the conferral by the news media of status and legitimacy on policy could be quite important, in effect contributing to the "biased pluralism" discussed earlier. Groups that have obtained large amounts of legitimizing coverage should find they have more access to the policymaking process and more impact on policy outcomes.

Agenda-Setting by Policymakers

The news media are as much the target of agenda-setting as they are the source. Because of the value of legitimizing news coverage to the goals of both policymakers and organizations, these parties will make efforts to influence the amount and kind of news coverage they and their initiatives receive. They are successful much of the time. One reason that much of news coverage is so supportive of the political mainstream is that most new sources are elected or appointed public officials (Brown, Bybee, Weardon, & Straughan, 1987). In addition, a surprisingly large proportion of news originates from press releases (Turk, 1986).

As Bernard Cohen (1963) notes, the more the press sees itself as a neutral conveyor belt, "the more easily it lends itself to the uses of others, and particularly to public officials whom reporters have come to regard as prime sources of news by virtue of their positions in government" (p. 28). As an example, Linsky (1986) describes the successful efforts of the Carter administration to distract media and public attention from the failed Iranian hostage rescue mission simply by not discussing it. "The networks and leading newspapers found themselves with much less to report with the government quite. As a result, for a long period of time the coverage, particularly in the front pages and as the lead news items, virtually disappeared" (p. 91).

Pseudoevents, trial balloons, leaks, press conferences, and press releases are all examples of efforts on the part of these actors in the policy process to obtain extensive media coverage that is framed correctly from their perspectives. Their goals may be several: to broaden public support for an initiative, to prevent wider public involvement in the process, to force actions on the part of other actors, and even to "test market" ideas. Linsky (1986) quotes Stuart Eizenstat, an aide to President Carter, as referring to the press as a "useful testing device, sort of a litmus test" for policy. "If they [the press] couldn't be convinced that something was a good idea then maybe it wasn't such a good idea and certainly the administration was going to have a tough time convincing the public" (p. 43).

Entman (1989) has developed a model to predict what he terms "news slant" in covering presidents that is driven by assessments by journalists of presidential competence and popularity. These assessments themselves are derived from members of political elites who provide journalists with information. He writes, "Without elite sources to spill some dirt, even the premier news organizations seem rarely to investigate a potential scandal....Journalists rely heavily upon the very elites they are supposed to hold accountable, not only for legitimate facts, but for political action and talk that can fuel coverage. Elite responses to news events heavily shape the journalist's agenda" (p. 73). Therefore, even critical coverage is from an "insider" point of view.

And as a British diplomat quoted by Yoel Cohen (1986) notes, this can easily lead to de facto control of the press by the foreign policy establishment. "By its control of the sources of information, with the implied threat that criticism of policies would lead to a less full flow to that correspondent, by co-opting all of us diplomatic correspondents into a cozy club of those in the know, I fear that the government (under both parties) did manage the news of our foreign policy" (p. 20).

Bernard Cohen (1973) has also identified a "feedback loop" that gives some structure to this cozy club. In his examples, the policymakers in the executive branch use the press to "sell" policies to the Congress, or directly to the public. The Congress then translates this "public will" into judgments on the policies, often using home district newspaper articles and editorials, which have already been strongly influenced by government policymakers, as the basis of the "public will." Simply stated, government "public relations activity results in press coverage, which is then interpreted as significant public opinion" (p. 179).

Policymakers' Perception of Public Opinion

Historian Ernest R. May has noted that "American political leaders have hearkened to the voice of the people as their 17th century forebears did to the voice of God. Perhaps scholars, instead of listening for these voices themselves, ought to begin by inquiring what it is that these men thought they heard" (in Benson, 1967, p. 545). Given that policymakers may use press reactions to their own public relations efforts as evidence of public opinion, some of the voices of "public opinion" they hear are simply their own echoes. In their classic study of the determinants of U.S. representatives' votes, Miller and Stokes found that the most important determinant of a legislator's vote was not constituent opinion, but the representative's *perception* of constituent opinion, and that these perceptions were often far off the mark. And perhaps more to the point, public officials may operate as if public opinion exists on an issue and is attentive to the decisions they make. Erikson, Luttbeg, and Tedin (1988) make the following point: "Indeed, we may have a major political linkage between mass opinion and leader response that is often overlooked—although the public is not watching, leaders sometimes do what they think the public wants because they mistakenly believe the public is paying attention!" (p. 307).

As has been noted, public officials often use the news media as a surrogate for public opinion. Yoel Cohen (1986) notes that in the absence of public opinion polls—and few are conducted concerning foreign affairs—"the views expressed in the media are equated with public opinion" (p. 59). Bernard Cohen (1973) quotes a state department official to the same effect: "We all read the press carefully; not only *The Washington Post*, but *The New York Times*, *The Baltimore Sun*, the Louisville papers. So we know pretty well what the country is thinking" (p. 106).

To the extent that the media report on professionally conducted opinion polls, such an assumption *might* be warranted. But as has already been noted, the stories reported in the news and the views expressed in those stories are not a representative sample either of all possible stories or of all possible views, even of the attentive publics.

The upshot is that public officials may entertain perceptions that may have been derived by unsystematic means, that may not be independent of themselves, of a public opinion that may not really exist. When people, even elite policymakers, hold "unwarranted assumptions about the thoughts, feelings, and behavior of other people," they are said to exhibit "pluralistic ignorance" (O'Gorman, 1975). Thus, as Benson (1967) has pointed out, there is no one-to-one correspondence among the distribution of opinion and the perceptions of opinion by government officials, let alone among their decisions.

Closely related is Noelle-Neumann's discussion of the "spiral of silence" (1974, 1977). She has raised the possibility that individuals'
perceptions of the opinions of others may be a critical factor in determining their willingness to express those opinions. If a person perceives
little support for his or her position, she predicts that the person will
refrain from talking about the issue. This in turn removes this perspective from the public discussion of the issue, thus magnifying the
dominance of the opposing position. However, the dominance may be
more apparent than real, based as it is on the distribution of the willingness to express opinions, rather than the actual distribution of opinions. Thus, pluralistic ignorance may be a frequent outcome.

The news media may interact in this process in a number of ways.
Katz (1982) has noted the potentially "liberating" impact of the mass
media in literally letting the public know what it (the public) thinks,
thus breaking through pluralistic ignorance and ending a spiral of silence, or perhaps reversing one. This potential seems to be especially
clear in Merton's (1968) description of two patterns of pluralistic ignorance: "the unfounded assumption that one's own attitudes and expectations are unshared and the unfounded assumption that they are
uniformly shared" (p. 431). Breaking down these assumptions seems
to be an example of linkage in the broad sense that Dominick uses. The
media can connect people and help create groups or publics simply by
communicating the existence of people with certain ideas or behaviors.
The result, as Katz also points out, can be dramatic social change.

Despite this potential, because of their place in the political and social
mainstream, their reliance on legitimated institutions and individuals,
and their vulnerability to manipulation, the media may be at least as
likely to maintain traditional assumptions "about the thoughts, feelings,
and behavior of other people" that serve to support and preserve currently legitimated institutions and individuals. This may explain, at
least in many instances, the "biased pluralism" that is said to characterize the policy process.

There is no reason to think that public officials are any less prone to
both the pluralistic ignorance and the spiral of silence than anyone
else, and in fact they may play a major role in both. The versions of
opinion that they hear may be the product of the spiral of silence, and
to the extent that they take public opinion into account, they may do
so in a state of pluralistic ignorance. In addition, an organization may
decide on a course of action and then seek to characterize public opinion as supporting it in order to legitimate it, thus contributing to both
processes. Cohen (1973) explains, "When a policy maker is attributing
a decision to the dictates of public opinion, he may be explaining away
a variety of complicated, delicate political constraints on his or his
colleagues' behavior by passing them off onto the one 'legitimate' po-

litical actor that cannot answer back, defend itself, or take offense at the charge" (p. 21). In this way, they may try to use the media to maintain or create perceptions of opinion that serve their own policy goals.

In addition, policymakers may find themselves part of a situation described by Katz (1983) as "the curious case where everybody knows something, and everybody knows that everybody knows, and yet communication of that piece of information will have an effect nevertheless" (p. 93). The examples Katz gives all involve policymakers who have adopted policies, perhaps in pursuit of legitimate goals, that if publicly communicated would have created—it was assumed—public uproars. Examples come most readily from international relations, where one must sometimes talk to countries or organizations that one does not recognize officially as existing. All relevant parties know that the two sides are dealing with each other, but widespread public knowledge of it would lead to the termination of contact. As Yoel Cohen (1986) writes, "The use of news media rather than, say, formal diplomatic contacts is not just a choice between one channel of communication and another. There is a real difference in the outcome of the communication exposed to the public and that not exposed" (p. 69). The major difference is that the public communication brings additional actors into the process, among them the public or its surrogates, and the policymakers must deal with them.

Policy Process, Policy Outcomes, or Policy Public Relations?

As was noted earlier, there are potentially two effects public opinion can have on public policy: effects on the process of policymaking and effects on the actual policy choice. Evidence can be marshalled for a media impact on both.

Linsky (1986) notes in several examples that media coverage, especially negative coverage, both accelerates the process and bounces it to a higher level of the bureaucracy. With the press and various interest groups clamoring for change or action, policymakers may find that their best-laid plans for slow and careful analysis and implementation are no longer appropriate or even possible. Linsky also notes that the media, especially television, tend to nationalize a problem. Thus the story of a toxic waste dump in one area can easily become a story of toxic wastes everywhere. National officials take over from local and state officials in this case. The videotaped beating of a black traffic offender in Los Angeles in 1991 created a local outcry, but, partly because of the barrage of media attention it received, it placed the issue of the use of unnecessary force by police brutality onto the public agenda in many communities.

These process impacts can easily have impacts on policy outcomes, since as the time frame for decision decreases, so do the number of possible policy options. Initial framing of issues has much the same impact, since certain definitions may lead to certain sets of policy choices. Yoel Cohen (1986) notes that public opinion and the media "play a negative role of limiting the options open to the policymaker" (p. 61). An official told him, to illustrate, "If anyone had wanted to be nice to Idi Amin public opinion would have reacted" (p. 62). As this implies, one effect of public opinion and the media on policy is that reaction of the media to a policy may be considered during the policymaking, thus limiting the options. In fact, a good public relations consultant would insist on just such an analysis before decisions are made.

These two outcomes do not exhaust the ways in which public officials can deal with public opinion information. A third option is available to policymakers, particularly in the face of negative public opinion. They may decide that they have not "packaged" the policy correctly. The negative public opinion or press feedback will cause them to change the way they present their policy decisions, but not the decisions themselves. As a result of his extensive interviews with foreign policy officials, Bernard Cohen (1973) concluded, "Policy makers' responses to public opinion fall as often into the information policy range as they do in the substantive policy range" (p. 132).

Evidence for all these reactions is provided by a series of studies conducted at Northwestern University on the impact of investigative reporting on policymakers and policy outcomes. These are summarized in Protess and others (1987). These researchers identified investigative reporting efforts before they were aired or published and attempted to measure the perceptions of members of the public and the relevant policymakers before and after the programs or series were presented. While the exact impact varied by issue and problem, the reporting of the problems did seem to change the attitudes and actions of policymakers concerning the issues. In addition, they found that reporters were directly involved in the policy process: "It was not the members of the public who were so aroused by the report that they pressured their representatives to act. Rather it was the active collaboration between journalists and policymakers during the prepublication phase of investigation that generated the policy outcome" (Protess, Cook, Curtin, Gordon, Leff, McCombs, & Miller, 1987, p. 180). In some cases, responses were "symbolic," in that the investigative reports provided an opportunity for politicians or interest groups to exploit. They point out that the exact nature of policymaker action may depend upon "the timing of the publication in relation to political exigencies, the extent of journalistic collaboration with policymakers, the level of general public and interest group pressures, and the availability of cost-effective solutions to the problems disclosed" (p. 182).

CONCLUSION

Why should the linkage between public opinion and public policy be so difficult to unravel? Perhaps it would be easier if another pillar of normative democratic theory were not so unsteady—the existence of very large numbers of involved and informed citizens who regularly vote, even in off-year and local elections, who actively hold public officials accountable for their deeds and misdeeds, and who regularly and directly make their feelings known to them. Evidence of linkage in such a society would be unambiguous, since much of it would be public and direct from citizen to official.

But such publics exist only spasmodically and fleetingly in American society, and probably in other democracies as well. This may explain Brooks's findings that little relationship exists between mass public preferences and governmental policy. Mass publics clearly have less to do with the policy process than normative democratic theory would predict. Attentive publics and the media seem to have a great deal of influence, however. The normative expectations that mass publics *should* exist and *should* have policy input persist, however, and play a critical role, if not in how policy is determined, then at least in how it is justified. Benson (1967) writes, "The claim that public opinion supports one side has considerable potency, and the question of 'who' constitutes the public represents, therefore, more than a scholastic exercise in concept clarification" (p. 522). A vacuum in the policymaking process is created if citizens are by and large apathetic but public officials feel they need public support to legitimize policies—a vacuum that special interest groups, the media, and policymakers themselves either rush to fill or are pulled into.

Since everyone assumes public opinion is important, therefore it is important. So some people go looking for it, while others try to tell them what it is. And all the while it may not be there to be found. This is an extraordinarily ambiguous situation. It has been understood, at least from the publication of Lippmann's *Public Opinion*, that it is in such situations, where clarity is demanded from ambiguity, that the media can have their most important, yet most subtle, effects.

THE PLAN OF THE BOOK

The preceding pages have been intended to give a broad sense of the many ways in which the news media may affect policymaking by translating public opinion to policymakers. The following chapters are intended to illustrate in detail a number of them.

In Chapter 2, "The Public's Knowledge of Politics," political scientists Michael Delli Carpini and Scott Keeter report on a program of research concerning levels and kinds of political and public issue knowledge among national, state, and local publics. It interprets the meaning of the levels of knowledge that are found in terms of expectations for democratic models of government and the assumption that public opinion has a systematic relation to public policy.

James Lemert contributes Chapter 3, "Effective Public Opinion." This chapter provides a definition and analysis of the public opinion that is organized, mobilized, and oriented toward public policy. He includes a discussion of the ways standard journalistic practices may discourage the formation and mobilization of such publics.

In Chapter 4 of this volume, Lucig Danielian's "Interest Groups in the News," moves the analysis a step further by focusing on interest group participation in politics through the mainstream mass media. In particular, she looks at the determinants of interest group access to the media, and media treatment of interest groups of varying distance from the "mainstream."

Dan Berkowitz contributes Chapter 5, "Who Sets the Media Agenda? The Ability of Policymakers to Determine News Decisions." In this chapter he attempts to establish some order among all the terms that have been used to describe agenda-setting and discusses the power relationships among journalists and policymakers.

In Chapter 6, "The News Media and Public Policy Agendas," David Pritchard gives an overview of theory and research on the ways in which news coverage changes or shapes policy agendas. Many of the examples are taken from the criminal justice and judicial system. Chapter 7, by Jack Doppelt, is titled "Marching to the Police and Court Beats: The Media-Source Relationship in Framing Criminal Justice Policy." It takes up where the previous chapter leaves off with a report of research on the frequency and kind of relationships that exist among policymakers and journalists in the criminal justice establishment in Chicago.

The final three chapters concern the ways in which policymakers perceive the opinions of the public. In Chapter 8, "Reporting on the Public Mind," Leonard Tipton discusses the various means by which the news media report, assess, and evaluate public opinion, thereby making it available to policymakers, among others.

Charles Salmon and Chi-Yung Moh, in Chapter 9, "The Spiral of Silence: Linking Individual and Society through Communication," describe Noelle-Neumann's influential spiral-of-silence theory of public opinion and investigate its ideological assumptions, historical context, and implications for individuals and institutions.

The final chapter by Dominic Lasorsa is titled "Policymakers and the Third-Person Effect." The third-person effect simply means that people tend to overestimate the effects of media on other people while perhaps underestimating these effects on themselves. Lasorsa relates this to policymaker assumptions concerning the effect of media on the public and the implications of that for policy decisions concerning the media themselves.

2

The Public's Knowledge
of Politics

Michael X. Delli Carpini and Scott Keeter

I know of no safe depository of the ultimate power of the people themselves, and if we think them not enlightened enough to exercise their control with a wholesome discretion, the remedy is not to take it from them, but to inform their discretion.

Thomas Jefferson

To say that much of the public is uninformed about much of the substance of politics and public policy is to say nothing new. Few serious observers of politics have ever thought the public was highly informed. While the advent of modern survey research provided ample evidence to confirm the views of the skeptics about the public's competence, sweeping generalizations about public ignorance of politics accomplish little. Even a modestly democratic society, in which regular elections still take place, would benefit from whatever competence the citizenry can muster. And so the more relevant question is "Who knows what about what?" Or "How many people are how informed (or ignorant) about what topics?"

Answers to these broad questions provide important evidence for assessing the quality of democracy in contemporary society. Hardly any democratic theorists specified the particular levels and types of knowledge the public needs for democracy to work best, but nearly all theorists, implicitly or explicity, hold that "more knowledge is better" and that some minimal level of citizen knowledgeability is essential.

Answers to the "who knows what" question address concerns of democratic theory in several ways. First, as citizens we can judge whether we think our peers ought to know a particular fact or understand a particular issue. For example, most observers of politics might agree that a responsible citizen ought to have known basic facts about the geopolitical situation in the Persian Gulf prior to the war against Iraq, since the president sought a resolution of support from Congress, which in turn professed an interest in the views of its constituents. And most might agree that a responsible citizen should know which political party has a majority in the U.S. House and Senate, since this information is essential if citizens are to be held to hold leaders accountable through the mechanism of elections. Indeed, it is difficult to understand how a citizen could fathom the domestic politics of the Gulf crisis—or most other national issues—without knowing that the president's party did not have a majority in the legislature.

Second, knowing how political information is distributed among the public—just as we know how wealth is distributed—allows us to see how "democratically" distributed is the potential for competent participation in politics. If most people are ill informed and a few are very well informed, a very different type of democracy is implied compared with one in which most people are moderately well informed. Related to the question of equality and inequality in the distribution of knowledge is the question of what kinds of people are well informed. If the distribution of knowledge parallels the distribution of income, not just in its shape but in terms of the actual people who possess more or less of each (as we might expect), then the materially disadvantaged of our society also lack a resource that could help them to use the political system to change their situation.

Third, characterizing the public's knowledge of politics is necessary for making intelligent use of public opinion data. Public opinion polling is ubiquitous, with most major journalistic organizations conducting or subscribing to regular opinion surveys. Polls are a key element in the public opinion–public policy linkage. Yet the extent of the public's competence to offer opinions on issues is directly related to its understanding of both the issues and the political system that deals (or doesn't deal) with them—and public competence varies among people and among issues. Public ignorance of certain issues means that slavish obedience to polls by policymakers would be foolish, but cavalier dismissal of polls as irrelevant to "true" public opinion is also foolish since a portion of the public *is* reasonably well informed on many issues. It is important to remember, however, that on some issues the interests of the "informed public" may diverge from those of other segments of society. In such cases, attending only to "informed opinion" may simply reinforce other inequities in the political system. We will return to this point later.

This chapter will describe the level and distribution of public information about politics and discuss the implications for democracy. Using a wide variety of surveys including several we conducted, we will characterize the level and distribution of the public's information about public officials, selected policy issues, and the political process itself. Our discussion will focus primarily on information holding. We will pay little attention to other aspects of democratic citizenship such as "rationality" in political thinking, not because such topics are not important but because we believe that factual knowledge is the base upon which citizen competence is built. It is a necessary—even if insufficient—condition for a properly functioning democracy.

LEVELS OF PUBLIC KNOWLEDGE ABOUT POLITICS

Though less well studied than other aspects of mass behavior, the question of political knowledge has been addressed for as long as public opinion surveys have been conducted. Research by Lazarsfeld, Berelson, and Gaudet (1944); Hyman and Sheatsley (1947); Berelson, Lazarsfeld, and McPhee (1954); Campbell and others (1960); Converse (1962, 1964); and Erskine (1962, 1963a, 1963b, 1963c) all provided evidence concerning the extent of political knowledge held by the American public. Since the early research was conducted, the measurement of political knowledge has played a role in many studies (see, e.g., S. E. Bennett, 1988, 1989, 1990; Delli Carpini, 1986; Delli Carpini & Keeter, in press; Entman, 1989; Ettema & Kline, 1977; Gaziano, 1983, 1984; Glenn, 1972; Inglehart, 1977; Keeter & Zukin, 1983; Kessel, 1988; Kuklinski, Metlay, & Key, 1982; Lovrich & Pierce, 1984; Nie, Verba, & Petrocik, 1976; Neuman, 1986; Owen & Stewart, 1987; Sigelman & Yanarella, 1986; Smith, 1970; Smith, 1989; Tichenor, Donohue, & Olien, 1970; Zeigler & Haltom, 1989). Yet despite this attention over the years, serious gaps exist in our understanding of political knowledge. A major reason for this is the relative paucity of systematic data. Erskine (1963a) noted this as early as 1963, commenting that "concern [in the polling field] about how much people know has decreased almost to the vanishing point in the last few years" (p. 133). Even when questions about political information are placed on contemporary surveys, relatively few questions are asked and the specific information asked about usually varies from survey to survey. No standard measure of general political knowledge exists. An important reason for the lack of data is the general belief among survey researchers that testing respondents can damage or destroy the rapport that is critical to the completion of a successful interview (Neuman, 1986).

We have attempted to address some of these gaps by designing and conducting several surveys devoted to measuring political knowledge. The largest and most comprehensive of these was a national survey of 610 adults conducted during the spring of 1989. The questionnaire contained approximately 100 items, about half of which were factual questions about government and politics. Selection of knowledge questions for inclusion was a multifaceted process that involved a review of dozens of previous surveys, relevant works on political theory and civic education, and a survey of members of the American Political Science Association asking political science teachers and scholars what kinds of things they thought citizens should know. The questions we selected were designed to tap factual knowledge in three broad areas of politics: (1) political institutions and processes, which included "rules of the game" (e.g., knowing who appoints Supreme Court justices) and civil liberties (e.g., knowing something about the First Amendment); (2) contemporary officeholders (e.g., naming the respondent's U.S. Representative) and party alignments (e.g., knowing which party controls the Senate); (3) policies and issues of the day (e.g., being able to describe the "Superfund" or knowing what percentage of the U.S. work force is unemployed). There were also questions on topics that contribute to one's understanding of current politics, for example political history and principles of macroeconomics.[1] Even with this relatively broad array of questions, we acknowledge that some areas of politically relevant knowledge were ignored (in particular, information about local politics, comparative politics, and political geography). We do think, however, that our questions provide a reasonable test of factual knowledge about the major domains of politics.[2]

We also conducted six surveys in Virginia, two of which were statewide polls designed to measure the public's knowledge of state-level issues and officials. A third statewide study dealt with knowledge and opinion about the Persian Gulf crisis, and a fourth looked at several issues of special relevance to women. While no state is a microcosm of the United States, Virginia is a highly diverse state whose demographic composition is similar to that of the United States as a whole. We believe that much of what we assert about state-level knowledge in Virginia would apply in many states. We also conducted two short surveys addressing local issues in the Richmond metropolitan area. An overview of the data sources can be found in Table 2.1.[3]

Knowledge about National Politics

Of the three major areas of national politics mentioned above—institutions and processes of national government, political parties and

Table 2.1
Description of Surveys Conducted by the Authors

Dates	Population	Sample Size	Content
January - March 1989	Members of the Am. Pol. Sci. Assn. (mail)	115	Opinions regarding what the public should know about politics
March - May 1989	Adult residents of the U.S. (telephone)	610	Knowledge of institutions and processes, issues, political leaders, history
January - February 1990	Adult residents of Virginia (telephone)	805	Knowledge of state elected officials, national institutions and processes, state issues
July - August 1990	Adult residents of Virginia (telephone)	875	Knowledge of state elected officials, national institutions and processes, state issues
October 1991	Adult residents of Richmond, VA (telephone)	400	Knowledge of local political issues, elected officials, government processes
December 1990 - January 1991	Adult residents of Virginia (telephone)	814	Knowledge and attitudes about the Persian Gulf crisis
March - April 1991	Adult residents of Chesterfield County, VA (telephone)	329	Knowledge of local issues, party control of county board, superintendent of schools, U.S. representative, national institutions and processes
July - August 1991	Adult residents of Virginia (telephone)	804	Knowledge about *Rust v. Sullivan*, Clarence Thomas, public schools, Sandra Day O'Connor, Bill of Rights, presidential veto, term of office for senators

Source: All surveys were conducted by the Survey Research Laboratory at Virginia Commonwealth University.

leaders, and current issues—respondents were most knowledgeable about institutions and processes, which is not entirely surprising since much of this information is presented to students as part of their primary and secondary education. Table 2.2 shows that knowledge that a presidential term is four years was nearly universal (95 percent), and 90 percent knew that persons accused of a crime had a right to a court-appointed lawyer if they cannot afford one (a product of television crime shows as much as education, perhaps). Over 80 percent could define a presidential veto and believed that Congress could override it (though only 35 percent could state that a two-thirds vote of both houses was required). A majority of the public had at least reasonable familiarity with certain civil liberties. Three-fourths thought that students could not be required to recite the Pledge of Allegiance, while 72 percent said that states could not prohibit abortions. Two-thirds chose the Supreme Court when asked which branch was responsible for determining the constitutionality of laws passed by Congress, and 58 percent said the president appoints federal judges. Fifty-seven percent could name at least one right guaranteed by the fifth amendment to the Constitution (almost all of the correct answers cited the protection against self-incrimination), and half said that a Communist had the right to run for president. Just under half (46 percent) knew that the first ten amendments were called the Bill of Rights, and 43 percent could name one right guaranteed by the first amendment (22 percent could name two rights). About one-third correctly said that the Congress has the constitutional responsibility to declare war (in light of post–World War II history, it is perhaps understandable that a majority incorrectly thought the president had this responsibility).

In all, responses to these questions suggest that a solid majority of the public has some familiarity with the basic institutions and procedures of U.S. government, and that a solid minority of citizens (if not a majority) have at least a rudimentary understanding of basic principles of civil liberties.

The extent of a citizen's familiarity with contemporary politicians and political alignments is mostly a function of their interest in and attention to current politics. Accordingly, knowledge in this area provides a measure of the extent of public engagement in politics. Of course, some political figures are highly visible because of regular and prominent media coverage. About three-fourths of respondents (74 percent) could name Dan Quayle as the vice-president[4] and 73 percent could name the governor of their state (see Table 2.2). A little over half (55 percent) could name one of their two U.S. senators. However, other politicians were less visible. Only 29 percent could name their U.S. representative, and 25 percent could name both of their U.S. senators. Only 30 percent described Supreme Court Chief Justice William Rehnquist as a conservative. And, as described below, elected state officials below the level of governor were named by one-third or fewer of our Virginia respondents.

Knowing which party holds a majority of seats in the U.S. House and Senate is a basic fact for understanding the current political terrain in Washington, and potentially would be important in the voting decisions of citizens. A majority of respondents correctly identified the Democrats as controlling the House (68 percent) and Senate (55 percent), but the

Table 2.2
Knowledge of National Issues, Leaders, and Institutions

SUBJECT	%	SUBJECT	%
Knows length of presidential term	95%	Says a Communist can run for president	50%
Says accused have right to counsel	90%	Says federal budget is closer to a trillion dollars than a billion or million	49%
Knows women's suffrage was not always guaranteed in the U.S. Constitution	90%	Knows first ten amendments are called "Bill of Rights"	46%
Can define presidential veto	89%	Says Sandinistas are government of Nicaragua	44%
Says veto can be overridden	83%	Can describe one First Amendment right	43%
Says U.S. has a trade deficit	82%	Says U.S. supports El Salvador government	43%
Says U.S. has a budget deficit	80%	Knows percent needed for veto override	35%
Says Nixon is a Republican	78%	Says Congress declares war	34%
Says schools can't require pledge of allegiance	75%	Says Rehnquist is a conservative	30%
Can name vice-president	74%	Can name U.S. representative	29%
Can name governor	73%	Knows percent unemployed	27%
Says states can't prohibit abortion	72%	Can name both U.S. senators	25%
Says Democrats control U.S. House	68%	Can describe two First Amendment rights	22%
Says U.S. supports Contras	66%	Knows percentage of federal budget spent on education	19%

Table 2.2 continued

SUBJECT	%	SUBJECT	%
Says Supreme Court determines constitutionality of laws	66%	Knows percent poor	18%
Says FDR was a Democrat	63%	Can describe the New Deal	15%
Says Truman was a Democrat	58%	Knows percent black	13%
Knowledge of *Roe v. Wade*	58%	Can describe Superfund	12%
Says president nominates judges	58%	Knows approximate dates of New Deal	12%
Can describe one Fifth Amendment right	57%	Can describe three First Amendment rights	11%
Can define recession	57%	Knows approximate date of women's suffrage amendment	10%
Says Democrats control U.S. Senate	55%	Knows percent with health insurance	9%
Can name one of their U.S. senators	55%	Knows percentage of federal budget spent on defense	8%
Says Contras are rebels in Nicaragua	54%	Can describe two Fifth Amendment rights	5%
Can describe effects of high tariffs	52%	Knows percentage of federal budget spent on Social Security	5%
Aware of arms control agreement	51%		

fact that over 15 percent incorrectly said the Republicans were in the majority strongly suggests that many were guessing, in which case some proportion of those who answered correctly did not actually know the correct answer.[5] Accordingly, it is probably safe to say that less than a majority of citizens are aware that the Democrats control both houses of Congress.

The third area of national political knowledge—information about current political issues—appears less familiar to the bulk of citizens. Some important (even if remote) facts are publicized repeatedly by the press and eventually make their way into the public's consciousness. For example, 66 percent of our respondents could correctly say that the United States' policy at the time was to support the Contras in the struggle in Nicaragua. The significance of this fact was probably understood by considerably fewer citizens, since less than half (44 percent) correctly identified the Sandinistas as the group controlling the government, rather than trying to overthrow it. Regarding another problem area in Central America, 43 percent correctly said that the United States supported the government of El Salvador against those trying to overthrow it.

Sixty-one percent of the respondents said they had heard or read something about the recent arms control treaty between the United States and the Soviet Union, the INF agreement (Intermediate-range Nuclear Forces), and 51 percent knew that the treaty involved nuclear weapons. However, only 34 percent said that the weapons were missiles, and only 18 percent specified that they were intermediate-range missiles. Only four percent said the missiles were located in Europe.

Although interest among the public in environmental protection grew during the 1980s, one of the major government programs to deal with environmental problems was almost completely unknown to the survey's respondents. Only 23 percent said they had ever heard of the "Superfund," which was created to provide money for cleanup of toxic waste dumps and other serious environmental hazards. Even among those who had heard of Superfund, only about half (12 percent overall) could identify its main purpose.

Surveys by other organizations have found similar patterns of knowledge of current issues. For example, a poll for the Times-Mirror Center for the People and Press conducted just after the budget agreement of October 1990 found 46 percent of the public recalling that an agreement had been reached. Thirty percent thought no agreement was reached, and 24 percent said they didn't know. Most of those aware of the agreement could name at least one type of tax that would be increased as a result of the plan.

Related to contemporary issues and policies are a number of social and economic indicators. Many of these statistics are reported regularly,

either by themselves or in conjunction with discussions of related issues. The vast majority of our survey's respondents correctly said that
the United States was currently purchasing more foreign goods than it
was selling abroad (82 percent) and that the U.S. government was
spending more money than it was collecting in taxes (80 percent). Half
of the sample correctly said the size of the U.S. budget was closer to a
trillion dollars than to a billion or a million. Relatively small minorities
of respondents could correctly estimate the unemployment rate (27
percent provided an estimate between 4 and 6 percent; 5.3 percent was
the correct answer), the poverty rate (18 percent placed the number
between 10 and 15 percent; 13 percent was the correct answer), or the
percentage of black citizens (13 percent placed the number between 10
and 15 percent; 12.4 percent was correct).

Two questions about macroeconomic concepts related to recurring
issues were answered correctly by a little over half of the survey's
respondents. Fifty-seven percent provided an acceptable definition of
a recession (at a time when no recession was occurring), while 52
percent could describe correctly at least one consequence of high tariffs.

The great variability in the extent of public knowledge about contemporary issues makes it difficult to generalize about the public's
competence in this domain. On some issues of sufficient prominence
and moment, a majority may be very well acquainted with basic facts
about the situation. For most topics of current politics, however, an
average of perhaps one-fourth to one-third of the public appears to pay
attention and become informed.

Case Study in Knowledge of a Significant Issue:
The Gulf Crisis

No single issue attracted greater public attention in recent years than
the invasion of Kuwait by Iraq and the subsequent military action undertaken by allied forces led by the United States. Unlike some crises
that develop suddenly, requiring rapid response that leaves little time
for public debate and input regarding policy options, Iraq's invasion
of Kuwait led to a relatively orderly and progressive response by other
nations, in which many of the major decisions—including the one to
begin the war—occurred following considerable public debate in the
news media and by elected officials. President Bush's ultimatum to Iraq
to leave Kuwait by January 15 focused attention and debate on the issue
of allied forces initiating military action. The president sought and
obtained, by a narrow margin, a resolution of support from the Congress,
approved just days before the deadline.

The Persian Gulf crisis was thus a classic case of an issue about which
the public had both an interest and an obligation in being informed.

Table 2.3
Knowledge about the Gulf Conflict

Subject	%	Subject	%
Knows that U.S. troops make up most of allied troops in Middle East	59%	Knows that Kuwait borders Iraq	35%
Knows that Iraq's army is larger than the U.S. army in the Middle East	53%	Knows that Jordan borders Iraq	21%
Can name at least one nation that borders Iraq	52%	Knows that Turkey borders Iraq	19%
Knows that Iran borders Iraq	38%	Knows that Syria borders Iraq	11%
Knows tht most Arab nations were supporting the allied efforts	36%	Say that % of oil used in U.S. imported from Middle East was closer to 10%	10%
Knows that Saudi Arabia borders Iraq	36%	Knows that Kuwait supported Iraq in the Iran-Iraq war	10%

The means for becoming informed about some aspects of the crisis were generally available, as the news media provided a daily diet of information and commentary about the issue. How informed were citizens about the situation? To provide a partial answer to this question, we conducted a statewide survey of 814 adult Virginians between December 6, 1990, and January 13, 1991. The questionnaire included several knowledge and opinion questions regarding the Gulf crisis. Table 2.3 shows the results for the knowledge questions.

About half of the survey's respondents were able to answer several basic questions correctly. For example, a majority (59 percent) said that most of the troops stationed in Saudi Arabia were from the United States. Thirty-six percent of respondents said that "most" Arab nations were supporting the U.S. actions in the Middle East (the correct answer), while 42 percent said "some" were. A fourth of the sample said Iraq's army was "much larger" than the U.S. deployment (the response that best conformed with official estimates at the time), and 29 percent said it was "a little larger."

Other facts were known to only a small minority of respondents. Nearly half of the sample was unable to name even one of the six countries bordering Iraq; another 10 percent could name only one. However, many topics about which the public was poorly informed were not given regular coverage by the news media. Despite the obvious significance of these topics, it was very difficult during the period leading up to our survey to find any regular discussion in the media of the recent military and political relations among Iraq, Kuwait, and Iran, and there was little information about the scope of current and past oil imports from the region. As a consequence, perhaps 42 percent of the sample believed that the United States imported at least half of its oil from the Middle East prior to the crisis (the correct percentage is estimated to have been between 10 and 15). Only 10 percent of the sample said the figure was close to 10 percent, and 22 percent said the figure was about one-third. One-fourth of the respondents said they didn't know. Similarly, only 10 percent of respondents said correctly that Kuwait had supported Iraq in the Iran-Iraq war.

The survey's results suggest that even when confronted with an issue of obvious significance and interest to most citizens, the amount of information collected and held by many of them is relatively small. Nevertheless, a significant minority of citizens was very well informed, as measured by our survey. Thirty percent could name three or more of the nations bordering Iraq. Approximately 10 percent provided very sophisticated explanations of why Saddam Hussein might have invaded Kuwait (including, for example, his charge that Kuwait had engaged in economic warfare against Iraq by overproducing oil and driving prices down), while another 20 percent demonstrated with their answers a good grasp of the geopolitical problems that may have motivated Hussein.

State and Local Government

Some observers have argued that many citizens pay little attention to and know little about national and international affairs because such matters are often remote from everyday experience (Boyte, 1980). State and local politics are more likely to affect citizens directly; in turn, citizens may have more influence over politics closer to home and, thus, more incentive to stay informed.

Even though it is difficult to make precise comparisons in the knowledgeability of citizens about national versus state or local politics (e.g., what issues at each level should be compared?), our data suggest that the level of public knowledge of state and local politics is not significantly higher—or lower, for that matter—than knowledge of national politics. Comparable portions of citizens we surveyed knew which party controlled the legislature at the state and the national levels. Awareness of basic facts about significant state- and local-level issues was comparable to awareness of national issues.

To compare state and local knowledge we conducted two statewide surveys in Virginia and two local surveys in the Richmond metropolitan area (see Table 2.1). In the statewide surveys, we asked a number of factual questions about state-level political topics, and we also included

Table 2.4
Knowledge of State and Local Politics

SUBJECT	%
Heard about historic designation controversy in Richmond	83%
Could name governor (state survey)	77%
Said Richmond mayor is appointed by city council	66%
Heard about controversy over minority set-asides in city contracting	57%
Aware that state faced a deficit (state survey)	56%
Knew party in control of House of Delegates (state survey)	51%
Could name one U.S. senator (state survey)	49%
Aware that general assembly (state legislature) is in session (state survey)	45%
Knew party in control of State Senate (local survey)	39%
Could name U.S. representative (state survey)	37%
Could name Virginia attorney general (state survey)	37%
Could name Chesterfield County school superintendent (local survey)	36%
Said mayor is selected by city council (local survey)	33%
Could name U.S. representative (local survey)	33%
Said Chesterfield County does not charge an impact fee (local survey)	30%
Could name the mayor of Richmond (local survey)	29%
Aware that governor had proposed no tax increase to deal with deficit (state survey)	26%
Could name lieutenant governor (state survey)	22%
Aware of pension fund controversy (state survey)	21%
Could name both U.S. senators (state survey)	19%

several items from our national survey to serve as a basis for comparison.[6] In the local surveys, we focused on local issues, officials, and partisan alignments. Table 2.4 shows the results from the state and local surveys.

Comparable percentages of Virginia residents said that the Democratic party held a majority of seats in the U.S. House and the Virginia House of Delegates (48 and 51 percent, respectively) and the U.S. and Virginia Senates (42 and 39 percent). Somewhat fewer Chesterfield County residents (33 percent) said correctly that Republicans held a majority of seats on the Board of Supervisors (the elected governing body of the county).

Attention to the ongoing affairs of state government was apparently episodic for a majority of the surveys' respondents. Less than half could correctly state whether the state legislature was in session or not (the question was asked on two state polls—the legislature was in session during one poll but not the other). Regarding current issues, a minority showed familiarity with basic facts. A little over half of the state survey respondents were aware that the state was facing a budget deficit, but only one-fourth of the respondents correctly said that the governor had proposed no tax increase to deal with the deficit. In an earlier state survey, one-third of the respondents were aware of a highly publicized controversy over the state's handling of tax exemptions for the pensions of retired federal government employees.

Awareness of local issues varied considerably. Majorities of respondents to one of the local surveys reported reading or hearing about two racially charged issues in the city of Richmond—controversy over a proposed "historic designation" of a neighborhood (83 percent) and the U.S. Supreme Court case regarding "minority set-asides" in local city contracting (57 percent).[7] And two-thirds of the respondents correctly said that the mayor of Richmond was selected by the city council, rather than through direct election (a recurring controversy in city politics). A mundane, though ongoing, issue in Chesterfield County was less known to respondents in that jurisdiction: only 30 percent said that the county presently does not charge developers an impact fee for new construction. This is in one of the nation's fastest-growing counties, where issues of development and growth are constantly on the public agenda.

Elected public officials below the level of governor were known to only a minority of respondents. Just over a third of the state surveys' respondents could name the state's attorney general, who was in her second four-year term in office (to which she was elected with over 60 percent of the vote). About one-fifth could name the lieutenant governor, a newcomer to state politics. In Richmond city, 29 percent could name the mayor, while 36 percent in Chesterfield County could name the superintendent of the public schools.

This review of public knowledge about state and local politics paints a picture similar to that of national political knowledge. Highly publicized issues may become known to a majority of citizens, but for the most part, knowledge of basic facts about issues, partisan alignments, and names of politicians are the province of only a minority.

THE DISTRIBUTION OF POLITICAL KNOWLEDGE

Our extended review of specific survey items documents the extent to which the public knows certain facts about political issues, processes, and leaders. While we do not claim to have selected for our surveys *the* most important facts a citizen should know, we do believe our items are generally representative of the type of facts that are important for citizens to know if they are to understand and affect the process of government.

What our review thus far does not tell us, however, is how individual bits of knowledge are distributed in the population. Just as societies with very equal and very unequal distributions of income could have the same overall mean income, so too can societies have more or less inequality of information. While there are many theoretical ways in which political knowledge could be distributed in a society, it may be useful to compare the actual shape of the distribution of knowledge with two plausible hypothetical models, each of which has a very different implication for the quality of democracy. These distributions are shown in Figure 2.1.

One hypothetical model has knowledge distributed among the populace in the shape of a pyramid, with the base at the bottom and the peak at the top. In this model, a few individuals are very knowledgeable about politics, while most citizens are uninformed. This model may be called the "managerial" model, because it implies that a few individuals are in a position to make effective use of their democratic rights and thus to exercise disproportionate influence over the making of public policy. Gross characterizations of the public as inert, apathetic, and ignorant imply this type of distribution.

An alternative model of the distribution of knowledge is shaped like a diamond, suggesting that there are a few very informed people, a few totally uninformed people, and most people clustered in the middle ranges of knowledge. If plotted as a graph it would resemble the normal distribution (the familiar "bell curve"). This model can be called "pragmatic democracy," and would be the product of a political culture in which the acquisition of political information was a civic norm, political information was reasonably accessible (through the schools and the mass media), and most citizens had enough motivation and cognitive skill to gather and retain a moderate quantity of knowledge.

Figure 2.1 shows the hypothetical models, as well as the distribution of scores from our national sample. To create the display, the national knowledge scale was divided into ten equal segments and the percentage of respondents scoring in each segment was plotted in the figure, with each asterisk on the figure representing 1 percent of the sample.[8] The pattern of the actual data does not match either the managerial or the pragmatic model. While there is a "bulge" in the middle of the distribution, the overall shape is more "boxy" than the pure pragmatic model would call for, with a higher percentage of citizens scoring at the top and the bottom than would be expected in a normal distribution.[9] There is little suggestion in these data of the "managerial" model, in which the vast majority of the public is dis-

Figure 2.1
Hypothetical and Actual Distributions of Political Knowledge

	MANAGERIAL MODEL (HYPOTHETICAL)	PRAGMATIC MODEL (HYPOTHETICAL)	ACTUAL DISTRIBUTION (NATIONAL SURVEY)
High knowledge	*	**	****
	***	*****	*********
	*****	*********	***************
	********	***********	******************
	**********	****************	*******************
	************	******************	*******************
	**************	***************	****************
	****************	***********	***********
	******************	*****	*******
Low knowledge	************************	**	****

The figures display hypothetical and actual distributions of respondents, with the highest scores at the top of the figure and the lowest scores at the bottom. To display the actual distribution from the national survey, the scale was divided into ten equal parts based on the range of scores. The asterisks show what percentage of the sample scored in each of the ten segments of the scale. Each asterisk represents one percent of the respondents.

connected from politics and a few individuals are far better informed than the average. While most can answer at least a few political questions, and while a few are highly expert, there are substantial numbers of individuals at each level of knowledge. There is considerable inequality of knowledge, both in relative and absolute terms. Even when we exclude the top and bottom 10 percent of cases, the median score of the top quartile of cases in the national survey is twice that of the bottom quartile.

Those who lack political knowledge are also likely to lack other resources. Figure 2.2 illustrates this point by showing the distribution of family income at different levels of political knowledge. Respondents to our national survey were divided into five groups (or "quintiles") according to their knowledge scores, and also categorized as high, middle, or low income (sorted into thirds according to family income). Figure 2.2 shows, for each quintile of knowledge, the distribution of income. Approximately 60 percent of individuals in the lowest quintile of knowledge were from the lowest third of the income scale; by comparison, only about 20 percent of the highest knowledge group were individuals with the lowest incomes.

HOW DOES KNOWLEDGE MATTER?

Our underlying assumption in this review has been that public information is the currency on which democracy operates. The more information the public has, the more equitably that information is distributed among citizens, and the less it is tied to economic resources, the more democratic the political system is. Given this assumption, the evidence presented in these pages raises the question "How democratic is contemporary U.S. democracy?"

However, not all students of contemporary democracy share this underlying assumption. Many observers believe that, despite relatively low levels of public knowledge, the U.S. government is broadly responsive to the will of its citizens. This conclusion is based in part on evidence that the winners of elections tend to be those candidates closest to the "mean" sentiment of the public at the time, and that legislators tend to act in ways consistent with public opinion in their districts (see, e.g., Fiorina, 1981; Key, 1966; Miller & Stokes, 1963). Converse (1990) and Page and Shapiro (1989, 1991), among others, argue that this seemingly magical outcome results from the aggregation of opinions and preferences through elections and public opinion surveys, which tend to remove most of the "noise" in public opinion produced by large masses of uninformed citizens. The key assumptions here are that many of the least informed ultimately do not make their preferences known, while the net effect of the uninformed who do

Figure 2.2
Distribution of Family Income at Different Levels of Political Knowledge

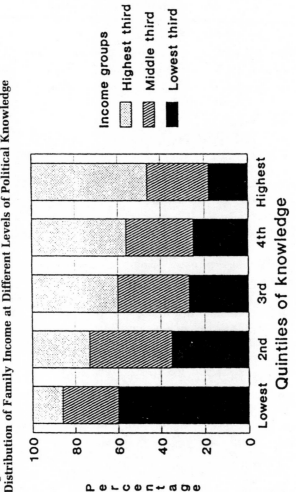

participate is to cancel one another out, leaving the "signal" of the informed to come through.

Arguments regarding the collective rationality of the public are normatively unsatisfying on a number of levels. First, the notion of collective rationality connotes minimal democracy achieved inadvertently. Not only are most citizens effectively disenfranchised by their ignorance, but they aren't even aware of it. In essence, the system works because the uninformed are randomly distributed, apathetic, or both. A second point, following from the first, is that there is no particular reason why the system should continue to work, especially if the mass of uninformed citizens can be pushed in a particular direction by interests opposed to the general good (or to their individual or group interests). This is, of course, a very old concern (see, e.g., Lippmann, 1925), but the development of the mass media along with modern techniques of advertising and persuasion suggest that this may happen more frequently and easily now than in the past.

Third, there is no guarantee that the interests of the informed and the uninformed are the same; indeed for many issues there is a strong presumption to the contrary. Unless one is willing to accept the dubious proposition that policymaking is essentially a technocratic exercise in which expertise would lead all citizens to the same policy judgments, it is likely that public policies will often favor better-informed citizens, who have more income, greater wealth, better jobs, and so forth.

Finally, even if the system—working through the mechanism of elections and surveys—is broadly responsive, a lot of politics goes on in what James Lemert, writing in the next chapter, calls "the influence framework." Much of this activity does not directly or palpably affect the broad social indicators upon which many citizens base their votes (e.g., the rates of inflation and unemployment, or the perception of U.S. military strength). Nor does it always involve the broad issues about which citizens are commonly polled. Thus, this aspect of politics is not subject to democratic control through the process of "collective rationality."

There is an air of unreality surrounding discussion of the public's rationality in evaluating government performance: poor performances by public officials in key policy areas are often not recognized as such in the electoral arena. As an example of this unreality, consider the national government's economic policies of the 1980s. By any reasonable standard, the performance of incumbents in the making of economic policy during the past decade should have been the subject of vigorous debate in the 1988 elections, and probably should have resulted in a great deal of electoral turnover. Analysts from all bands of the political spectrum felt that both the president and Congress had taken many actions that seriously weakened the U.S. economy and will result in lowered living standards in the future. The distributional consequences of economic policies were significant as well, and largely negative for the majority of citizens. For example, middle-income taxpayers gave substantial electoral majorities to Ronald Reagan in 1980 and 1984, in part on the promise that taxes would be cut. Despite the great show of tax cutting in the 1980s, by 1988 these citizens faced higher effective tax rates than in 1979. More generally, from 1980 to 1988 only the top quintile of Americans gained in income or wealth, while the greatest losses (in both absolute and relative terms) were suffered by the poorest 20 percent of Americans (Phillips, 1990). Yet in the elections of 1988, discourse about economic policy was muted and unenlightening, and voters returned high percentages of incumbent legislators to office and elected the sitting vice president, George Bush, to the White House.

PUBLIC OPINION POLLING AND THE MASS MEDIA

Citizens sometimes disagree with a favored candidate on particular issues. Even if they choose not to base their vote upon these issues, they may still prefer that government act according to their wishes and are entitled to try to influence the policy process. In addition, organized interests have become increasingly sophisticated at having their grievances addressed regardless of which party controls government. For a growing number and range of public issues, campaigns and elections have become secondary to the political processes occurring between elections (Ginsberg & Shefter, 1990). As a result of this shift, public opinion polls have arguably become the most prominent manifestation of the public's will.

However, public opinion surveys are double-edged swords in a democracy (Ginsberg, 1986). In theory, "biased pluralism"—as described in Chapter 1, the upper-status bias of those who contact legislators, belong to interest groups that lobby, contribute significant amounts to political candidates, or even those who vote regularly—is counteracted by public opinion taken from polls, because the respondents are more representative of the population than are the collection of individuals public officials usually hear from. However, public opinion polls are not always free from the biases that distort other aspects of the democratic process. As surveys play an increasingly important role in the authoritative allocation of goods, services, and values, political elites of various stripes have become increasingly effective at using public opinion polls to their own advantage (Ginsberg, 1986; Margolis & Mauser, 1989).

A key actor in both the use and abuse of public opinion surveys is the media. There has been an explosive growth in media-sponsored polls, and in the attention paid to nearly any poll by the media. Public opinion polling represented a major advance in the mass media's long-standing desire to become the preeminent linkage between citizen and government. Polls have provided journalists a means of liberation from other mediating institutions such as political parties, interest groups, and "bosses," to which the media have been hostile since the Progressive era. For these reasons, the press has a strong vested interest in having polls taken seriously.

However, the wide variations in what people know about politics also mean that caution must be taken when using polls to characterize "public opinion." The enthusiasm of journalists for public opinion polls may lead, unconsciously, to the misuse of polls and the consequent misrepresentation of public opinion by journalists. One such danger is that public opinion will be portrayed as more settled and substantial than it is—what Lance Bennett calls the "state of consciousness fallacy" (1980). Ironically, this misrepresentation often unwittingly serves the purpose of the very elites to which journalists profess hostility.

Despite this potential for abuse, we believe that polls can provide a useful perspective on public opinion about particular issues. In order to be meaningful, however, opinion polls need to measure more than just opinions. Pollster Daniel Yankelovich, in offering a distinction between "mass opinion" and "public judgment," suggests the use of one or more simple tests: for example, asking questions in slightly different ways to detect volatility in attitudes, or asking respondents to react to the consequences of their preferences (Yankelovich, 1991; see especially Chapter 3). We suggest that pollsters also make a greater effort to measure the public's familiarity with and knowledge of the issues involved.

Of course, distinguishing informed from uninformed opinions is not without its own potential for bias, especially given the differences between the types of people who tend to be informed and uninformed about politics. In the short run, informed opinion should be treated as a category within other relevant groups and classes, rather than a substitute for them. For example, if one is interested in knowing the public's views on the state of the economy, we would argue that a consideration of the opinions of informed citizens within each of several different economic classes would be illuminating. In the long run, however, the most effective way to assure that public opinion truly reflects the public interest is to assure that political knowledge is both widespread and equitably distributed among citizens. As Jefferson wrote, the remedy is "to inform their discretion."

NOTES

1. Questions varied in their degree of difficulty, their format, and whether they queried about facts that were likely to be learned in the classroom or that required monitoring the changing political landscape.

2. Our respondents agreed, with 94 percent saying that our questions were a fair test of what they knew about politics.

3. In addition to our own surveys, we drew on a number of studies conducted by mass media and academic organizations.

4. The survey was conducted a few months after Quayle took office in January 1989, following considerable (and mostly negative) publicity during the election campaign.

5. We would expect all of the questions for which respondents were presented with a finite list of alternatives to be affected by guessing.

6. Virginia is a very diverse state with several large metropolitan areas (including suburban Washington, D.C.), as well as a significant rural population. Our confidence in the representativeness of the state for the present research is bolstered by the similarity between the state samples and the national sample on several items asked of both groups.

7. Note that these percentages are for reported exposure to information, and do not test knowledge directly.

8. In the national survey, a scale was constructed using 51 separate knowledge questions. Some items were combined, with respondents being assigned fractional scores based on their answers. Scores on the scale ranged from 3 to 44 with a mean of 24.4 and a standard deviation of 9.1. Two-thirds of respondents scored between 15 and 34. Half of the sample fell between 17.5 and 31.5. Details of the construction of the scale are available from the authors.

We believe that political knowledge is fundamentally a unidimensional phenomenon, and thus a single measurement scale, properly constructed, can measure it adequately. For evidence regarding the dimensionality of political knowledge, see Zaller (1986) and Delli Carpini and Keeter (1990). For an alternative view, see Iyengar (1990).

9. We recognize that the nature of the testing instrument can influence the shape of the distribution of scores. While we designed the survey to include questions covering a range of political topics and with varying degrees of difficulty, the comparison of hypothetical and actual distributions presented here is meant to be a general characterization rather than a precise mathematical specification.

3

Effective Public Opinion

James B. Lemert

As we saw in the preceding chapter, popular knowledge can be so low about so many things that measuring *preferences* without first measuring *knowledge* can produce essentially meaningless percentages.

For example, the polls too often confuse knowledge with popularity by asking people for their candidate preferences instead of finding out first whether people even know the names of the candidates. Because of this failure to measure knowledge, if and when a previously unknown Democrat or Republican candidate makes a big surge in a preference poll, the poll-fascinated news media interpret the surge as reflecting a massive change in attitudes toward the candidates, instead of as the natural outgrowth of a gain in name familiarity.

A classic example of this misinterpretation occurred in Oregon during the 1990 campaign for the U.S. Senate between incumbent Republican Mark Hatfield and Democrat Harry Lonsdale. Lonsdale had been trailing Hatfield in a poll for *The Oregonian* by more than 40 percentage points in the late summer. Then, in late September and early October, Lonsdale, a wealthy businessman who had never before run for public office and was virtually unknown to Oregon voters, ran a series of "attack" ads against Hatfield. The hard-hitting ads for the first time caused much news coverage of Lonsdale's campaign against Hatfield. Many Democrats, once they knew something about Lonsdale, quickly fell in line behind him. Since there are more Democrats in Oregon than Republicans, Lonsdale quickly gobbled up most of Hatfield's lead. In effect, Lonsdale had simply become known to his natural constituency—Democrats. Meanwhile, Oregon news media had misinterpreted Lonsdale's surge in the polls as dramatic evidence that he had changed voters' minds.

Similarly, the polls often beg the question of knowledge by asking people directly about their policy preferences without bothering to find out, first, whether respondents have any knowledge about the policy area in question. Poll respondents can often choose among the several opinion responses the interviewer offers them—without knowing a blessed thing, other than what's implied in the question, about the issue area. (See Bishop, 1990, Bishop, Oldendick, & Tuchfarber, 1983, and Bishop, Oldendick, Tuchfarber, & Bennett, 1980, for a series of studies that clearly document this problem.)

Just as with candidate races, then, the polls often present a highly misleading picture of how much support there is for measures on state ballots or for policies that government officials are considering.

With ballot measures, what often happens is that early polls show huge majorities favoring the measures; as people actually acquire information about those measures, that majority often disappears. Those misleading early polls, at most, are showing support for something like "the general idea" of each measure, rather than for the measure itself. Later, as people learn about the actual measure, they often find less to like about it—and the percentage of support shrinks.

Similar things happen when we look, not at ballot measures, but at policy questions that will be settled without direct voting by the people. For example, the polls can be extremely misleading when used to assess public support—or lack of it—for policies that haven't been announced or implemented yet. Almost inevitably, after it happens, people react to the announcement or the implementation, rather than to the more abstract "general idea" that the poll question had asked them to consider beforehand.

Experienced politicians and policymakers know this, and thus are appropriately skeptical of a poll's preference percentages until there is some basis for assessing the level of information behind those percentages. It is this problem with the polls, along with several other problems with them and with public opinion measurement, that require us to distinguish between what we will term *effective public opinion* and some other concepts.

EFFECTIVE PUBLIC OPINION

We define effective public opinion as *opinion that reaches decision-makers as they try both to discern public opinion and decide how to react to it.* Another way of putting the idea of effective public opinion is that it is those expressions of opposition or support that reach and influence policymakers' ideas about what "public opinion" is (Lemert, 1981). Given this basic definition, we need to differentiate between effective opinion and (1) *mass opinion* and (2) *majority opinion.*

Mass Opinion

The idea that there is often a difference between "public opinion" and the policy views of a "mass" of people goes back a long way (e.g., Blumer, 1946, and Key, 1961). What's a "mass"? In brief, Blumer and other sociologists say that a "mass" is a large number of people who happen to be doing—or thinking about—something at roughly the same time. Thus a "mass" of people read *Newsweek* yesterday; another mass watched "60 Minutes" last Sunday night; a third mass bought disposable razor blades last Thursday, and so on. Members of the *Newsweek* "mass" may or may not be members of the "60 Minutes" mass or of the razor-purchasing mass, and so on.

One essential characteristic of a mass is *coincidence.* People choose to do the same thing at roughly the same time—each person for her or his own individual reasons.

A second essential characteristic of the mass is that its members are doing or thinking about the same thing *without awareness of how many other people are doing or thinking about the same thing.* In other words, at the time of the activity, individual members of a mass are cut off from almost all other members of that mass. Direct communication among members of a mass is minimal or nonexistent *at the time of the mass behavior.*

Finally, the people in a mass are *disengaged and separated from the political system.* In contrast, the retail and marketing system surrounds us with consumer products, facilitating mass purchases. Even direct mail marketing, which doesn't exactly surround us with the products, nevertheless makes it extremely easy for us to make a purchasing commitment by placing a check mark on a card in a postage-paid, preaddressed envelope. In other words, the retail and marketing system is set up for the convenience of mass consumer behavior. Even when a mass of people is attending to (say) a televised political campaign debate, the debate itself provides them no way comparable to the marketing system to "connect" with the candidate they prefer. Even when the debate "sells" the candidate, what if the viewer isn't registered or isn't eligible to vote? What if the election is two months later, not "open for business" the next day, the way the marketing system is?

Mass opinion, then, can be thought of as the views of people about some psychological object they have in common. Their views toward the object may or may not be the same, but presumably they all know enough about the object to have an opinion about it. The object may be a consumer product, a composer's music—or a million other things that have nothing to do with a public affairs *issue* object. An issue object is the subject of a public controversy, for example, President Bush's energy policies, whether the state can and should intervene in abortion decisions, whether the government should do more to protect American industry from foreign competition, and so on.

When mass opinion does concern a public issue, mass opinion is the raw material out of which policymakers construct their impressions of public opinion. Raw material? What does that mean? Recall that the mass is disengaged from the political process—and policymakers' constructions or perceptions of public opinion on the issue are very much the result of political processes. Only some members of a mass—many of us would say far too few—feel willing or able to *participate*. Generally, political participation of some kind is necessary to make one's opinion visible to policy decision-makers.

Political participation includes relatively easy things, like voting. But easy doesn't mean everybody with opinions votes. We are having trouble getting 50 percent voter turnout, even in the November presidential elections. In fact, in most elections, in most states, voter turnout is much less than 50 percent. Almost always, *effective opinion in an election is expressed by a majority of those who vote.* A majority of a minority in other words!

Participation also may involve a huge variety of not so easy things, like writing letters to legislators, participating in demonstrations, signing petitions, putting yellow ribbons around trees, and so forth. Let's consider that letter-writing example in more detail. Try writing your legislator if you don't know the office address, or if you feel you don't know enough yet about the issue, or if you don't have confidence that you can write an intelligible letter. Those feelings are major obstacles to making your opinion *visible* to a policymaker. Roughly 10 percent or less of Americans claim they have *ever* written their legislator, let alone written concerning any specific policy issue. Policymakers' constructions of public opinion will rely on those opinions that are *visible* to them. If only a few constituents wrote U.S. Rep. John Q. Zilch about what to do concerning Iraq's invasion of Kuwait, those constituents' opinions at least had a chance to reach, and be visible to, Representative Zilch. To be sure, there are other ways in which opinions can reach Zilch—phone calls, petitions, bumper stickers, demonstrations, letters to the editor in newspapers he reads—but all of these other ways also require an act of political participation that usually leaves every other member of that mass behind—behind, and invisible to the policymaker.

To repeat a point made earlier, the marketing system makes it far easier for people to participate as consumers than the political system does for them to participate as citizens. As we'll see in this chapter, the general mass media also make it easier for citizens to act as consumers than the news media do for citizens to act as political participants.

In principle, there is one nonparticipatory way that opinions of the members of a mass may become visible to policymakers: if and when a telephone or personal-interview poll is done and the findings made known to the policymaker. Agreeing to be polled by a survey interviewer is essentially *passive* and nonparticipatory. As we've already seen, you can respond to opinion questions without knowing—or caring—anything about the issues asked.

Policymakers generally know this, of course. A number of studies done at the University of Oregon show that state legislators, city council members, and other policymakers do *not* rely on poll-based data in forming conclusions about public opinion (e.g., Cundy, 1973; Wilkins, 1976; Lemert, 1971; and Lemert, 1986), and a series of studies of members of the U.S. House of Representatives also show the polls far down the list of ways these legislators discern public opinion, and these preferences don't seem to have changed much over time. (For how unchanging these House of Representatives findings are over time, compare Kriesberg [1945] with Erikson and Luttbeg [1973] and an American University survey of House aides reported in 1981 [Constituents, 1981].)

Majority Opinion

The polls seem to portray whatever response gets a majority as "public opinion," ignoring the problem of participation. A president may get a majority of those voting, but when even the president is elected by (say) 30 percent of all eligible voters, how is it possible to believe that effective public opinion and majority opinion (in a poll) are automatically the same? Further, even if we continue to limit our argument to elections, what if the losing side in an initiative election refuses to accept the majority verdict of those who voted, and keeps bringing the same ballot measure back until it finally wins? That recently happened in Oregon, where a property tax limit initiative finally passed narrowly after being beaten four straight times.

And, of course, we shouldn't limit ourselves to elections in distinguishing between majority and effective opinion. Many times in the past, a determined minority has used better organization and effort to make itself appear as the dominant public opinion on some policy controversy. Obvious examples of this phenomenon include opponents of abortion—before the Supreme Court's "Webster" decision alarmed the pro-choice forces—and, perhaps even now, the anti-gun-control forces.

Remember our definition of effective public opinion: opinion that reaches decision-makers as they try to discern public opinion and decide how to react to it. Resources are not equally distributed in our society; some people have much greater ability than others to make their views visible to policymakers. In other words, to calculate a majority is to miss the point. Policymakers respond to intensity, resources, and organization in constructing their ideas about "public opinion."

As one such decision-maker put it, "Opinions need to be weighed, not counted."

PERCEIVING PUBLIC OPINION

Effective public opinion reaches policymakers in two rather distinct perceptual situations: the *Election Framework* and the *Influence Framework* (see Lemert, 1981, especially Chapter 2).

The Election Framework

Three sets of information reach policymakers in the Election Framework: (1) the *voting outcome* (e.g., percentages for and against a measure, or for candidates A and B), (2) the *turnout* (a higher percentage of turnout signals greater interest and concern), and (3) *exit poll* interviews with voters leaving their precincts (an extremely useful set of information that allows clarification of voting outcomes, when the exit poll is used for analytical purposes, rather than for projecting winners). Unlike information in the Influence Framework, there is a strong consensus among policymakers about the relevance of each of these three forms of information to their assessment of public opinion.

The Influence Framework

In effect, the Election Framework occurs only on election days. All other opinion input reaches policymakers in the Influence Framework. As a perceptual situation, the Influence Framework differs from the Election Framework in many ways. In contrast to the Election Framework, information about public opinion on an issue in the Influence Framework

• comes in over a longer and more indefinite period of time;
• comes in a huge variety of forms;
• can change dramatically over the time period;

- is less standardized and more subject to dispute;
- can include essentially "passive" poll data (remember, exit polls interview *voters* only);
- lacks the kind of historical records that enable easy comparisons (e.g., whether this was an unusually high or low turnout is easy to see in the Election Framework; it is far harder to determine whether a crowd of demonstrators or last week's volume of letters was unusually large); and
- is characterized by relatively few resources devoted to processing it (many millions of dollars are spent on gathering and very quickly processing millions of votes; in contrast, 150 letters on the same issue in one day might easily overwhelm the office resources devoted to processing constituency mail); as a result, a relatively small number of participants can "overwhelm" resources set aside to process information about their opinions and can make a devastating impression on policymakers in the Influence Framework.

Additionally, the political system, unlike elections, imposes relatively low expectations on policymakers to devote large resources to processing Influence Framework opinion input (several studies by political scientists suggest that legislators spend far more of their staff resources on processing constituent "service" mail than on opinion mail).

HOW THE PERCEPTION PROCESS OPERATES

Already we have seen why most legislators seem to base their perceptions of public opinion on participation-based expressions of opinion, rather than on polls. However, not all policymakers are elected or are legislators, and very little research has been done on whether these other policymakers prefer poll or participation-based data.

However, we are pretty sure that, when processing opinion mail, legislators and their office staffs make a quick distinction between *organized* and *spontaneous* opinion mail.

Organized mail usually is recognized easily because the mail may use identical phrases; it may all arrive suddenly, with no particular reason evident for its arrival then, not before or after; and almost certainly the mail uses the same arguments. Legislators and their staff tend to *weigh* such mail, rather than read it. Nevertheless, the greater the "weight" (numbers of letters) of the mail, the more impressed policymakers may be, because someone obviously has been able to mobilize and energize a lot of people. Typically, organized mail is regarded as special-interest mail, but the greater its weight, the closer to constituent opinion mail it is thought to be.

Spontaneous mail is individually written, with no apparent guiding hand lurking in the shadows. If spontaneous mail arrives in spurts, the spurts will very likely be in response to some development in the news. Otherwise it tends to arrive more evenly. Not all spontaneous opinion mail reaches policymakers, by any means. Often it is heavily screened by staff, who may be asked to summarize it and pass along only the most lucid letters or the letters written by "important" constituents and campaign contributors.

Legislators and their staffs also distinguish between letters and other contacts from *inside* and *outside* the legislative district. Generally, opinion contacts from people living inside the district are given more weight because these are people who have the power to vote for or against the legislator. However, if a U.S. representative has ambitions to run for the Senate, contacts with people living inside the state but outside the district may gain in importance.

Policymakers often use the *amount* of participation as an index to how *salient* (important) an issue is. The greater the salience, the riskier for policymakers will be (a) misjudging what "public opinion" wants and (b) any obvious attempt to ignore or override the public's wishes. The greater the amount of participation concerning an issue, the more likely policymakers will think the issue is salient. Generally, it takes a much bigger increase in the numbers of participants to signal salience in the Election Framework than in the Influence Framework. In the Influence Framework, increased participation may quickly overwhelm resources devoted to process it. Furthermore, turnout records routinely are kept for all past elections; therefore, the amount of turnout always can be compared with the highs and lows of the past. In contrast, no such formal records of the almost infinite variety of types of participation are kept in the Influence Framework. What all this means is that *salience impressions are easier to create in the Influence than in the Election Framework.*

JOURNALISTS, EFFECTIVE OPINION, AND MASS OPINION

A number of things print and broadcast journalists do—or fail to do—enlarge discrepancies between mass opinion and effective public opinion. Much of the rest of this chapter will consider some of these things done—and left undone—by journalists.

Besides the fact that each of these actions and inactions widens the discrepancy between mass and effective opinion, all these journalistic choices have at least two characteristics in common.

1. They are deeply *traditional* patterns of behavior in journalism, so traditional and conventional that journalists rarely think much about them.

2. They *distance* politics from ordinary citizens in a variety of ways,

interfering with citizens' ability and willingness to make their opinions visible through participating in either the Election or the Influence Framework. As a result, the field of battle to establish what "public opinion" supports is largely left to skilled individuals and organized groups, both of whom already have the will and the skill to participate.

Let us consider now some of these things done, and left undone, by journalists.

Withholding Mobilizing Information

Mobilizing information (MI) is any kind of information upon which people can act. (For a more detailed explanation of what is and is not MI, see Lemert, 1981, Chapter 6.)

Locational MI ranges all the way from dates, times, and places, such as in the daily television program listings in your newspaper, to the toll-free WATS line to reach your state legislature's switchboard. To be complete as Locational MI, the information should refer to both time and place.

Identificational MI ranges from a consumer product brand name to a physical description of a bank robber and the car he raced away in, to both the name and the office address of your own state legislator. Generally, Identificational MI involves both the identificational aspect and the locational aspect of place. Except for consumer product brand names, the *identification alone is not enough.* (Once again, the marketing system surrounds us; the brand name alone is sufficient without information about place, at least when the product identified is easily available at retail outlets.)

Tactical MI involves either explicit or implicit models of behavior. It can range from details about how a gas station was held up successfully to gardening tips to information about how one arranges to testify at a city council meeting.

In an unplanned but very predictable and systematic way, journalists withhold MI from news of politics and controversy while often providing it in "safe" kinds of news. For fear of appearing *partisan* (in other words, not "objective"), the office addresses of your state's two U.S. senators will usually be withheld from stories about how they might vote on a controversial bill, for example, but an address and phone number almost certainly will be reported in a story about a group organizing to rebuild the storm-damaged farm house of a 60-year-old widow. Journalists believe that to report such MI is implicit *advocacy* of some kind of action; nobody will become angry if you seem to advocate helping widows, so journalists don't feel exposed, with their necks on the line, in positive-context news stories. Notice, however, that the information itself—the address, for example—"advocates" nothing. It is the context in which that information appears that is confused with the information itself.

In any case, then, while it might not be "objective" to report the organizer's address and phone number, the journalist can be sure nobody will object. In contrast, quite a few people—especially the two senators—might object to giving the senators' office addresses in the more conflict-laden context of a public policy controversy. Even though an address or phone number urges no particular action, reporters and editors think they would be held responsible for whatever action results. MI in a story about controversy implies heated action on both sides; identical MI in a story about a needy widow implies only helping, charitable behavior. So we usually see plenty of MI in such safe or positive contexts—and little or none in stories about controversy (see especially Lemert, Mitzman, Seither, Cook & O'Neil, 1977). In addition, journalists risk the enmity of powerful elites such as the two senators only under very unusual circumstances. Those elites, after all, are potential news sources with whom the reporter will have to deal the day after the offending story appears. Reporters give up access to such sources with extreme reluctance.

Another obstacle to MI is that such things as addresses, room numbers, and telephone numbers are regarded as "dull detail" and will be left out of almost all newspaper stories that don't concern *local* events. The "dull detail" barrier is even higher in broadcast news, almost regardless of whether the story concerns local events. The presumption on the part of broadcast journalists is that such details cannot be communicated effectively to audiences. (See Lemert, 1981, chapter 6, for a more complete discussion of MI as "dull detail.") As a result of both the print and broadcast obstacles to "dull detail," whenever the controversy concerns policymakers who are located outside the local area— say, way off in Washington, D.C., or in the state capital—addresses, phone numbers, room numbers, ZIP codes *all* disappear from the news. Ironically, citizens at least have phone books for their own localities, but how many of us have a directory of state or federal offices?

In summary, MI disappears from the news precisely when controversy is involved. And it disappears precisely where ordinary citizens have the fewest other resources to obtain political MI—that is, when policymakers are located out of town.

Audiences seem to want MI, both in political news and in consumer news. But, tellingly, they have the very accurate belief that their newspaper won't provide it. These results are reported in a study where interviewers showed respondents two versions of a given story, identical except that one version had MI and the other didn't. The concept of MI never was explained to the respondents, most of whom quickly noticed the difference between the two versions. Half read two versions of a political story about the state legislature; the other half read two versions of a consumer story about how to judge whether a cord of firewood had been delivered. In each case strong majorities said they wanted their newspaper to carry the MI version. But less than a third thought the newspaper would carry the consumer MI version and less than a tenth thought it would carry the political MI version (Lemert, 1989, pp. 111–114).

Non-Stories about Non-Issues

Another way in which the news media can discourage popular participation is through ignoring issues, since it is pretty hard to get excited about an issue if you don't know there is one. If only "insiders" know about a controversial practice or proposal, the rest of us will hear about it only after it is too late for our participation to make any difference— *if* that is, we ever hear about it at all. Long ago, Warren Breed (1958) argued that the most likely kind of story to be left out of local newspapers was one about a "politicoeconomic" issue that would have been highly controversial if only the local newspaper audience had known about it. In his study of what was left out of these newspapers, Breed broke new ground by showing researchers how they could study what did *not* happen. Among the several techniques Breed used was a comparison of local issues identified in a series of community studies by sociologists against what local news was covered by newspapers in each of those communities. To Breed, politicoeconomic issues seemed to be cases where private industries were given special political advantages at the expense of the public. Breed's examples of such issues included unregulated pollution from a local power plant and a city killing a plan to put traffic signals in a dangerous intersection, allegedly because the signals might slow traffic flow during employee shift changes at a manufacturing plant.

Since Breed's pioneering study, numerous writers and researchers have provided more examples of stories not covered. Hirsh (1976), for example, reported that the Chicago print and broadcast news media virtually ignored a major Federal Trade Commission administrative law trial of Sears for consumer fraud. Chicago is the world headquarters for Sears; Sears occupied Chicago's (and the world's) tallest building; Sears employed nearly 30,000 people in Chicago; untold thousands of Chicago residents might have been among the victims of the alleged fraud—and Chicago was where the trial was being held! In other words, it should have been a very big local story in Chicago. During 11 days of damaging testimony against Sears—often from its own employees— most of the Chicago news media failed to cover the story. Only when Sears changed its plea and settled out of court did the *Chicago Tribune* do a story—and even then the very short, nonlocally written story appeared nearly a week after the trial had ended. Journalism reviews such as the *Columbia Journalism Review* often will carry several examples, in each issue, of such nonstories.

That's Some Other Place's Problem

Closely related to the nonstory is the displacement of an issue to somebody else's locale. In effect, a story that might have been done about a local problem is a nonstory, but the same problem somewhere else is covered by the news medium. Print and broadcast journalists call this tendency *"Afghanistanism"*—doing stories or writing editorials about issues as if they occurred somewhere far away like Afghanistan, while ignoring similar issues in the medium's own locale. Hungerford and Lemert (1973) found that Oregon newspapers displaced environmental controversies to locales outside their own circulation zones, in contrast to other news stories about public affairs. Ironically, local staffers were actually more likely to write these displaced environmental items than the other public affairs items.

So what? How would displacing a problem outside of the immediate locale enlarge the discrepancy between mass opinion and effective opinion? Displacing the environmental problem away means that the problem is less *salient* (important, personally involving) and therefore reduces the audience's motivation to participate. A story about water or air pollution problems is far more important to most people if it is "their" air or water that may be polluted. If each newspaper practices "Afghanistanism," then it's always somebody else's air or somebody else's water that may be a problem—too bad, of course, but let those people work out their own solution. Meanwhile, political insiders and interest groups are well aware of where the problems are—and they have a smaller, more identifiable set of opponents to worry about. Thus, making elite opinion into effective opinion becomes easier.

Letting the Marketplace Settle the Issue

There is a huge, unspoken gap in American journalism between what the news media define as the public sector, which is presumably completely open to news coverage, and what is defined as the "private" sector, which is not as wide open to coverage. One of many symptoms of this division is easily spotted by looking at the news media "beat" system. Most beats, or areas of regular coverage, fall into what journalists think of as the "public" sector: police and fire, public schools, the local college or university, and a very large number of agencies or divisions of local, state, and federal governments.

To journalists, anything in the public sector presumably is subject to aggressive, adversarial coverage—at least when they think it is needed. In 1987 and 1988, even the love life of a public figure such as former senator and presidential candidate Gary Hart was fair game to be covered. So *Miami Herald* reporters staked out Hart's Washington-area home, keeping track of female visitors. Among Hart's many mistakes in this episode was the public challenge he threw at journalists to find any evidence that he was having an extramarital affair. The *Herald* took the challenge. Hart dropped out of the presidential race, tried an aborted reentry, then left the presidential scene, presumably for good.

The ethics of Neil Bush as a businessman and as a director of the failed Silverado Savings and Loan are "fair game" for news coverage almost entirely because he is George Bush's son. If anything, the range of what is "private" for public figures is narrower than ever in modern American history.

But unless government becomes involved in some way, a much broader definition of what is "private" does apply to such important and universal areas of American life as work, consumer behavior, and other kinds of economic activity. Instead, unless government intervention or inquiry redefines the behavior in question as falling into the public sector, the news media will tend to avoid unilaterally extending the definition of "public" to that behavior. To be sure, there are some business reporters and editors, many sports reporters and editors, and some "soft" news specialists whose beats sometimes will carry them into "private" areas such as labor, housing, leisure, lifestyles and so on. Nevertheless, the core focus of the news media is a very narrowly defined "public" sector.

Government, public policymakers, and debates regarding policy proposals tend to be the focus of public-sector news. In marked contrast, the individual with a bone to pick with a private firm is left either to take legal action or to express her or his opinion in a very impersonal economic marketplace. Other than through the essentially *political* process of organizing a consumer boycott or organizing an employee strike or other job action, individuals will tend to feel isolated and helpless if the only action possible is to withhold their consumer monies. Recall the nature of a mass here: a coincidence of action, taken without awareness of how many others might be doing (or willing to do) the same thing. Since the mass media are one of the few ways that members of a mass can become aware of their collective potential, the insensitivity of journalists to the private sector works systematically against the "marketplace" truly working as a functional substitute for political action.

In fact, one classic way to defuse pressure toward policy action is to suggest that the answer really lies in consumer choices. For example, one standard reply given by broadcasting interests to complaints about the quality of TV programs is to say that consumers can always switch channels or flick the "off" button. Sometimes this tactic is used in an affirmative way, as well. In the spring of 1990, environmental activists and the corporate sector joined in Earth Week, a nationwide anniversary celebration of Earth Day. Almost all of the teach-in activities and media communications seemed aimed at encouraging recycling and other mass consumer behaviors, rather than at participating in the Influence Framework.

Overemphasizing the Election Framework

The news media tend to frame politics in terms of elections and election campaigns, often even reducing Influence Framework policy decisions to how they might affect a politician's future electoral prospects. Further, one of the few times that the media overtly advocate political participation is with regard to election: Does there breathe a soul who hasn't heard local newscasters say, "We don't care how you vote, but be sure to get out and vote"? To some extent, this is understandable, since the legitimacy of the American political system ultimately rests on the legitimacy of popular elections (see Lemert, Elliott, Bernstein, Rosenberg, & Nestvold, 1991, for a discussion of this in connection with the legitimacy of presidential debates). And the legitimacy of the election usually is defined in terms of how large the turnout was.

Another symptom of the relatively greater news emphasis on elections is the greater extent to which the news media will provide mobilizing *information* (as distinguished from "please vote" urgings) designed to enhance turnout. Not only is the deadline for voter registration given routinely, but so will be voter registrars' phone numbers, addresses, and office hours. In addition, in special cases the MI given will go well beyond even these things. In Oregon, for example, many local elections now are being held by mail ballot. Since the mail balloting takes days to complete, we sometimes see stories in newspapers attempting to clarify confusions that mail voters have expressed during the voting about the meaning of the vote. A Eugene, Oregon, *Register-Guard* story by reporter Ann Portal (1991), for example, explained how, if confused voters now wished to retract or change their ballot, they could contact authorities to arrange for a replacement ballot.

Unfortunately, though, most of the public policy decisions are made in the Influence Framework (Lemert, 1981). The easiest way to see why this is so is to look at possible policy-voting alternatives to the Influence Framework.

1. The initiative, referendum, and recall are available only at the state or local level—and only in some states, at that. Even when voters have these opportunities available, the courts, legislators, and administrators usually have many chances to reinterpret and selectively implement voters' collective decisions.

2. At best, elections of candidates provide skimpy policy guidance to the winner, especially if no exit survey is done of the voters as they leave the polls. In fact, even the margin of victory does not imply a policy mandate: According to numerous exit polls, Ronald Reagan's 1984 landslide win came about, not because voters felt they agreed with most of Reagan's policy views, but because they felt he provided stronger leadership than Walter Mondale would have (see John, 1984, and Opinion Roundup, 1985, p. 42). Several of these exit polls explicitly offered voters the choice of saying they voted for their candidate because they agreed with most of his policies. Reagan voters rejected that alternative, while Mondale voters embraced it. Despite what politicians would like us to believe, the margin of a candidate's win is independent of the clarity of any policy mandate. It is quite conceivable that a huge winner has put together a coalition of quite different— sometimes even partly incompatible—policy groups, while a very narrow winner has a majority composed entirely of people with one policy view.

So the Influence Framework is where public policy is made. In emphasizing the Election Framework as the opportunity for citizen input, then, the news media enlarge the potential discrepancies between effective opinion (at least in the Influence Framework) and mass opinion.

Undercutting Elections

Even though the news media may focus too much on electoral politics and too little on what those we've elected are doing, many writers (e.g., Entman, 1989) have pointed out that the news media send out distinctly mixed signals concerning elections—especially candidate elections, and more especially presidential elections. At the same time that the media urge voters to turn out, campaign stories may imply that the candidates will say anything in order to get elected.

Lemert, Elliott, Bernstein, Rosenberg, and Nestvold (1991) also report that the importance of presidential debates to voters rarely figures in postdebate network news analyses. Instead, foremost in these analyses is the impact of the debates on the ambitions of the candidates. As one might expect, "focus group" and studio audience members were almost five times more likely than journalists to discuss the usefulness of the debate to voters. In effect, the voter tends to be shunted aside in coverage

of presidential campaigns while, at the very last minute, the media urge
everyone to Be Sure To Vote.

The Lack of "Accountability" News

Entman (1989, p. 4) argues that "despite their frequently bellicose
and suspicious stance toward [every president since 1964], the media
[have] failed to make the government's decisions visible and leaders
accountable at the very times spirited inquiry was most desperately
needed. News coverage challenging these presidents' most disastrous
decisions was too little, too obscure, too late."

Using the index to the Vanderbilt Television News Archives, Entman
showed that ABC, NBC, and CBS had spent far less time covering
government domestic policies "and ever more about heartwarming or
poignant events of emotional gratification but little political meaning"
(1989, p. 119).

While Entman never clearly defines what he means by "accountability news," it appears that what he means is news that has at least
these two properties: (1) it connects specific officials and agencies with
their actions (proposals, policies, etc.), and (2) it makes the connection
soon enough for other political actors—including citizens—to have a
chance to try to reverse, change, or otherwise modify the action.

Citizens' motivation to participate increases when they are allowed
a glimpse into the policy process *before the policy becomes fixed in
stone.* After the policy is firmly in place, members of the mass are forced
into a *reactive* mode, rather than a *proactive* one. Especially if one is
a little cynical about the willingness of government to change its policies, a constantly reactive frame of mind can discourage one's sense
of political effectiveness (see especially Downs, 1957, and Schattschneider, 1960). Clearly, it is in the short-term self-interest of politicians to avoid being held responsible for unpopular actions and to
obscure or delay mass awareness of the implications of such actions,
so that the lack of accountability news cannot be blamed entirely on
the news media. Nevertheless, since it is the self-proclaimed role of
the media to hold public officials accountable for *their* actions, we may
be entitled to hold the news media responsible for their own inactions.

Once again, the result of a lack of "accountability news" would be
to enlarge the discrepancy between mass and effective opinion. We
turn now to a closely related inaction or "nondecision" (a decision *not*
to do something) by modern journalists.

Waiting outside the Lobby

Journalists covering the U.S. Congress and federal executive agencies,
as well as journalists covering state government, are far more likely to

report the *results* of interest group lobbying than they are to cover the lobbying *process* itself (see Lemert, 1981, chapter 7). When there is no coverage of the lobbying process, those members of the mass who depend on the media are once again denied a chance to participate until it seems to be too late to make any difference.

What might "process" coverage be like? One example would be a story about a "mobilization alert" sent to supporters by (say) the National Rifle Association, the banking industry, or the beer industry. Each of these groups has used such a mobilizing message (Lemert, 1981, pp. 122–133) in recent years. Typically, the interest group is trying to mobilize letters and telegrams from constituents to legislators or administrators, whose names and addresses usually are provided the recipients of these essentially *private* messages. These calls for participation are sent directly (via U.S. mail and other means) only to people who are already members of the interest group or are otherwise identified by the interest group as generally supportive of the position it wishes to see enacted (see Morin, 1991). In some cases, the effort to mobilize supporters goes well beyond merely providing names and addresses; some interest groups provide toll-free numbers and operators who will convert the phone call, free, into a lettergram to the appropriate legislator.

Since the mobilization messages to supporters ultimately are designed to influence public policy, they are private only in the sense that they are *covert*. They ought to be fair game for news coverage, and it is hard to believe that any competent political journalist couldn't easily tap into the mobilization process while it is still going on. Among many ways this can be done is to check with targeted legislators or their staff members to see if they are *currently* receiving a wave of "organized" (interest-group-stimulated) mail. As we've already seen, legislators almost automatically keep separate tallies of "organized" and other constituent mail.

Such a news story about the mobilization process almost certainly would alert media-dependent members of the mass who disagreed with the interest group's goal and would give them the chance to express their own opinion to the same "targeted" policymakers. As a result, if enough members of the mass expressed an opinion opposing the one mobilized by the interest group, *effective opinion* would be *changed*.

Ironically, we often see news coverage of the impact of interest-group mobilization after the policy decision has already been made. At least two things can result from such after-it's-too-late coverage: (1) the interest group's reputation for power is enhanced (a reputation it can and probably will use) and (2) citizens' feelings may be reinforced that they are left out in the cold—not even inside the building. And certainly not in the lobby.

The "Official Source" Syndrome

One of the ways journalists define "objectivity" in their news coverage is by narrowly defining who can be a source for controversial public-sector news stories. As a result, there is a strong bias toward giving sources with status and official positions a much greater opportunity to initiate, and react to, public issues. Since such sources generally will hold more or less conventional policy views, a further result is that radical and/or unconventional views ordinarily will not have the same chance to be introduced into public policy debates (see Gans, 1979).

How and why does this bias favoring "official" sources occur? Journalists' "craft attitudes" (Lemert, 1970) draw a clear distinction between news and editorial (opinion) content. Opinions are not allowed in the news unless they are attributed to a source who is "qualified" to express them. (In contrast, the media can express their own opinion, without attribution, on the editorial page or in a broadcast editorial.)

Given this starting point, when opinions are expressed in the news the reporter needs to worry primarily about (1) the accuracy of the quotes and paraphrases, and (2) the qualification of the source to have and express those opinions. In practice, the reporter reduces his or her vulnerability to accusations of bias by selecting the most obvious sources. Assuming that obvious (to journalists) sources are used, then the only vulnerability the journalist has concerns the accuracy of the statements attributed to sources. Being "objective" thus is reduced to being an accurate note-taker.

Many researchers have documented this "official source" bias in the news, most of them through analysis of actual news content (e.g., Gans, 1979; Atwater & Fico, 1986; and Brown, Bybee, Wearden, & Straughan, 1982) and a few by eliminating other explanations through an experimental design (Schwantes & Lemert, 1978).

We've already described the problem of non-issues, where certain issues never reach the public agenda because there is no news coverage of them. Activists who would like to create awareness of an issue have a major problem if they lack the credentials to be obvious, "official" sources. Lacking ready access to the news because they lack credentials, they are strongly tempted to create events, such as protest demonstrations, that compel news coverage. When they do this, however, they are likely to find that the reasons for the demonstration are not covered while the demonstration-as-public-disturbance is. Journalists are preoccupied with whether arrests were made, what the demonstrators looked like, and so on, not with what policy arguments (if any) were made by demonstrators. In effect, this kind of "disturbance" coverage transforms the demonstrators into the issue, rather than the cause they are advocating. As the Vietnam War protests demonstrated, this issue transformation can isolate protestors from the larger body of people who might have agreed with their cause (see Gitlin, 1980; and Scammon & Wattenberg, 1970) if only the news focus had been on the reasons for the demonstration instead of on the tactics of the demonstrators.

IMPLICATIONS FOR JOURNALISTS

This chapter sets forward a variety of ways that journalists discourage both political interest and political involvement. It is in this context that public affairs journalists should consider several ominous facts, all of them concerning signs that more and more members of the mass are deciding that it isn't worth their while to attend to the news. (1) Both newspaper readership and per-household subscriptions have been in decline for decades (see Meyer, 1985). (2) The reliable audience for network television news has gotten progressively older, and even fewer Americans say that "yesterday" they watched network news than say they read the newspaper (*American media*, 1990, p. 3). (3) More young people than ever before are avoiding public affairs news (*Age of indifference*, 1990).

These trends suggest that both print and broadcast news media have a vested economic interest in increasing the proportions of the mass who will follow news about government.

Then why the many journalistic acts of commission and omission that discourage political interest and involvement? The answer probably lies in the power and apparent usefulness of journalists' long-unexamined craft traditions, combined with both journalists' and management's equating of their short-term interests with their long-term ones. They are not the same; in fact, they may very well be in direct conflict.

For example, we've already reported some evidence, earlier in this chapter, that audience members want—but do not expect—their newspaper to change its practices regarding the reporting of mobilizing information. Yet journalists seem afraid to provide MI when doing so might bring complaints from their news sources or other influential interest groups.

It is true that politicians and other elites can bring intense, short-term economic and political pressure on journalists. But these elites have shown repeatedly that they can and will adjust to what the news media do, because they literally can't live without the media. In contrast, the adjustments being made slowly by more and more members of the mass audience suggest that they, at least, think they are learning to live very well, indeed, without the public affairs news media.

The rhetoric of journalists often invokes their role as a kind of representative (the word often used is "surrogate") of the people and an agent acting on behalf of the people's "right to know." However, research into journalists' actual behavior suggests very strongly that journalists more often *act* as if they were part of the political system toward which many Americans feel alienated. From the point of view of the audience, political journalists are part of the problem, not part of the solution.

In this section, we have tried to outline an argument that journalists need to look beyond protecting their short-term relations with other elites and consider both the ethical and long-term economic reasons for changing their behavior, which often can best be described as elitist. It is hard to say how many more readers, listeners, and viewers will drift away from public affairs news if journalism continues its long-established habits. As we've seen, television news and newspapers already are seeing massive numbers drifting away. The longer public affairs journalists wait to reconsider these habits, the harder it will be to win back the audience that, through advertising and other revenues, pays their salaries.

IMPLICATIONS FOR POLICYMAKERS

Because they generally rely on participation-based expressions of opinion, policymakers can readily assess the relative *salience* (importance) of issues by comparing the amount of participation each issue arouses. The more salient the issue, the riskier and more dangerous it is to make policy choices when expressed opinion is divided, since that means opinion is very polarized.

However, those policy choices have the best chance to succeed when policymakers can find opportunities for compromise and consensus. Does relying on participation-based expressions of opinion, rather than the polls, provide policymakers with their best chance of finding ways to frame issues to win the maximum amount of support? True, the polls mix together the non-opinions of the inert and uninformed mass citizenry with the opinions of (1) the active and the informed plus (2) the passive but informed. But somewhere in that larger mass of people there may be opportunities not so easily found among polarized activists.

Policymakers need to be aware that, like journalists, they have a vested interest in improving levels of mass interest and public participation. The legitimacy of popular government depends on public participation in both the Election and the Influence Frameworks. As even the turnout in elections continues a long slide downward, more than a few people have begun to notice. A president elected by a majority that converts into fewer than a third of voting-age Americans is resting her or his legitimacy on a minority that is outnumbered two to one by people who are essentially uncommitted spectators with a weakened sense of the legitimacy of that office. The legitimacy problem may be even more extreme for state and local politicians, who are often elected by even smaller numbers of participants.

Legitimacy, the law, and force are ways that government can govern citizens. Legitimacy is a precious commodity, since it leads to unforced acquiescence or cooperation. If legitimacy fails, ultimately the law fails without the use of armed force. In very cold-blooded terms, legitimacy is the cheapest way to gain citizens' cooperation. Clearly, then, it is in the long-term interest of policymakers to encourage legitimacy through increasing popular interest and participation. Once again, we have the short-term advantages of minimizing popular participation in conflict with long-term vested interest—this time for the policymakers.

What can policymakers do to encourage interest and participation? Policymakers can help journalists provide political MI more often by encouraging them to put it in their news stories—and not complaining if and when phone calls and floods of letters come in during a controversy. Policymakers also ought to be looking at the ways that ritualized opportunities for public input, such as public hearings, are conducted. For example, why can't government offices provide "tip sheets on testifying to us" ahead of time to people who are planning to testify at such hearings? Maybe both policymakers and participants would gain from such a service.

Both journalists and policymakers need to take a hard look at their ways of doing business. Both they—and the people they serve—would gain from that new look at old habits.

4

Interest Groups in the News

Lucig Danielian

An underlying and important guarantee of pluralism in a liberal democracy is the availability of diverse information that allows citizens
to understand policy issues so action can be taken and social change
can progress smoothly. These mostly unstated pluralist assumptions of
access to information and access to the means of production of information underlie much of the study of the mass media and research in
the social and political sciences in the United States. When these assumptions are closely analyzed, a better understanding emerges of media processes in relationship to social change.

This chapter begins with a review of interest group politics—a research domain that is central to analyses of policymaking and yet is
mostly left untouched by mass media scholars. The bulk of the chapter
is a discussion of the literature on how interest groups are represented
in the news media, why access is limited, and the effects of this on
political participation.

INFORMATION AND INTEREST GROUPS
IN DEMOCRACIES

Interest groups are important to the realization of democratic ideals
because "once the political community grows beyond the manageable

boundaries of the town meeting, some kind of private associational life becomes essential to democracy" (Schlozman & Tierney, 1986, p. 4).

Because a plurality of interested voices taking stands on various issues is an important assumption of our democratic state, one necessary question for analysis is whether or not such pluralities do indeed exist in the various forums for political participation, especially in the mass media. But such an evaluation of just what constitutes an adequate or sufficient representation of interests is not easy. When the basic individualistic assumption of "one person, one vote" is applied to other forms of political activity such as interest group membership, the resulting ideal formulation is that all citizens should be able to be equally active on all issues (Schlozman & Tierney, 1986). Such a formulation, however, is no more of a guarantee for participation through interest group representation than is "one person, one vote" a guarantee for participation through enfranchisement.[1] The question of equality is made even more complex when individual preferences and their intensities are included. Moreover, all groups are not equal; for example, some groups are made up of members with more political skills and contacts.

Democratic theory postulates something like the following: Individuals should have equal opportunity for participation in organized interest groups on issues about which they care, all organizations representing any stance on any issue should have equal opportunity for participation in politics, and the ideal state of equality for organized interest group participation in political spheres through the mass media should lead to at least a balanced representation of groups in the media, regardless of whether or not the groups representing various interests are themselves equal.

But what constitutes satisfactory levels of balance in media representations? McQuail (1986) has proposed criteria for defining and determining levels of diversity in the media product. These criteria include examining the quantity of channels, the range of sources in channels, and the volume of various channels and sources of political communication. That is, both the quantity and quality of source representation are necessary components to determine "whether the media offer opportunities for politically diverse audiences and/or audience interests to flourish" (1986, p. 143).

McQuail proposes two general media structures that are possible within pluralist frameworks: "external diversity" and "internal diversity." External diversity exists when there are strong differences between channels but homogeneity within channels; internal diversity exists when channels are homogeneous and the content within channels is diverse, that is, impartial and balanced. He further distinguishes between two forms of balanced representation of sources, "open" and "reflexive." Open media channels provide equal access to all "serious and legitimate" viewpoints and are associated with the external model of diversity. In reflexive media channels, access reflects proportionately the distributions of existing public opinion; such access is associated with the internal model. The open model promotes social change while the reflexive model leads to the mainstreaming of public opinion, according to McQuail.

Democratic theory assumes that political discourse through the mass media meets one or more of the criteria of access for sources, diversity of opinions, and/or a balance in the representation of interests.

INTEREST GROUPS IN PLURALIST STATES

Even before the advent of television as a dominant medium for political discourse, Truman (1958), one of the founders of interest group theory, concluded that the activation of these potential groups depended upon the mass media. But it is Schattschneider's (1960) analysis of the modern democratic state, in which a powerful conceptualization is developed, that still remains to be extended to theories of the mass media. He postulates that conflict is at the center of politics and that "the outcome of all conflict is determined by the scope of its contagion" (1960, p. 2). The spectator audience is as important as the actual dueling political participants because the potential always exists that the public will be brought into the conflict and, thus, will broaden the scope of discourse and change the political outcome. Therefore, the best political strategy, in cases where influence through direct access to decision-makers is possible, is one in which an interest group manages to control the scale of conflict on an issue by keeping decision-making private and behind closed doors.

Extrapolation of Schattschneider's thesis to the mass media suggests that still other groups may use media access as a strategy for bringing public opinion into decision-making.[2] And in a society in which mass media outlets are increasing in number, the potential importance of public opinion—and how it is formed—may also be increasing.

The fact that most decision-making, in deals that can be performed with a narrow range of participants, takes place outside the scope of the media spotlight must also be taken into consideration. In another powerful insight, Edelman (1964) explains that while positive and sympathetic political rhetoric is often produced by politicians on behalf of those interests with the least influence, political decisions about the actual distribution and redistribution of limited resources generally are made quietly on behalf of well-organized and influential interests. (See Lemert's discussion of the "Influence Framework" in Chapter 3.)

It is the media spotlight that can activate public opinion. And activating public opinion is not the same difficult process as activating formal and organized interest groups. Indeed, it is likely that some of those groups that seek mass media access are doing so in order to broaden the scope of conflict and to change political outcomes because they do not have the resources necessary for direct access to decision-making that takes place behind closed doors. Public opinion (and the mass media impact on its formation) must be analyzed for its own potential political power.

Interest group politics can be defined as "the wide variety of organizations that seek joint ends through political action . . . with collective goals that are politically relevant" (Schlozman & Tierney, 1986, p. 10). One useful way to analyze the representation of interests in politics is to divide them into two broad categories: economic, private interests versus noneconomic, citizen or public interests (Schlozman & Tierney, 1986; Danielian, 1989).

Although the organized interest group community in Washington, D.C., has grown substantially during the past 20 years, groups tend to be skewed toward the predominant representation of economic interests (Schlozman & Tierney, 1986).[3] This business group bias has been noted by other researchers (e.g., Olson, 1965; Key, 1958; Lindblom, 1968), but no one sums it up better than Schattschneider: "The flaw in the pluralist heaven is that the heavenly chorus sings with a strong upper class accent" (1960, p. 35).

Both economic and noneconomic groups consider media relations as central to lobbying. Although there is an unfortunate paucity of research in this area, Schlozman and Tierney (1986) found that 86 percent of those groups represented in Washington, D.C., indicated that they used talking with the media as a technique of influence. When asked which of 27 various influence techniques were used more than in the past, talking with the media ranked first: 68 percent of all groups used this technique more than in the past. However, when the distinction between economic and noneconomic interests is used, other significant differences emerge. Seventy-two percent of corporations and only 46 percent of citizen action groups employ public relations experts on staff. However, 50 percent of citizens' groups and only 19 percent of the groups representing corporate interests consider journalists an important channel for information and consultation.

Such findings support the importance of taking into consideration the scope of issues and who controls how issues are presented. Business interests may directly control news media coverage of issues through paid media access or through the direct financial support of "independent" think tanks that produce experts used as "objective" sources by the news media. And citizen action groups may be more dependent upon contacts with newsworkers who, through various gatekeeping and selection processes, ultimately control the news product.

Whatever the form of media relations, or management, groups consider media representation an important source of political influence— the mass media are at least perceived as being central in decision-making processes.

INTEREST GROUPS AND THE MASS MEDIA

Questions of Access

Unlike the presumably easily attained direct democratic participation of the past, individuals today often gain access to others through organizations, and it is assumed that this access to others is generally achieved through the mass media. The mass media can even be thought of as "a functional substitute for concrete group contact, for the now impossible meeting of the whole" (Alexander, 1982, p. 18).

However, groups and the issues they promote can gain access to this public "meeting place" only if the mass media are willing to communicate them. For example, most citizen interest groups do not gain access to the news media easily, and the access that is achieved is tempered by how the media choose to cover groups and the issues they promote. There are two primary factors in determining news coverage of interest group sources: (1) the ways in which the mass media produce news and (2) the levels of media-related resources that organized interest groups possess.

The news media's gatekeeping and agenda-setting functions can play important roles as barriers, or facilitators, in the political process, as can newsmaking's ideological assumptions, economic imperatives, practical constraints, and professionalism. Meanwhile, a group's ability to be newsworthy requires specialized skills and resources that go hand in hand with economic power (Gans, 1979). Therefore, it is important to analyze the mass media themselves as powerful institutions in our social and political processes. As McQuail explains, the media are not "merely neutral 'message-carrying' networks," but are, rather, "themselves separate institutions with their own objectives to pursue, their own power and institutional dynamics" (1979, p. 77).

In this regard, Lemert (1981) provides a useful definition of power. It is the

relative ability to block or initiate public discussion of potential issues, to influence perceptions of public opinion held by key decision-makers once an issue "goes public," to define issues and options under discussion, to influence participation by others, and to induce decision-makers to adopt the desired policy. (p. 163)

Players in the political arena have such power to the extent that they "consciously or unconsciously create or reinforce barriers to the public airing of policy conflicts" (Bachrach & Baratz, 1970, p. 8). Both the mass media and organized interest groups have the potential, depending on their status, for wielding such power in defining the range of discussion on issues.

The importance of the mass media role in how society does or does not change can be seen clearly within the context of questions surrounding the mechanisms for defining what is and is not a newsworthy issue, what aspects of an issue are appropriate for reporting, how prominently and with what consistency an issue and surrounding events are covered, which sources and therefore interests are used to define an issue, and how these sources are covered in the news. These points of focus have implications for ascertaining the scope of issues and, hence, how members of the public participate in decision-making through the mass media.

Although it may occur directly or indirectly and through mechanisms not yet fully understood, the public does participate in decision-making processes through its opinions. V. O. Key (1961) reviewed the various evolving conceptualizations of public opinion up to his own analysis— from democratic theory's ideal of rational democracy, to Lippmann's insights destroying the "straw man" of public opinion, to the psychological work on manipulation, and finally to C. W. Mills's formulation of public opinion tagging behind elite consensus.

Key insists that governments cannot ignore public opinion, which he defines as "those opinions held by private persons which governments find it prudent to heed" (1961, p. 14). Democracy, proclaims Key, is not a hoax. And, indeed, some important recent research described below lends some credibility to the notion that public opinion does affect public policy, as well as the idea that the media affect public opinion.

Public Opinion and the Mass Media

Benjamin Page and Robert Shapiro have been involved during the past several years in an important and ongoing research project focused on public opinion, its effects on policy, and mass media effects on public opinion (1982, 1983; Page, Shapiro, & Dempsey, 1987). Much of their research is based on a large collection of polling questions that have been used at least twice using identical wording. Their first study

(1982) analyzed the public opinion responses to several hundred repeated policy items from the years 1953 to 1979. The researchers found no significant changes in public opinion for half of the items, and half of those items that did change significantly moved less than 10 percentage points. Those policy items that changed more than 10 percent mostly represented gradual shifts in policy preferences involving trends toward a general liberalization of social attitudes linked to changes in the social and economic environments. Most notable were policy items focusing on the issues of civil rights, abortion, civil liberties, capital punishment, and social welfare programs. Public opinion was found to be generally stable and quite rational.

Page and Shapiro (1983) next analyzed the amount of congruence between those issues with statistically significant opinion changes and actual policy changes. They found that there is substantial congruence between opinion and policy when opinion changes are large and sustained and when issues are salient. They also found evidence that opinion tends to move before policy. However, they tempered this conclusion: "Even to the degree that policy does react to public opinion, one should be cautious about bestowing the normative imprimatur of 'democracy' without taking account of the quality of that opinion: what kind of information it is based on, what has influenced it, and perhaps how closely it corresponds with objective standards of citizens' interest" (p. 189).

In order to begin addressing these questions, Page, Shapiro, and Dempsey (1987) next examined how the media affect public opinion change. They selected 80 pairs of identically worded polling questions representing a variety of foreign and domestic policy issues from 1969 to 1982 and created a database of all sources used in network news coverage about the policy issues from two months before the first polling time through the second polling time. Using regression analyses, they found positive media effects on public opinion for three of 10 news source types: editorial commentary, experts, and popular presidents. Interest groups tended to produce negative effects on public opinion; that is, public opinion on issues actually changed in a direction opposite those stances taken by interest groups. The researchers concluded that they had identified the main influences on short- and medium-term opinion change; the news sources alone accounted for almost half the variance in public opinion change for the 80 issues studied.

While such findings may be new to political scientists, strong media effects on the public have been established by communication researchers during the past 20 years or so. However, mass communication researchers have taken an interesting and fruitful detour from directly analyzing opinion changes (and, one might conclude, have yet to find their way back to the main road), resulting in a large body of research on media agenda-setting.

Agenda-Setting and Interest Groups

Maxwell McCombs and Donald Shaw (1972) circumvented the argument about the minimal effects of the mass media on opinions and attitudes by focusing their research on what they defined as the first steps of opinion change, awareness and, especially, cognitions. Agenda-setting borrowed from Bernard Cohen (1963) the simple idea that "the media may not be successful in telling us what to think, but they are stunningly successful in telling us what to think about." And, indeed, nearly all agenda-setting research supports just such a notion.[4]

Shanto Iyengar and Donald Kinder (1987) have produced a series of studies that support strong agenda-setting effects for television. In a series of experiments in which issue saliences in national network news broadcasts were manipulated, the researchers found that subjects regarded the target issue as being more important for the country. They "cared more about it, believed that government should do more about it, reported stronger feelings about it, and were much more likely to identify it as one of the country's most important problems" (p. 112).

Also, issues presented in lead stories were more influential on personal issue saliences than nonlead stories. And in a reversal of previous findings by others, Iyengar and Kinder found agenda-setting to be stronger for issues considered obtrusive, or issues with which subjects had personal experience.

By asking subjects to rate the objectivity and accuracy of the national newscasts viewed, Iyengar and Kinder discovered that viewers who think that the networks are authoritative sources for information were more influenced by the news stories than were those who rated the network newscasts less highly. It is important to determine in future research whether or not this finding holds up for specific news sources. As Page and Shapiro explain, it could be that those sources positively affecting public opinion are presented in a more credible manner in the news. Iyengar and Kinder's finding of stronger television agenda-setting effects for as simple a factor as placement in news broadcasts is a case in point. Such findings should lead social scientists away from the idea of the news media as "neutral transmitters." Indeed, when sources such as interest groups do gain access, the way in which they are presented may be as important as, or more important than, anything they have to say.

There does seem to be a growing sense among mass communication scholars that agenda-setting research is, at worst, at a stalemate or, at best, at a challenging crossroads.[5] But the sheer weight of the evidence supporting agenda-setting effects seems to ensure its central role in research and theory, especially if research cataloging intervening effects at the individual level is left behind in favor of broadening the agenda-setting hypothesis in the spirit of its own original agenda.[6] Although agenda-setting theory is rarely invoked in this context, it may be possible to think of it as a useful bridge between communication research and political theories: Agenda-setting assumes that mass communication is central to political and social processes. As McCombs and Shaw (1977) explained in an earlier work:

In a society as large as the United States, if a group does not have access to an interested mass medium—either through the intrinsic appeal of its special interest or through the availability of extensive financial resources—we simply will never learn of its concern. Or, as was the case with Vietnam and civil rights, concerned groups will have to take to the streets to convert their concern into an event that the news media will translate as an issue. Unfortunately, the news media are more attentive to news events than new ideas. So, the study of the agenda-setting process is crucial to our attempts to achieve a better interchange of ideas and a smoother process of social change within our society. (pp. 150–151)

They set the agenda for quite a bit of research in this passage. Most importantly, research that determines the news media agenda and specific sources on issues is one way to determine how some of these processes work, including what and who impacts the news media agenda, and therefore public agendas.

ORGANIZED INTEREST GROUPS AND THE NEWS MEDIA

Organized interest groups are important for pluralist theory, and although most communication research works under the unexamined assumptions of pluralism, little attention by mass communication scholars has focused on interest groups as news media sources. However, there is a small body of important work with findings on why certain groups attempt to gain access (Goldenberg, 1975; Tichenor, Donohue & Olien, 1980), the effects of news coverage on group processes (Gitlin, 1980; Tuchman, 1978), the effects of news coverage on the public and on newsworkers' perceptions of groups (Shoemaker, 1982, 1984), and the representation of interest groups on network television news (Danielian, 1989).

Organized Groups and Access

In her study of resource-poor groups, the political scientist Edie Goldenberg (1975) researched the conditions under which groups attempt to gain access. Distinguishing between factors such as the properties of the group, the target audience, and particular situation, Goldenberg found that the greater a group's resources, the greater its ability to "make the papers."

Resource-poor groups seek access to the press in order to achieve a variety of goals, including establishing the group's identity; projecting specific images; conveying information; publicly identifying the group's enemies and targets; building credibility; and building resources such as visibility, funding, moral superiority, and reputation.

Groups are most likely to seek access when goals are widely shared by a group's members; when the group possesses key resources such as experience, a sense of efficacy, and funds; and when group leaders are willing to exploit these resources in order to gain access. These groups seek press coverage in order to access different target audiences. Resource-poor interest groups mostly attempt to reach large, distant, and geographically dispersed audiences, elected officials, and the newspaper's readers. Goldenberg found that press coverage was attained successfully when the group's goal deviated from the social norm, when it affected many people, when it was a variation on a theme already established by the media, and when the goal was specific but not technical.

A more recent survey of ten organized interest groups in the Los Angeles area found that those groups that have positive attitudes toward the news media and that rate themselves as successful in gaining media access also have high levels of media-related resources. Their issues and goals also fit within the mainstream of political activity (Danielian, 1986). All ten groups included the public at large as part of the audience they wanted to reach through media access, but most groups were also trying to reach more narrowly defined publics such as elected officials and past supporters. Nearly all of the groups named personal contacts with the media as the most important strategy for successful access, and named credibility as the most important group attribute for access.

Tichenor, Donohue, and Olien (1980) collected data on 19 small communities that were embroiled in controversial issues. The researchers began their work with the assumption that the press "is an integral subsystem within the total system, and its strong linkages with other system components impinge upon it as much as it impinges upon them, if not more" (p. 217).

They found that in small communities, groups use the press as a device for defining problems and for creating awareness about issues for the community at large in order to affect decision-making. However, they also found that the small town press played its own significant role in these political communication processes. In fact, the performance of the press "typically becomes part of the controversy." This controversy stems from the fact that community media tend to reflect the perspectives of business and other dominant elites and tend to back the winners in conflicts, rather than less powerful citizen interest groups. The researchers conclude that the power to influence policy decisions is in the hands of elites, and not citizen action groups, both in business and in the press.

Based on their findings, Tichenor, Donohue, and Olien tentatively hypothesize that interest groups probably go through stages of experimentation with various media strategies based both on their resources and on their experiences with what works in gaining access to the press and, therefore, the policy-making process.

Media Effects on Organized Interests

Tichenor, Donohue, and Olien (1980) also conjecture from their data that groups may "become more conservative in their tactics as they widen their organizational base. Todd Gitlin (1981) found just such mainstreaming effects in his study of the news media and the Students for a Democratic Society (SDS). Gitlin notes that the news media are potential political weapons of the disenfranchised, but he warns that groups begin to perform according to journalistic standards as soon as they begin to discover the media's power to amplify their concerns.

However, following media conventions in order to attain access often undermines groups and compromises their "power to determine their own destinies, their leadership, and even their politics" (p. 53). There are several specific ways in which the media affected the SDS. For example, the media generated a membership surge that attracted individuals who identified with the antiwar image portrayed by the media rather than persons who might identify with the grass-roots SDS ideology of participatory democracy (which was not a focus of media coverage); the media certified leaders and transformed them into celebrity figures, a process that alienated leaders from the rank and file membership because it contradicted the goals of equal participation in decision-making; and the media helped to inflate the rhetoric and militancy of the SDS by providing the most coverage to its most outrageous activities.

Through its coverage of the SDS, the media were able simultaneously to amplify and to contain the group's images. Interest groups are concerned about this power of the press. In the survey on ten Los Angeles groups (Danielian, 1986), more than half of the groups noted the difficulties that emerge because of the contradictions inherent in attempting to both promote the group's goals and obtain positive media access. The director of one group explained that he was successful in gaining media access only when he diluted his group's stances on the issues, but then he had to respond to accusations from the membership that he was pandering to the media.

In Gaye Tuchman's analysis (1978), social movements pass through distinct phases, progressing from informal groups to complex voluntary organizations. As groups evolve, coverage of their activities changes "inasmuch as news organizations coordinate their news nets with legitimate institutions" (1978, p. 134). That is, the more legitimate the organization, the more positive the news coverage. Tuchman's research on news coverage of the women's movement is a good example of this access problem because, as she explains, there was a definite discrepancy between the approaches of newsworkers, who were men, and the participants of the women's movement. This gap contributed to the media's ability to transform the movement and its issues as they were shaped into news stories. And because news is centered around the male concern for a hierarchy of events rather than the articulation of issues, much of the early work of the women's movement, such as consciousness raising, was left uncovered. When the movement was covered it was with such traditional news techniques as the "first woman to _____ (fill in the blank)." Such coverage portrayed the movement as reformist in nature rather than as a revolutionary movement aimed at altering the fundamental relations between women and men.

Once it was successfully institutionalized, Tuchman found that the women's movement was limited in its ability to carry forth radical issues. As with SDS, the women's movement was co-opted by the frames of the conventional news narrative. "Once framed within the web of facticity, a social movement cannot undercut the news net by challenging the legitimacy of established institutions" (1978, p. 154).

Monica Morris predicted as early as 1973 that the media's treatment of the feminist movement would lead to "co-optation through respectability" and that the result would be only slight and slow changes in the status of women. Morris correctly predicted that the media's strategy in the long run would begin with a general blackout of the women's movement, followed by frivolous treatment when the movement persisted, and ending in a stage in which the news media would publish those goals that least threatened the status quo while deemphasizing the movement's more revolutionary aims.

A more recent study compared Los Angeles Times coverage of the Los Angeles chapter of the National Organization for Women (NOW) with the group's own newsletter coverage of key events from 1970 through 1983 and found her prediction to be accurate (Danielian, 1988). The Los Angeles Times coverage of the events became more similar to that of the newsletters as the NOW chapter's purposes became linked to mainstream political processes. For example, the Times no longer refers to women protesters with such sexist adjectives as "buxom lasses," as it did in front-page coverage in 1970. When NOW endorsed Walter Mondale for his 1984 presidential bid (the first NOW approval of a mainstream presidential candidate), the front-page story focused on the strength of NOW and the value of its political work.

Media Effects on the Public Perception of Groups

Determining differential media effects based on the type of news coverage accorded to groups is another important research focus. Outside of the work of Pamela Shoemaker, little research has been performed on how news stories about interest groups may affect public attitudes toward groups.

In two experiments, Shoemaker (1982) found that varying news treatments of deviant groups can affect individual perceptions of group legitimacy. Four dimensions of group legitimacy emerged from her factor analysis: evaluation, legality, viability, and stability. Those groups portrayed in a serious and fair manner in news stories were given higher scores by subjects on the measures of legitimacy than groups that were ridiculed and portrayed as eccentric.

Shoemaker (1984) also studied the relationship between newspaper editors' perceptions of deviant groups and media treatment of groups. This study is based on data culled from a survey of 56 editors and a content analysis of news coverage of 11 groups with differing levels of deviance. Shoemaker found that those groups perceived to be deviant by editors were also the groups with the least favorable newspaper coverage and that the coverage portrayed the groups as illegal and nonviable.

It can be assumed that a group's ability to affect public opinion positively is linked to the public's perception of the group's legitimacy and that this public perception is affected by the media. However, in the only study linking sources in the news to public opinion, Page and his colleagues (1987) found that interest groups tended to produce negative changes in public opinion. Shoemaker's results lend credibility to the notion that the type of coverage given to groups is another important factor in this process.

Interests in the News

A mapping of the representation of interest groups on network television news programs was performed recently in a secondary analysis of the Page, Shapiro, and Dempsey data described earlier (Danielian, 1989). The data include all sources presented by network news broadcasts for 80 diverse foreign and domestic issues covering a 15-year time span beginning with 1969.

Interest groups make up 10 percent of network news coverage of all sources, with the groups most covered being business and, surprisingly, citizen action interests. However, there are some differences in how these interest groups are covered in the news. Citizen action groups are covered as representing more extreme stances on issues and are the group type most associated with acts of civil disobedience. Business interests, in contrast, are most often associated with neutral statements and are the sources that present virtually all statistical information. These specific differences have implications for the ways in which these groups and the various interests they represent are perceived by the general public and elite decision-makers. One hypothesis is that groups portrayed in acts of civil disobedience are perceived as less credible or legitimate than those groups associated with neutral statements, suggesting, in turn, that these groups would have differential effects on public and elite opinions on policies.

Although numerous interest group sources are used by the networks in their nightly reports, the result is not balanced coverage. In nearly half of the 80 issues, the networks covered either only economic interest groups or only noneconomic groups. The result is that many issues are presented to the public through the news media within a limited framework of political discourse.[7] Moreover, those interest groups covered in the news are not representative of the population at large. For example, business interests are overrepresented and the interests of the working class are underrepresented in network news broadcasts.

Journalistic norms of what constitutes an appropriate source on an issue are at play when reporters decide who to select from their Rolodexes. It is not yet clear if the voices of less well established sources are heard by reporters and editors. In fact, it may be the case that the journalistic norms of newsworthiness stand in the way of more balanced reporting. As just one example, by seeking out sources that are authoritative and dependable in order to meet the journalistic norm of credibility while working on deadline, reporters may be ignoring voices not already established unless they are unusually loud or distinctive.

NEWS MEDIA CONSTRAINTS AND INTEREST
GROUP ACCESS

Although radically dissenting opinions do gain access (whether or not the resulting coverage is balanced and accurate), the news media tend to exclude those issues and sources that seriously conflict with the status quo or sources that are extremely controversial and outside the mainstream of political discourse (Hall, 1979; Gitlin, 1980; Tuchman, 1978).

There is a definite contradiction between the democratic ideals of the free marketplace of ideas, for example those ideals represented in the social responsibility theory of the press, and the media's overriding purpose of profit-making. This contradiction tends to lead to news coverage with an overwhelming bias in favor of the prevailing social order. But according to Miliband (1969), "There is nothing particularly surprising about the character and role of the mass media in advanced capitalist society" (p. 236). The media fulfill an intended conservative purpose, "given the economic and political context in which they function" (p. 236).

Hall (1979) defines three key ideological functions of the media: (1) the selective construction of social knowledge; (2) the production of a constant inventory of society's plurality in order to define that which is legitimate and that which is not, rather than to advance the public's knowledge with diverse information; and (3) the production of consensus and the construction of legitimacy, "not so much the finished article itself, but the whole process of argument, exchange, debate, consultation and speculation by which it emerges" (1979, p. 342).

However, economic and ideological explanations are not sufficient explanations for answering questions of media access. News production also establishes its own image of society's order through a myriad of social, professional, and practical pressures.

Television news stories focus on reporting "facts" by filtering most information through "the two sides" or what is defined as "both sides" (Altheide, 1976; Nimmo & Combs, 1983). Because competitive organizational and economic imperatives necessitate stories that can maintain large audiences, newsmakers believe that images should be easily consumed, and this emphasis leads to stories that best fit into traditional and easily recognized narrative plot lines (Epstein, 1973). The resulting coverage tends to focus on the event rather than on the issues and underlying conditions involved, the individual rather than the group, conflict rather than consensus, and the facts that advance the story line rather than those that explain the situation (Gitlin, 1980).

According to Epstein (1973), television news frames tend to reduce complex issues so that change seems relatively easy to accomplish. The more complex reasons for change, such as economic feasibility, minority interests, or political reverberations in other social, economic, and cultural areas, are not easily portrayed in television's visual presentations, and therefore, are mostly left uncovered.

There are also purely practical constraints on who gets to make news in both the press and on television. Powerful sources such as leading public officials are most depended upon by reporters because they are quickly available, reliable, productive, articulate, able to supply suitable information, and authoritative (Gans, 1979). The use of such sources is also efficient, another essential component of deciding what is news. Nevertheless, the news value of "journalistic balance" persists as a central factor in the selection of sources (Gans, 1979). Reporters attempt to achieve balance through story mixture and through variety in subjects, geographic locations, demographics, and political affiliations or stances. But such techniques can result in news that is fundamentally unbalanced. The result is news that reports on those at the top of the social hierarchy and those at the bottom who may threaten the prevailing power structure (Gans, 1979; Danielian, 1989). The resulting array and placement of sources on policy issues that are presented for public and elite consumption can therefore lead to the blocking of fundamental policy change at structural levels in society.

IMPLICATIONS FOR POLITICAL PARTICIPATION

The focus of this chapter has been on interest group participation in politics through the mainstream mass media. But from a mass communication perspective, it is essential that we better define what is meant by the "mass media." For example, are new formats for information such as C-SPAN and cable access programming included in our assumptions about the mass media and their effects? There is also a need to define how the alternative media and alternative definitions of news affect group access and, therefore, decision-making.

But it is more complex still. There is a reciprocity in all of these processes: Public opinion also affects the mass media; public and elite opinion must surely affect interest groups and other sources of news; decisions about policy should affect groups, public opinion, and news media practices and norms. It may even be appropriate to conceptualize public opinion itself as a form of "feedback" to groups and decision-makers in these processes. There is a definite need to elaborate these various political processes more rigorously and to develop mass communication theories that can make sense out of our increasingly complex global societies.

Fundamental questions and answers about democratic states are made more possible when the mass media are included centrally in theories of political participation and social change. Certainly, in order for citizens to participate more fully in today's modern state and to promote democratic values, the mass media must do more than merely meet some minimal requirement for balance in reporting information to citizens. Nor can the media assume that all those who want meaningful access to decision-making processes can achieve it if they just try hard enough.

Rather, in today's world, the only resolution to critical problems is through more information and not less, participation of more voices and perspectives not usually heard and not fewer, and more diverse and creative thinking in decision-making on policy and not the status quo.

NOTES

1. Even the individualistic formula "one person, one vote" needs close examination in order to determine real levels of equality. There have been instances in the recent past when the right of access to the polls was unequal, and the policy of gerrymandering is still hotly debated in some states.

2. In their study of Watergate, Lang and Lang (1983) found that public opinion played just such a role for those actors trying to impeach Richard Nixon.

3. Schlozman and Tierney (1986) found that of all organizations with a formal Washington, D.C., presence, 77 percent can be categorized as representing business and professional interests. Statistical information, culled from the Census Bureau, revealed that only 16 percent of the general population could be defined as businesspersons or professionals at the time of the study.

4. In their review of the published agenda-setting research, Rogers and Dearing (1988) identified 138 studies as of early 1987.

5. See, for example, the Langs' concept of agenda building in The Battle for Public Opinion (1983): the typology outlined by Rogers and Dearing (1988); and the critiques from Gandy's study of information subsidies (1982); and from the political scientists Iyengar and Kinder (1987).

6. Some researchers are attempting to expand the agenda-setting model. For example, see the ongoing research project by the Northwestern University team focusing on the news media's agenda-setting effects on decision-makers and public policy (Cook et al., 1983; Protess et al., 1985; Leff et al., 1986; Protess et al., 1987) and the research on intermedia agenda-setting (Reese & Danielian, 1989; Danielian & Reese, 1989).

7. Newspaper coverage is very similar. An unpublished pilot study of front-page stories in the New York Times found very few interest groups used as sources (reported in Danielian, 1989).

5

Who Sets the Media Agenda? The Ability of Policymakers to Determine News Decisions

Dan Berkowitz

Who sets the media agenda? Nobody really. Most literally, the news agenda is not "set" in the same way that the agenda-setting tradition considers the *transferral* of a set of issue priorities from the mass media to the public mind. Instead, the creation of a news agenda is the result of a *process* that depends on much more than a loosely linked transferral of one group's priorities to another. A more useful question then becomes, "How does the news agenda take shape?," which is followed by the question, "What is the ability of policymakers to influence news decisions?"

When considering the impact of *policymakers* on the news agenda, the focus is actually on a portion of a larger group called *news sources*, who supply news items and story information to journalists. Put most simply, news sources exert a stronger influence over the news agenda than do journalists. Over and over, studies have found that source-originated stories comprise the majority of a newspaper's or television station's news mix. Further, policymakers have been found to be even more influential than the overall group of news sources.

The journalistic tenet of objectivity is largely responsible for this source influence, because it requires a journalist to attribute information to a legitimated source before it can pass muster as "objective" (Entman, 1989; Schudson, 1978; Tuchman, 1978). Objective journalists, then, cannot work from their own priorities for what should be news. Instead, they must wait for potential news items to somehow surface. To accomplish this, journalists cast what they see as an appropriate size and weave of "news net" and then periodically haul it in to see what they have caught (Tuchman, 1978). Journalists then choose from among the "fish" in the net to decide what should be "the news." Most often, though, the catch amounts to news sources who have intentionally jumped into the net with the motive of promoting their own points of view. In a nutshell, most of journalists' news choices end up being based on what news sources have to offer (Gans, 1979; Sigal, 1973).

Sigal (1986), for example, argues that news is basically what sources say, although he adds that sources' efforts to shape the news agenda are tempered somewhat by the routines of journalism and by the demands and constraints of media organizations. Similarly, Cutlip (1988) describes a "national public information system" composed of government officials, public relations practitioners, and the media, concluding that government officials and their public relations people have the upper hand over the mass media. The outcome, Cutlip believes, is that the media end up as servants of government, accepting news handouts and publishing them almost uncritically. Entman (1989) uses a market analogy, where journalists work under economic market pressures to turn a profit, while policymakers face political market pressures to protect their own political interests. As a result, policymakers strive to manage news, and journalists eagerly seek their low-cost news in order to minimize costs and maximize profits.

Despite the intuitive appeal of these conclusions, the process is not so simple. The journalist-policymaker relationship really is much more complex than a simple domination of one group by the other. Further, the language of the debate among scholars has become considerably muddled, so that what has been learned is difficult to integrate. This chapter therefore begins to lay a foundation by delving into terms that have added both understanding and confusion to the study of journalists and news sources: *agenda-setting*, *agenda-building*, and *information subsidy*. With those preliminaries aside, the chapter then considers the meaning of *power* over the news agenda, adding up the evidence from several studies to empirically document the most commonly considered kind of power. It also expands the discussion of power beyond the ability to determine *what* will become news.

To only *describe* policymakers' influence over the news agenda does not clearly lead to an understanding of *why* they are influential. A theoretical perspective based on role theory provides a framework for analyzing the journalist-policymaker relationship. This contrasts with the traditional normative or descriptive views that call the relationship either adversarial or symbiotic. Implications of this role theory perspective are also outlined here.

Power relationships among journalists and policymakers are not static, however. Two groups of mitigating factors shape the relationship dynamics. The first group, environmental factors, takes into account conflict, crises, and disasters. The second group, newswork factors, suggests that organizational and social constraints of journalism limit *both* the extent of journalistic decision-making and policymaker influence.

Finally, the chapter attempts to consider how these discussions might be taken all together to develop an overview for assessing who, after all, sets the news agenda.

CLARIFYING A MUDDLE OF RELEVANT CONCEPTS

A common language does not exist for discussing key concepts related to news agendas, yet such a language is crucial to shared understanding. The terms *agenda-setting*, *agenda-building*, and *information subsidy* have helped solidify thinking about the role of the mass media in society, and about how mass media content takes shape. These terms' usage has not been consistent, however, so that scholars are sometimes left in an "agenda-" maze. Rogers and Dearing (1988) differentiate between agenda-setting and agenda-building, where "setting" refers to the effect of the media agenda on society. "Building," in contrast, is concerned with a broader picture, where media and public agendas influence public policy. Lang and Lang (1981) have taken this broader view, suggesting that agenda-*setting* is too media-centric a term. Agenda-*building*, however, identifies a collective process that includes "some degree of reciprocity" between the mass media and society. Others have made similar observations about the distinction between agenda-setting and agenda-building (McCombs & Gilbert, 1986; Weaver & Elliott, 1985).

The main problem is deciding when to apply the agenda-setting label and when to base a discussion on agenda-building instead. For example, is the media agenda "set" or "built"? The following discussion attempts to consolidate the language in order to unify future work.

The Range of Relevant Concepts

To begin, key concepts will be isolated and a set of neutral labels applied. Then, commonly used terms will be matched up to these labels. Initially, these concepts will be referred to as *Concept A* through *Concept D*. Finally, usage guidelines will be offered.

Table 5.1 summarizes the four agenda concepts and their applications. Concept A refers to the effect of mass media content on the *public's* perceptions of a news agenda. Concept B focuses on *policy-*

maker's perceptions, which may in part be shaped by the media agenda, but also by other sources such as opinion polls and informal contacts. Concept C concerns *media content* and how the media agenda is formed. Concept D is similar to Concept C, except that it emphasizes the importance of *social power* in the shaping of a media agenda. Rather than referring to a cognitive list of ideas, Concept D is related to a process involving journalists and policymakers.

The term *agenda-setting* has most consistently been applied to Concept A. This usage is commonly attributed to Cohen (Cohen, 1963), Lang and Lang (1981), McCombs and Shaw (1972), and people who have followed in their footsteps. Rogers and Dearing's (1988) examination of agenda-related research acknowledged the conceptual muddle in agenda language, and used the phrase *agenda-setting* plus a modifier to distinguish among the first three concepts. For Concept A, then, they apply the term *public agenda-setting*.

Looking closely at Concept B suggests that it is really a variation of Concept A. In some instances, it considers how policy issues evolve, while at other times it has considered only the media-policymaker linkage. Concept B moves away from the traditional emphasis on *public* opinion and instead considers a specialized segment of society: policymakers. Concept B has been labeled as *agenda-setting* by some (Cohen, 1973; Leff, Protess, & Brooks, 1986; Pritchard, Dilts, & Berkowitz, 1987), although scholars with a political science orientation have called this concept *agenda-building* (Cobb & Elder, 1983). The term *policy agenda-setting* has also been applied (Rogers & Dearing, 1988).

Concept C most clearly corresponds to the thrust of this chapter and is perhaps the most muddled of the four concepts. Because the research question in this line of inquiry often asks, "Who sets the media agenda?" or "How has the media agenda been set?," the term *agenda-setting* again has been applied here. Sometimes, though, it has been labeled as *media agenda-setting* to emphasize the process it refers to (Rogers & Dearing, 1988). One problem, though, is that the phrase "media agenda-setting" has also been applied to Concept A, referring to the effect of media agendas on the public. Further dashing any hope for conceptual clarity, the term *agenda-building* has been applied to Concept C, as well (Berkowitz, 1987; Berkowitz & Adams, 1990; McCombs & Gilbert, 1986; Weaver & Elliott, 1985). Recall that political scientists have most often attached the agenda-building label to the society-policymaker relationship. As this chapter argues in several places, the media agenda is not simply set, but instead evolves from the interaction of people and organizations in society.

There has been less confusion about the use of Concept D, although it, too, is somewhat muddled. *Information subsidy* is the term most often applied to Concept D. The term's inception highlighted how in-

Table 5.1
Concepts and Terms Commonly Used in the Study of Agendas

Concept	Model	Terms in Use	Recommended Term
A	Media --▶ Public	Agenda-setting Public agenda	Agenda-setting
B_1	Media --▶ Policymakers	Agenda-setting Policy agenda-setting Agenda-building	Policy agenda-setting
B_2	Media + Public --▶ Issues	Agenda-building	Policy agenda-building
C	Sources --▶ Media	Agenda-setting Media agenda-setting Agenda-building	Agenda-building
D	Source + Power --▶ Media	Information-subsidy	Information-subsidy

formation serves as an economic commodity bartered between journalists and news sources (Gandy, 1982). For media organizations,
reporting the news carries several costs (Entman, 1989; Epstein, 1973;
Gaunt, 1990). Key among those is the cost of maintaining a news staff
of reporters and photographers, and of making the commitment of their
time for gathering the raw materials of news stories. It follows, then,
that news sources who are able to reduce the costs of reporting the
news will be able to exert greater influence on the news agenda. In the
United States, greater financial resources usually (but not always)
equate with greater social power, enhancing news sources' ability to
package information into an economic commodity most valuable to
journalists.

Although Concept D seems relatively straightforward, it has been
muddled by the necessity of operationalization. One way to examine
the concept is through case studies (Gandy, 1982). A more quantifiable
or more generalizable methodology, though, has used content analysis
to examine the agenda-shaping competition among representatives of
a specific kind of news source, such as state government public information officers (Turk, 1986). A similar approach has been to examine
the sources appearing in the news produced by one or more media
organizations (Berkowitz, 1987; Berkowitz & Adams, 1990; Brown, Bybee, Weardon, & Straughan, 1987; Sigal, 1973). Content analysis, by
necessity, must rely on visible information subsidies, the most visible
among them being the news release. For this reason, information subsidy has been interpreted by some (Wilcox, Ault, & Agee, 1989) as only
a euphemism to sanitize the word "news release."

Toward a Solution

How should the conceptual muddle of "agenda-" terms be resolved?
The decision for Concept A is fairly straightforward. Concept A, the
transfer of the media agenda to the public agenda, is most clearly and
commonly represented by the term *agenda-setting*. When used in a
discussion solely concerning the media-public effect, the term will do
best without any qualifiers or modifiers that would likely raise more
questions than would be answered. However, when discussed in combination with the other concepts, the term *public agenda-setting* will
add clarity. It is important to keep in mind, however, that Concept A
likely involves a reciprocal effect between media and society (Lang &
Lang, 1981; Pritchard & Berkowitz, 1991; Rogers & Dearing, 1988).

Concept B really has two faces and its label depends on which context
is under study. When discussion is limited to the media-policymaker
linkage, the term *policy agenda-setting* offers a good fit. Although it is
similar to the traditional usage of the agenda-setting concept, the focus

has shifted from the public to policymakers. When the focus is not on policymakers' personal agendas, but instead on the broader societal context where public issues surface and gain salience, the mass media become only one indicator of public sentiment, and the term *policy agenda-building* is more accurate. Most often, though, mass communication scholars have considered the transferral of agendas (agenda-setting) rather than the evolution of issues (agenda-building).

Choosing an appropriate term for Concept C—how the media agenda is formed—requires further consideration of this concept's meaning. Concepts A and B are most closely analogous to the meaning of the word *agenda*, which can be seen as a list of items that has been prioritized and transferred. Both public agenda-setting and policy agenda-setting are processes where either members of the public or policymakers develop a mental list of what to think about, based partly on their encounters with the mass media. Concept C, however, does not really focus on the transferral of priorities. Instead, this concept concerns the interactive, give-and-take process of *shaping* media content. This shaping goes beyond the impact of policymakers or journalists alone, and is constantly reshaping rather than becoming a discrete knowable entity. As such, the media's list of priorities does not really follow any particular group's priorities (except perhaps from a macro-level perspective as cultural hegemony). Because Concept C does not focus on agenda transferral as much as it does on agenda *creation*, the term *agenda-building* most appropriately provides a good match to its meaning, much as the term has been used for discussions of the policy agenda. In discussions of the evolution of both the media and policy agendas, the label *media agenda-building* can add clarity.

Concept D does not really require relabeling. *Information subsidy* provides an accurate portrayal of this concept. The main concern for clarifying Concept D is that the actual process involves more than news releases alone. When used correctly and when clearly defined in advance, this term does not really pose a problem.

In sum, studying the question of who shapes the news agenda has been approached through a variety of terms that generally correspond to four main concepts. With a common language now delineated, the discussion turns to policymaker power.

AN ASSESSMENT OF POLICYMAKER POWER OVER THE NEWS AGENDA

As David Pritchard argues in the following chapter, the activities of policymakers are often *political decisions* tied to public opinion. When policymakers decide to take a certain stance or propose a particular action, they first try to develop an understanding of constituents' sentiments, either from opinion polls or from reflections of public opinion presented through mass media content or from other less formal means. And when policymakers attempt to influence public opinion, they often see the mass media as a convenient channel for transmitting their messages. Sometimes, they intentionally attempt to place stories, while other times, they position themselves as useful news sources whom journalists can come to depend on. They also develop a sense of how to avoid the media agenda. When policymakers become more successful at shaping the media agenda through any of these means, they will wield greater social power.

A starting point for assessing the social power of policymakers is to examine their ability to gain media coverage for their stories. An analogy to a classroom provides a close fit to this situation. Imagine a professor leading a discussion in a group of active, interested students. These students' grades are determined in part by class participation, so that it benefits them to raise their hands and be called on. Although many students regularly raise their hands, a smaller number of them do so with extra flourish and are called on more regularly. Further, some of those charismatic handraisers express themselves eloquently, while others have a difficult time making a coherent point out loud. The professor, cognizant of this, tends to call on those students who can build the most interesting discussion, so that concepts will be clearly illuminated. In sum, although practically the entire class attempts to participate in discussions, only a few students have the knack to become regular participants who can offer what the professor is looking for.

The same is true for policymakers attempting to influence the news agenda. Most are interested in news coverage for publicizing their own interests, and most are able to produce a basic news release, stage some sort of public event, or hold a news conference. Overall, though, many policymakers are not particularly savvy about journalists' needs, and therefore are not especially effective in gaining journalists' "permission to speak." A smaller group of policymakers knows how to attract journalists' attention and have their news covered. And a smaller group yet actually meets journalists' expectations for "good class participation" that can be packaged as news. Again, although most of the policymakers in the "class" regularly raise their hands, only those who promote the liveliest "discussions" will be called on regularly.

Quite a few studies have attempted to assess who are the most frequent "class participants." Because of the relatively small number of studies focusing exclusively on policymakers, the discussion builds on the body of knowledge about news sources in general. Two main research approaches have been used. First, *success rates* have been analyzed by documenting journalists' use of sources' subsidized information. Second, studies have looked at the *outcome* of these information-subsidy efforts to examine sources' prominence in the overall news mix.

Tallying the Score for News Source Success

To study success rates, researchers have examined the proportion of news releases or other information-subsidy efforts that are kept and discarded by media gatekeepers. Overall, sources have little success in gaining coverage. Typically, 5 to 10 percent of source-originated news items are used by print or broadcast media organizations (Baxter, 1981; Kopenhaver, 1985; Morton, 1986). Sometimes, a two-stage filtering process takes place, where nearly a quarter of all releases are retained, but the number finally used is still less than 10 percent (Berkowitz, 1990a). The bulk of those discarded news items come from organizations outside of the station's viewing area that hoped to gain low-cost publicity through airtime (Berkowitz & Adams, 1990). That point has been re-iterated by a myriad of studies: Attempts to influence the media agenda often lack relevance to a media organization's audience (Abbott & Brassfield, 1989; Aronoff, 1975; Baxter, 1981). Essentially, a large proportion of news sources do not effectively understand the journalist's needs or their definitions of news.

The case for government information-subsidy efforts—the place where policymakers can often be found—appears somewhat different. Generally, policymakers have a greater proportion of their news items selected for coverage in the mass media. In part, journalists see the actions and decisions of this group of news sources as impacting society, so that policymakers gain legitimacy as newsmakers—providing news about government is a basic tenet of U.S. journalism. It also seems likely that policymakers would see it as more important than other sources to understand journalists' needs and would therefore better learn how to participate in the news agenda. In a study of information-subsidy efforts by state government public information officers (PIOs), for example, about half of all information subsidies became news stories. Not all of these took the form of a news release, however, but included agency reports, memos, and other forms of communication from PIOs to reporters (Turk, 1986). A study of information subsidy at the federal level found that nearly 20 percent of White House information subsidies were used by the media (Turk, 1987). In either case, these figures are much greater than for news sources overall.

Looking at Visible Source Impact

Studying the role of sources in the news mix provides a somewhat different picture. Despite the relatively low *success rates* of news sources in general, a large proportion of the news mix is nonetheless built from source-initiated news items. This stems not so much from source power as it does from the role of the journalist in a media organization (Weaver & Wilhoit, 1980). As in many other fields, everyday life in a media organization becomes a series of strategies designed to efficiently and predictably create a product that will meet the needs and demands of the organization's consumers (Tuchman, 1978; Zimmerman, 1970). In this case, those constituents are advertisers and media audiences.

One strategy that journalists use to meet organizational expectations is to find news items that can be gathered and reported predictably, that allow careful rationing of resources, and that can be completed within organizationally expected deadlines (Bantz, 1985; Breed, 1955; Tuchman, 1978). Items from news sources about planned events meet this need most successfully. Sources who therefore become good providers of this kind of raw material can readily become part of the news agenda, provided, of course, that their stories coincide with the commonly accepted news definitions and formats (Altheide, 1991). In the end, journalists turn to source-initiated stories with regularity. News stories of this type have been labeled *routine channel news*, those stories based on news releases, news conferences, and official proceedings (Sigal, 1973).

Frequently, half or more of the stories in newspapers are routine channel news (Brown et al., 1987; Sigal, 1973; Soloski, 1989b). The proportion of source-initiated news in television—a medium with greater constraints and resource demands—is higher, even as much as three-fourths of all news stories (Altheide, 1976; Berkowitz, 1987; McCombs & Becker, 1979). An estimate of overall source impact based on media content paints a picture of greater overall source influence than does a view based on success rates. Narrowing the definition of news sources to those in government shows even greater impact on the news agenda. Government-affiliated news sources have higher success rates and have been found to be the most frequently appearing of sources at the local, state, and national levels (Berkowitz, 1989; Brown et al., 1987; Sigal, 1973; Soloski, 1989b).

A Deeper View of Source Power

The preceding discussion has suggested that power over the news agenda can be evaluated by examining the ability of sources to place stories. However, the ability to join the news agenda is not the only measure of the power of policymakers.

Two levels of influence are more subtle and more powerful, but also less visible (Gans, 1979; Gaventa, 1980; Lukes, 1974). Beyond the ability to become part of an existing policy debate, news sources can provide situation definitions of issues that establish the boundaries of future discussion (Lemert, 1981). This is a higher level of power than simply joining the existing news agenda. If policymakers can define their stand on an issue, *as well as the alternatives available for discussion*, then they have defined the situation in more "winnable" terms. Not only can they bring out their side more effectively, but they have delimited the general arguments that the opposition can make. Clearly, this ability brings more clout for swaying a policy debate than only the ability to have a say in others' arenas. If the first level of power was analogous to *winning* a fight, this second level of power corresponds to *choosing the terms* of the fight.

Beyond these two levels, very powerful sources can influence *whether an issue even receives media attention* (Gans, 1979). The classroom metaphor used earlier serves again. In most classes there are students who do their best to *avoid* contributing to discussions, because they are unprepared, have done something wrong, are shy, or too hung over to do more than occupy a seat. By avoiding attention, they also avoid public disclosure of their real or imagined inadequacies. So too can sources, particularly powerful ones, avoid media attention when it suits them.

This kind of source power is less detectable than the first two levels because there are no stories to observe. Fishman (1980) illustrates this with an example about media efforts to cover an apparent crime wave. In one case, police were interested in promoting a program aimed at crimes against the elderly. By placing a feature story about the program and then supporting the story with instances of crimes, the media began to report an increasing city crime wave, even though the number of crimes was actually decreasing. In a second case, a police official denied the existence of a crime wave when asked. After a few unsuccessful attempts at gaining information about a crime wave's existence, the reporter dropped it, it became a non-story, and the "crime wave" disappeared. In both cases, public officials were able to influence the media agenda in a way that enhanced their positions in the public policy arena.

Reconsidering source power through the previous discussion has shown that at the most basic level, source power constitutes the ability to speak out with a particular position in an ongoing media debate. At least as important, however, is the ability to define an issue's dimensions, or better yet, whether an issue will even surface. Most often, studies have focused on the lowest of the three power levels, because measuring source impact on the news process is most easily accomplished by looking at what *has* been published. In contrast, although anecdotal evidence abounds concerning the ability of sources to "kill" or deemphasize negative press coverage (see any issue of *Columbia Journalism Review*), it is next to impossible to quantify the frequency or impact of something that *has not* surfaced.

A ROLE THEORY PERSPECTIVE ON
JOURNALIST-SOURCE INTERACTIONS

The journalist-source relationship has been depicted in two contrasting ways by the mass communication literature. The first way suggests that the two groups are *adversaries*. This is a normative perspective stemming from classic democratic theory that portrays journalists as watchdogs over business and government, a role where the media serve as a fourth branch of government (Graber, 1984). A second depiction serves mainly as a descriptive view, where the relationship between journalists and news sources is portrayed as a mutually beneficial exchange. There, each party comes into the relationship seeking something and each also gives up something in return (Blumler & Gurevitch, 1981).

The problem with these two perspectives is that a number of examples can be found to both support or negate either one. Because neither adversarial nor exchange conditions exist as a static state, portraying them as one or the other is an inaccurate oversimplification of a much more complex relationship. In the end, then, these two common perspectives fall short of real utility (Swanson, 1988).

An Alternative to Traditional Perspectives

Another, more versatile way of assessing the journalist-source relationship is to examine *why* and *how* these parties act as they do. Role theory (Biddle & Thomas, 1966) becomes useful for this pursuit, because it portrays journalists and sources as social actors who generally define their relationships according to socially prescribed expectations, and more specifically base individual actions on the role expectations that might exist in any particular situation. The journalist-source relationship, then, is best understood not through normative assumptions or a description of typical interactions between the groups, but instead by focusing on a shared culture defined by the two groups and their social environment. Although role theory has traditionally been a microlevel theory where a role is personally defined by the social actor, this discussion moves it into an organizational- or societal-level perspective as well.

Taking a macrolevel approach suggests that journalists as individuals do not have the most important impact on defining their roles. Instead, journalists mainly fit into role "slots" that have been predefined by higher-level social forces, including the media organization and the journalism profession. It is important to emphasize, though, that the role definitions of this shared culture are not *officially* prescribed by each group's organization. Rather, role prescriptions are based on internal and external *social expectations*. Internal expectations are those unique to the subsystems and larger-order systems within which each group independently functions; external expectations, in contrast, are those that cross the boundaries between journalists and news sources.

Role prescriptions, however, cannot clearly be connected to a single source, such as the media organization. Considering specific levels of analysis helps make both internal and external influences more explicit. Although several level-of-analysis schemes appear in the mass communication literature (Dimmick & Coit, 1982; Hirsch, 1977; Whitney, 1982), four levels are most useful here. These are (1) individual level, (2) organizational level, (3) professional level, and (4) societal level.

Certainly, individual journalists will see their roles somewhat differently. For example, a large national survey (Weaver & Wilhoit, 1986) found that most journalists saw themselves in an interpretive role, but many others saw their functions as either information disseminators or adversaries of business and government. Individual-level interactions between journalists, however, generally do not exert much influence over their role prescriptions, because the social forces of media organizations strongly limit individual differences (Bantz, 1985; Shoemaker & Mayfield, 1987). Regardless of how one journalist might sway another journalist's beliefs about news, the media organization's requirements will be stronger influences about what can be done (Breed, 1955). Similarly, individual beliefs are likely overshadowed by organizational expectations. Even journalists working at "alternative" news organizations are constrained by the organization in their range of news alternatives and interpretations (Eliasoph, 1988).

Organizational-level influences are likely to be strong shapers of journalistic role prescriptions because of the close linkage between role performance and a journalist's livelihood. If a journalist sees his or her mission as distinctly different from the organization's views, organizational pressures to conform can threaten perceived job security (Breed, 1955). Organizational role prescriptions are, in turn, significantly shaped by an organization's linkage with its financiers and its need to remain financially viable (Shoemaker & Mayfield, 1987). As a result, organizational role performance concerns story selection, story treatment, production quotas, and quality standards that shape the character of news as an organizational product designed to please audiences and draw advertisers (Bantz, McCorkle, & Baade, 1980). Social prescriptions are learned as journalists observe meetings, engage in reporting and editing of news, and otherwise interact with their peers and supervisors in a media organization (Bantz, 1985). Over time, a journalist becomes enmeshed in the organizational culture and begins to subconsciously act according to its norms. The incentive to conform to organizational expectations is the avoidance of conflict, which could hamper effectiveness, and, ultimately, career advancement.

Professional-level role expectations focus on ethical concerns and standards of quality. They moderate those of the organization, but are not likely to override them (Soloski, 1989a; Weaver & Wilhoit, 1986). In other words, professional journalistic beliefs often must yield to the organization's bottom line. As economic pressures become greater for a media organization, professional-level role expectations decrease in the effect they have on journalists' behavior.

There is also an interaction between professional and organizational expectations. In general, the closer organizational role expectations are to professional expectations, the less tension will exist within the news organization and the greater the likelihood that journalists will base their behaviors on organizational prescriptions. Professional expectations in this case will be less conscious and less visible in journalists' interactions. In contrast, as organizational expectations become based on productivity and efficiency rather than on thoroughness and completeness, professional-level expectations will explicitly play a greater part in journalists' own role prescriptions (Bantz, 1985). Accompanying this will be a greater amount of conflict within the organization.

Societal-level role prescriptions relate mainly to commonly accepted beliefs about social power and social structure, what has been termed "ideology" (Bennett, 1982). Because these prescriptions come from a higher level than the media organization or the profession, their influence on role expectations is difficult to detect. Yet, societal-level prescriptions become important because they create or "reify" what journalists come to see as a natural social order, even though it is actually a human creation (Soloski, 1989b).

Policymakers also face *internal* role prescriptions, and again, individual variation among policymakers will likely be overridden by higher-level expectations. Either officially or unofficially, policymakers belong to specific political parties or are members of particular ideological factions. These serve as the functional equivalent of journalists' organizational influences. Much as journalists' role prescriptions are shaped by a media organization's external economic pressures from advertisers and audiences, policymakers face organizational pressures that rise from below through the opinion of important publics that have put a policymaker or a policymaker's superiors into office. Policymakers' professional and societal role expectations also offer a close parallel to those of journalists.

What this discussion of internal sources of role prescriptions has suggested is that the way journalists and sources view the mandate for doing their job is the result of several levels of forces in constant interaction. Further, this interaction is dynamic, so that each level—individual, organizational, professional, societal—might be more or less influential at any particular instance. These dynamics extend beyond the internal elements, as well, to interact with external social forces.

External role expectations between the two groups must be considered to fully understand why they interact as they do. Although *dyadic relationships* between journalists and policymakers account for some variation in social role prescriptions, a higher level of analysis again seems more meaningful. Essentially, a journalist cannot practically or effectively establish a different set of rules for each policymaker. On one hand, this would be difficult to remember. On the other, it is unlikely that policymakers would accept explicitly preferential treatment for some. If journalists are led by objectivity to depend on source-originated news, then explicit preferential treatment would likely cut off the pipeline on which they are so dependent (Entman, 1989). In sum, a basic set of role expectations must be used as a starting point for journalist-policymaker interaction. As a bottom line, *external* role prescriptions must be negotiated to allow effective *internal* role performance for each party.

At the *professional* level, external influences surface when policymakers publicly criticize media performance or when journalists' stories express concern about treatment by policymakers. External role prescriptions also come at the *societal* level. This influence is for all purposes the same as internal societal-level forces, because most mainstream news organizations and most policymakers share the same assumptions about society, and actually both constitute elements of the ideological apparatus that governs society (Althusser, 1971).

As journalists' and policymakers' social roles become more clearly defined and apparent to members of each group, they not only will base their actions more and more on these roles, but they will also increasingly develop expectations for how the other party should act in any situation, what could be called a *shared culture*. In essence, this shared culture becomes an *unofficial* set of ground rules for journalist-source interaction. Although both parties might not be fully satisfied by the constraints and obligations related to their role prescriptions, they nonetheless learn that meeting expectations of these externally prescribed roles is crucial to effectiveness and success within their respective organizations.

Implications of a Role Theory Perspective

The role theory framework clearly shows why the journalist-policymaker relationship must be viewed as dynamic rather than static, because both groups face situations that accommodate role performance expectations to varying degrees. Essentially, the degree to which each group is able to follow a role prescription will determine whether a relationship will be basically adversarial or based more on an exchange at any given time.

When performance of an internally prescribed role can be accommodated by mutual cooperation, the relationship becomes more of an *exchange*. When one party's actions, however, do not allow the other to fulfill internal expectations, the relationship likely will become more *adversarial* instead. Further, when one party is not even aware of externally negotiated role expectations or intentionally chooses not to follow them, the relationship also becomes adversarial.

A *first implication* of this role theory perspective is that since journalists must meet internally prescribed expectations related to productivity and efficiency, policymakers will gain the opportunity to impose situation definitions leading toward their own preferred interpretations of issues and events. This is because, as a bottom line, journalists must return to their media organization with *a* story, even if it is not *the* story they originally wanted. Similarly, when policymakers engage in an encounter with journalists in order to seek publicity for their views, journalists are more able to succeed with their own situation definitions. The alternative for policymakers is to miss out on any publicity at all.

Implicit here is the notion that *each* party regularly attempts to skirt the boundaries of *externally* defined role performance in order to be more responsive to *internally* placed demands. Some degree of mismatch between journalists' and policymakers' goals is therefore likely but still acceptable under the external role prescriptions of the journalist-source subculture (Bantz, 1985). In most situations, then, the exchange relationship appears as "a bit of sport" between the two groups. When one of the groups attempts to lead the relationship toward a gross mismatch of role fulfillment, however, it becomes more like "war," what is commonly termed an adversarial relationship.

To explain the dynamics of the journalist-policymaker relationship by looking only at role performance, though, would be too much of an oversimplification. Adversarial and exchange conditions also depend on the *social power* of each party in an encounter. Social power in this context translates to "influence," which in turn is built on factors such as prestige, visibility, size, and resources. A *second implication* of the role theory perspective, then, is that a party with greater social power in a journalist-policymaker encounter will be able to more greatly stretch the limits of that party's role performance without bringing on an adversarial response from the other party.

Reese (1991) offers a typology representing the possible relationships between journalists and news sources. Both media organizations and social institutions can hold relatively higher or lower social power. Journalists affiliated with national television networks, for example, would have greater social power than those affiliated with community newspapers. Similarly, federal policymakers would have more social power than those in city government. Relative status within an organization would also influence social power, so that a network anchor would have more social power than an unknown network reporter.

This power view suggests that if a high-level federal official was meeting with journalists from a local media organization, the federal official would have a greater ability to depart from the usual rule system within which the local journalists worked, and would therefore have greater control over the news agenda. If both parties were of equivalent status, however, influence would be more balanced and the usual working rule system would be followed more closely (Reese, 1991). Conversely, national journalists would have more influence over the news than the local officials they would be reporting on. In sum, the party with the greater social power can better control the developing news agenda.

A *third implication* of this role theory concerns the relative ability of different policymakers to shape the news agenda. The power dimension suggests that policymakers with greater social power will influence the news agenda more than less powerful policymakers. There are two reasons for this. One reason follows from the preceding discussion, and suggests that greater power corresponds to greater source agenda control.

A second reason is closely related, but bears an important distinction. If external role expectations are shaped by mutual interaction between journalists and policymakers, then those policymakers with greater social power will have greater impact on how the *rules for social interaction* are shaped. It is also likely that more powerful policymakers will have shaped these rules more closely *to their own needs*. Less powerful policymakers, in contrast, might not even understand the rules of the culture and might therefore deal with the media in ways that unknowingly violate cultural norms. This inappropriate behavior would trigger an adversarial relationship with journalists and would reduce those sources' influence on the news agenda.

A *fourth implication* of this role theory also concerns the consequences of a power differential. As policymakers attempt to place news stories, not all news favorable to a policymaker's interests will meet the expectations of the shared culture. In these cases, policymakers who understand the rules of the culture the best will be most capable of transforming a news item's appearance to conform more closely to the culture's current news definitions. When policymakers do so, journalists can cover the news item and still remain within the boundaries of their internal role expectations. In this way, more powerful policymakers will have a greater degree of agenda influence, if not the exact news story that they want. Policymakers *less aware* of the culture's conventions, however, would be less likely to know how to tailor news, and would again have less impact on shaping the news agenda.

To understand this role theory perspective, then, requires an examination of two dimensions. The first is role performance. When both parties are allowed to fulfill their role expectations, the relationship will more closely correspond to an exchange; when one party's attempts for greater agenda control reduce the ability of the other to fulfill its role expectations, the relationship will become more adversarial. The power dimension, however, mediates this general situation: journalists or policymakers with greater social power are better able to stretch their agenda-shaping ability without creating adversarial circumstances.

FACTORS UPSETTING THE BALANCE OF POWER
BETWEEN JOURNALISTS AND POLICYMAKERS

In everyday news situations, the balance of source power over the news agenda follows a predictable order. Government sources have greater influence. Sources connected to larger corporations or interest groups have greater influence. Smaller organizations, nongovernment sources, and groups with narrower, self-interested goals typically have less ability to become legitimated news sources in a policy debate and therefore wield less influence.

The dynamics of some situations, however, shift the usual power relationships (Berkowitz & Beach, 1991). The balance of power shifts, for example, during a crisis or disaster situation, when normally powerful sources get caught unprepared or unaware. A second situation relates to community conflict. Although the character of a community shapes the roles and power of news sources, conflict-laden issues upset the social balance. A third situation flows from the newswork process, when external role performance must bow to internal demands.

Power Shifts during Crises and Disasters

If everyday news is commonly routine channel news, then it might be considered as "prepackaged" by news sources to accommodate the needs of journalists while simultaneously helping meet sources' objectives. For routine news, policymakers who become effective members of the journalist-source culture are able to build more influence over the news agenda (Molotch & Lester, 1974). For everyday stories that are not prepackaged, such as spot news, feature news, and stories about trends, journalists usually have a regular pool of news sources to call on. Again, policymakers most familiar with the journalist-source culture and its socially defined rules are most likely to become part of the regular source pool and thereby influence the news agenda. In sum, powerful sources are at their best in routine situations.

When a disaster strikes, though, regular news sources might not be at the scene or might not be informed about the situation (Sood, Stockdale, & Rogers, 1987; Waxman, 1973). This is especially true for official sources constrained by bureaucracies (Graber, 1984). Even though journalists might not be able to rely on their regular sources, media organizations still demand that they produce their regularly scheduled news product. This is the time when other news sources with a particular interest in an issue related to a crisis or disaster story can become part of the news mix, simply because of their immediate availability. As the situation develops further, though, regular sources such as policymakers eventually gain awareness of the story, collect information about the situation, and once again become the legitimated news sources to whom journalists usually turn for information.

Molotch and Lester (1974) provide an example of this mediating situation with their discussion of an oil spill at Santa Barbara, California. When the spill was first discovered, environmental groups quickly reached the scene and became news sources. At that point, they were able to convey messages about the impact of oil spills and the hazards of offshore drilling. By taking advantage of legitimated sources' slower response, they were able to upset the usual balance of power. Eventually, though, then-President Richard Nixon appeared on the scene. At a section of the beach that had been cleaned of oil, he declared the disaster to be over. In this example, a disaster led the balance of source power to tip first one way and then the other.

In a more recent occurrence, the Exxon Valdez oil spill in Alaska also showed a shift in source influence (Holusha, 1989). In the early days of the spill, policymakers from the environmentally conscious Alaska state government were able to speak as the main news source. Their messages focused on the serious environmental damage taking place. Exxon, caught off guard, responded weakly and slowly. As a result, the situation was defined by the state government's terms, and Exxon found little credibility for its version of the story.

Community Structure and Community Conflict

The character of a community influences the range and type of sources who will appear in its media (Tichenor, Donohue, & Olien, 1980). In general, greater community diversity is associated with a wider range of viewpoints and a more diverse news source mix

(McCombs & Becker, 1979). Diversity has often been equated with community size (Donohue, Olien, Tichenor, & Demers, 1990), where larger communities tend to be more diverse, although the economic base is also an important factor (McLeod, Sandstrom, Olien, Donohue, & Tichenor, 1990). More special-interest groups also develop within larger communities, and more stratification by social class takes place. As a result, a lower degree of consensus is common in larger communities. Conflict is not uncommon, and the everyday balance of source power would not likely be seriously shaken by a moderate degree of conflict.

Smaller communities, in contrast, are more homogeneous in nature. People have more commonalities, such as religion, occupation, and education. The power structure is therefore more narrowly defined in these homogeneous communities, and the sources appearing in local media are drawn chiefly from that power structure. In particular, local media in these homogeneous communities face a greater need to avoid conflict with the power structure for economic reasons. Most simply, there are relatively few advertisers to turn to (Donohue, Olien, & Tichenor, 1989; McLeod et al., 1990).

These community differences bring implications for the power of news sources. In larger communities, the more diverse range of viewpoints allows news sources with alternative viewpoints greater opportunity to present information and shape the news agenda. In smaller communities, the greater degree of consensus news means that alternative sources have fewer opportunities to present their views in the mass media. Further, fewer sources will be as familiar with the journalist-source culture and have the ability to successfully function within it.

The introduction of *conflict* breaks down the usual boundaries of news source diversity, where conflict can be defined as open disagreement between two or more parties. This disagreement means that opposing viewpoints have been made visible, even acceptable within the range of social discourse (Tichenor et al., 1980). In a conflict-related situation, the norm of journalistic objectivity leads reporters to try to cover the various sides of the debate. It follows, then, that conflict will expand the range of news sources in smaller communities. As a result, policymakers' power to shape the news agenda becomes diluted, as other news sources enter the fray.

The Impact of Newswork

The most traditional of studies about how the news agenda is shaped point toward the gatekeeper, that person who sifts through a host of potential news items and selects what will become news. Those studies have highlighted either gatekeepers' personal subjectivity or their news judgment as key factors (Berkowitz, 1991; Buckalew, 1970; White, 1950). The gatekeeping tradition has overlooked an important point, however: a fair degree of haphazardness actually pervades the news process, so that the news agenda is not completely shaped by either journalists or policymakers. This is because the work of journalists is largely dictated by the necessities of everyday life within a profit-seeking organization (Altheide, 1976; Bantz et al., 1980; Gans, 1979; Herman & Chomsky, 1988; Shoemaker & Mayfield, 1987). Management expects that newsworkers will turn out a product with the resources that have been allotted and within the time frames that have been prescribed. Because resources and time are almost always in short supply, newswork becomes a series of purposive, socially learned routines employed to expedite tasks (Eliasoph, 1988; Fishman, 1980; Tuchman, 1978) and avoid conflict with an organization's power structure and policies (Bantz, 1985; Breed, 1955; Soloski, 1989a).

In a sense, newswork most closely resembles many other scheduling activities (Bantz et al., 1980; Berkowitz, 1990b; Zimmerman, 1970). Possible news stories are somewhat analogous to patients waiting to see the dentist. A simple teeth-cleaning procedure requires a small amount of time and minimal expertise, while a root canal procedure demands greater dental resources in the form of time, personnel, and equipment. The dentist, however, has a set working time each day and the patients he schedules will depend on how much time each patient's procedure will entail: if there are a lot of root canals, the dentist can see fewer patients. Similarly, the task of journalists is to fill a predetermined amount of newspaper space or airtime with news. The effort that can be given to any one story depends on what else is available. If newswork is largely a strategic ritual designed to meet the dual demands of journalism and business, then these routines will likely favor some news items over some others. The most interesting, the most important, and the easiest to cover are likely to take precedence by simple necessity. In sum, what might be news on one particular day might not be news on another, so that the actual "odds" of entering the news mix will vary daily.

A FINAL ASSESSMENT OF SOURCE POWER IN THE MEDIA AGENDA

This chapter began with the idea that the news agenda is not really "set," but instead, "built." In general, most of the building materials are provided by news sources, especially policymakers. From there, the assessment becomes less clear. Few policymakers can expect to regularly shape the news agenda, because so much of the process is dynamic and depends on factors beyond their control.

The most basic reason for this assessment lies within the nature of American journalism and its mythical foundations in objectivity. Objectivity requires certain work practices if it is to be attained. A by-product of these work practices is that source-originated news from legitimated sources tends to be favored. Policymakers are among the most legitimated of news sources.

Beyond journalism itself, the shared culture of journalists and policymakers leads toward a dynamic relationship that is sometimes more adversarial and sometimes more of an exchange. Although many studies have taken a normative or descriptive approach that argues for one or the other, the role theory perspective presented here shows that understanding the journalist-policymaker relationship is not a matter of picking a stance and building an argument for it. Instead, the nature of the relationship tips one way and the other depending on the specific conditions of their interaction. The balance can be shaken by the degree to which organizational demands on a journalist or source allow the other party to meet internal expectations. The power balance of the journalist-source match-up is also important to consider.

Even an analysis of roles and power is not really enough to carefully understand the journalist-source relationship, though. An unexpected occurrence can change a source's usual ability to shape the news. The character of the community where news takes place is important, because the array of viewpoints and the tolerance for their expression are distinctly different as communities become more pluralistic or more homogeneous. After taking these factors into account, the process of newswork presents a set of conditions that varies from day to day: Sometimes competition for news space is keen, while at other times journalists must grasp whatever comes into view.

In the end, then, studying how the news agenda is "set" is to take a narrow view. What takes place is a process, a process that can be modeled according to several dimensions, but also a process with dimensions that can never be effectively nailed down to provide an exact answer of who has the lead in the agenda-setting competition.

6

The News Media and Public Policy Agendas

David Pritchard

As societies become more and more complex, the distance between citizens and government grows. This phenomenon poses difficult problems in political systems with representative forms of government. In a system in which policymakers are increasingly distant from citizens, how can public policy be responsive to the public will? And how can the public hold policymakers accountable for their actions?

This chapter focuses on such issues by examining the extent to which news media serve as a link between citizens and policymakers.[1] The implications of such a role for the news media are tremendously important, in terms of theory as well as in terms of the day-to-day workings of government. For what is the nature of "democracy" in a political system without a direct link between citizens and government—a system in which public policy may be more responsive to the agendas of the news media than to the priorities of the people, in which the responsibility to hold policymakers accountable rests more with the media than with the people?

The chapter begins with an overview of the relationship between citizens and government in the United States, using the familiar agenda

1. The author wishes to thank Professor David Weaver of Indiana University for thoughtful comments on a draft of this chapter.

metaphor as an analytical tool. Next, the nature of policy agendas is explored in some depth. The media/policy connection is reviewed with the help of examples drawn from research from a wide variety of policy arenas. The chapter concludes with some speculations about the future of the connections between citizens and policymakers in the United States.

LINKING CITIZENS AND POLICYMAKERS

The concept "public policy" can be defined as organized governmental action or inaction—"whatever governments choose to do or not to do" (Dye, 1984, p. 2). As such, policy is the result of conscious decision-making, even if the decision is to do nothing. Those who participate in the decision-making process are the policymakers, who may or may not be elected officials.

Responsibility for public policy in the United States is dispersed fairly widely. The federal government has major policy responsibilities, but so do the states and local units of government. And within each level of government, policy responsibility is apportioned among the legislative, executive, and judicial branches of government.

For much of the United States' history, the most important linking agent between citizens and policymakers in these various policy arenas were the major political parties. The parties essentially served as brokers, influencing not only the flow of political resources such as money and votes to favored (often hand-picked) candidates for public office, but also influencing the flow of resources from the government to favored segments of the populace through various forms of patronage. In all of these dealings, the political parties claimed to represent the interests of the people.

The major political parties declined in influence after World War II. Taking their place as the principal link between the people and the government were the news media, which also claimed to represent the interests of the people—especially the people's so-called "right to know."

The supplanting of political parties by the news media has changed the nature of the link between citizens and policymakers. To the extent that the present-day news media are brokers at all, they deal in information rather than in the more tangible resources of votes and dollars. The distribution of information by the news media may influence agendas of citizens and of policymakers, and those agendas may in turn influence the flow of resources, but the nature of the citizen-government relationship has changed in fundamental ways.

Gone is the overt partisanship of the political parties, gone is the overt patronage, gone is the need for citizens to publicly affiliate themselves with the broker. And gone is the relatively direct link between citizens and policymakers. In its place is a somewhat nebulous process featuring the modern news media, which are overtly nonpartisan and which tout independence from government and policymakers as one of the cornerstones of their professional ideology. With the news media as the principal link between the public and policymakers, the connection is more subtle, ambiguous, and indirect than was the case when political parties were the principal link.

The new arrangement can be seen as a departure from classical democratic theory, which holds that public officials and policymakers should be responsive to the will of the citizenry. If the news media influence policymakers at all, according to the classical notion, it should happen by way of a two-stage process: the media first influence citizens, who in turn influence the elected and appointed public officials who represent them. As such, classical democratic theory posits no direct news-media influence on the behavior of public officials and other policymakers.

In the late twentieth century, however, it is difficult to document the direct link between citizens and policymakers envisioned by classical democratic theory. Instead, there is considerable evidence of a direct link between the agendas of the news media and the behavior of policymakers. The underlying notion is that policymakers may use the news-media agenda as a surrogate for the agendas of the public (Sigal, 1973; Entman, 1989).

POLICY AGENDAS

As noted earlier, policy can be defined as organized governmental action or inaction. Policy agendas are lists of issues to which policymakers pay attention. Some issues on a policy agenda are more important to policymakers than are other issues on the policy agenda, and every issue that has a spot on a policy agenda is more important to the relevant policymakers than all of the issues that have not gained a spot on the policy agenda. These informal rankings of issues are generally widely understood within a given policy arena.

It is axiomatic that the more prominent a position an issue holds on a policy agenda, the more attention policymakers will pay to it. Accordingly, actors in various policy arenas expend considerable energy trying to improve the relative position of an issue in which they have an interest. Often, the challenge is not so much to improve the issue's position on a policy agenda as to get it on the agenda in the first place (Cobb & Elder, 1983; Hilgartner & Bosk, 1988; Rogers, Dearing, & Chang, 1991).

The concept of policy agenda can be broken down into two distinct subconcepts: symbolic agenda and action agenda. Symbolic agendas are those lists of issues that require visible, but not necessarily substantive, action on the part of policymakers (Edelman, 1964). Action agendas, by contrast, are those lists of issues that require substantive action that includes the allocation or reallocation of government resources to address a perceived problem.

The two kinds of policy agendas are conceptually distinct, and issues that have a prominent position on a symbolic agenda may not be prominent on an action agenda, or vice versa. Or an issue may occupy a similar position on both kinds of agendas. The shifting of government resources to address a perceived problem, for example, may well be accompanied by a great deal of symbolic activity. Also common, however, is symbolic activity without substantive action (Cook et al., 1983; Protess et al., 1985). And it should be clear that the policymakers make countless resource-allocation decisions each day without any concomitant public symbolic activity.

POLICYMAKING AS UNCERTAINTY REDUCTION

Policy—organized governmental action or inaction—is of necessity created and implemented in an organizational context. Two propositions are central to understanding organizational behavior. First, all organizations have limited resources to use in the pursuit of their goals. Second, all organizations experience uncertainty about how to allocate their resources (Stinchecombe, 1968).

It follows directly from those propositions that organizational decision-making is a process of uncertainty reduction through which organizations try to maximize the likelihood of achieving their goals (Dimmick, 1974). Such a process necessarily implies a judgment about the likely effect of an organizational action. And if, as Schutz suggested, action is the result of the projection of past experiences and current concerns into the future, then action takes place in the future perfect tense; one bases action on what one expects will have been the case (Schutz, 1962). In a policymaking context, this phenomenon has been demonstrated by Cook, who noted that members of the U.S. House of Representatives decide what to do in part "by anticipating what a reporter will find newsworthy" (Cook, 1989, pp. 7–8).

Organizations' continual attempts to reduce uncertainty mean that resource allocation is not a random process. Formally or informally, organizations develop sets of priorities that guide resource-allocation decisions; these sets of priorities are the action agendas referred to earlier. The priorities are structured so that tasks deemed relatively more important to the furtherance of the organization's goals receive a relatively larger share of resources (Emerson, 1983).

These priorities are not cast in stone, however. Changes in an organization's political environment may cause a reordering of the various issues on its agenda. Organizations constantly monitor their environments for cues that may help reduce their uncertainty. Organizations may take cues about the importance of certain issues—"important" defined in terms of how much risk to the organization is associated with the task—from other institutions or organizations. This may help explain why policymakers are such voracious consumers of news (Weiss, 1974).

This uncertainty-reduction approach to policy behavior is not inconsistent with classical democratic theory, in which the legitimacy of representative government flows from the consent of the governed. In theory, public officials in such a system are accountable to the public for the policy decisions they make, with frequent elections serving as a central mechanism of accountability. Elected officials who ignore policy issues of importance to the general public, or whose policy actions stray beyond the bounds of what the public finds acceptable, will be less likely to continue in office. Between elections, public officials are held accountable by opposition parties and citizen groups, by government agencies and bureaucracies that have interests of their own, and by the news media, all presumably ready to identify and expose officials' shortcomings.

In practice, the mere existence of such mechanisms of accountability no doubt constrains the behavior of public officials. Officials monitor their political environments closely for information about possible risks, and then tend to act in a manner that will reduce uncertainty and minimize the possibility of conflict with important constituencies. In this sense, public opinion, defined broadly as the opinion of important publics (or constituencies), is a legitimate factor for policymakers to consider.

The search for the link between public opinion and public policy often focuses on the press. After all, elected public officials and whatever nonelected policymakers they may appoint do not always (or even often) have direct measures of public opinion about issues that must be addressed. In the absence of direct measures of public opinion, policymakers may tend to use indirect indicators such as how much attention the news media devote to a given issue. This is the media-as-surrogate-for-public-opinion function outlined earlier.

Policymakers' susceptibility to news-media influence may vary from policy arena to policy arena (Lambeth, 1978). In addition, the role orientations of individual policymakers may affect their inclination to use the media as a surrogate for public opinion (Gibson, 1980; Drechsel, 1987).

Despite the fact that individual attributes of policymakers may make them more or less susceptible to media influence, it is important to keep in mind that policymaking is principally an organizational process. As such, the policy agenda-setting effect of the news media is quite a different phenomenon from the agenda-setting effect of the press on citizens (McCombs & Shaw, 1972; McLeod, Becker, & Byrnes, 1974).

The major difference is that policy agenda-setting is essentially a behavioral, rather than a cognitive, process; what matters is not what policymakers think about given issues, but rather what they actually *do* with respect to those issues. Citizen agenda-setting, on the other hand, is a cognitive process in which increased media attention to an issue makes the issue more salient to audience members. The increased issue salience that results from citizen agenda-setting may in turn influence citizens' attitudes and behaviors (Weaver, 1991), but the fact remains that citizen agenda-setting is a cognitive process.

EVIDENCE FROM VARIOUS POLICY ARENAS

Evidence in support of news-media influence on public policy comes from a variety of policy arenas. Perhaps not surprisingly, the effect of the media is strongest on symbolic agendas. Established resource-allocation agendas are hardier and more resistant to change (Pritchard & Berkowitz, 1989).

The news media have an influence on policymakers in some unexpected places. For example, there is considerable evidence that the Supreme Court of the United States responds to public opinion. Shortly before he was appointed chief justice of the United States, William Rehnquist gave a speech in which he acknowledged the influence of public opinion. "Judges, so long as they are relatively normal human beings, can no more escape being influenced by public opinion in the long run than can people working at other jobs," he said (Rehnquist, 1986). The effect of public opinion on the court—not only the cases it decides to hear, but also its decisions—has been documented by Gaziano (1978), by Kairys (1982), and most persuasively by Marshall (1989). Gibson (1980) has documented the effect among trial-court judges.

What is not entirely clear about the effect of public opinion on judges is exactly how judges learn about public opinion. It seems plausible that they use news-media agendas as a surrogate for the agenda of the public, but no carefully controlled studies have explored that possibility.

Nonetheless, it is striking that justices of the Supreme Court of the United States, whose lifetime tenure in theory should make them the least accountable of all policymakers, are among the most responsive to public opinion. Their susceptibility to public opinion may be somehow related to the fact that the Supreme Court has no role in administering the policies whose fates it decides. The fact that tradition and judicial ethics prohibit parties to a case or interest groups from contacting Supreme Court justices to lobby also separates the justices from most other policymakers, who have considerable job-related contact with various interest groups and constituents.

Another important set of policymakers associated with the judicial branch of government are prosecutors. Although they are technically part of the executive branch of government, prosecutors are lawyers and work in the judicial branch. There is evidence that prosecutors, like judges, are influenced by public opinion. There is also evidence that media attention to specific cases or categories of crime affects how vigorously prosecutors actually prosecute.

A Wisconsin study found that how prosecutors handle criminal cases was significantly predicted by the level of attention the press had given to the case (Pritchard, 1986). Specifically, the greater the amount of prior newspaper attention to a crime, the less likely prosecutors were to plea bargain the case. The relationship held even after statistical controls for factors such as the demographics of suspect and victim, their relationship, and the seriousness of the crime were imposed. A study of Indiana prosecutors found similar results: media attention to so-called victimless crimes such as obscenity was causally related to whether prosecutors took formal action against people engaged in such activity (Pritchard, Dilts, & Berkowitz, 1987).

Prosecutors may be influenced by the media only when media attention is targeted on specific cases or issues, however. Scheingold and Gressett (1987) found no relationship between the annual number of articles an urban newspaper published about national criminal-justice policy and the severity of the practices of the local prosecutor's office over a 14-year period. They concluded that policy leadership and resource constraints may be more important predictors of general prosecutorial policies than is media attention to crime.

In addition to their influence on the judicial system, the news media also seem to have an effect on policymakers in the federal executive branch. Lambeth (1978) found that executive policymakers were more likely than congressional policymakers to think the press was influential. Linsky (1986) found that most federal policymakers thought that the national media had a substantial impact on policy. A study notable for its measurement of actual behavior (albeit symbolic behavior) rather than self-reported perceptions showed that the national news media clearly helped set the agenda for the president's 1980 State of the Union speech (Gilberg, Eyal, McCombs, & Nicholas, 1980).

The executive branch is responsible for administering economic regulation in the United States, and there is evidence that regulated industries accept the hypothesis that media attention influences policymakers. Specifically, a study of pricing decisions by oil companies during the oil crisis of the late 1970s found that the major oil firms moderated their price increases when television coverage of the oil industry was high (Erfle, McMillan, & Grofman, 1990).

The legislative branch of government has been the setting for many studies of the influence of the press on policymakers. Newspaper crusades for reform are related in important ways to legislative outcomes, according to a review of research about the legislation of crime and delinquency in North America (Hagan, 1980).

Sutherland's research on laws dealing with sexual psychopaths shows a typical pattern. Michigan enacted the first such law in 1937; many other states adopted similar laws in the ensuing years. Sutherland identified a three-stage process of legal innovation. In the states where such laws were passed, the first stage was widespread media publicity about a few serious sex crimes. The second stage was government study of the phenomenon, and the third stage was adoption of a statute. The laws were seen mainly as a response to generalized fear, inspired largely by media content (Sutherland, 1951; see also A. Swanson, 1960).

Other studies that have documented a link between media attention to specific issues with statutory changes at the state level are Berk, Brackman, and Lesser's research into the relationship between *Los Angeles Times* editorials and changes in the California penal code (1977) and McGarrell's study of juvenile correctional reform in New York state (1988).

Perhaps more pertinent to the notion of an agenda-setting effect of the press on policy is research by Heinz, who showed that variation in day-to-day attention to crime by metropolitan newspapers predicted legislative activity with respect to crime in the United States after World War II (Heinz, 1985). Some scholars, however, have found no evidence, or only weak evidence, of an agenda-setting effect of the press on legislative policymakers (see, e.g., Walker, 1977; Lambeth, 1978; Kingdon, 1984; Hess, 1986).

The possible agenda-setting effect of investigative reporting on policymakers is something of a special case and also deserves attention. Available evidence for the effect is mixed.

When investigative reports focus on problems that are beyond the ability of individual agencies to solve (e.g., fraud in the delivery of home health-care services, impropriety in dealing with sexual assault by a variety of governmental agencies), policymakers' responses tend to be symbolic rather than substantive (Cook et al., 1983; Protess et al., 1985). On the other hand, when investigative reports reveal wrongdoing within a specific agency (e.g., brutality by city police officers), the policy response tends to be substantive (Leff, Protess, & Brooks, 1986).

This pattern of findings suggests that the news media's influence on policy varies according to whether an agency perceives that it has clear responsibility for the issue at hand. When responsibility is clear—prosecutors being responsible for processing criminal cases (Pritchard, 1986; Pritchard, Dilts, & Berkowitz, 1987), a police department being responsible for the behavior of its officers—media attention to an issue tends to influence what Cobb and Elder (1983) call the "institutional agenda" and what this chapter calls the action agenda.

In such situations, substantive action tends to be taken, essentially for reasons of accountability: only by taking such action can policymakers minimize the possibility of conflict with important constituencies, especially the public, who might see lack of action as a breach of responsibility.

On the other hand, when responsibility is diffuse—e.g., no single agency was responsible for regulating home health-care services, no single agency could solve the widespread problem of official indifference to rape victims—media attention to an issue tends to have little, if any, substantive influence on policy. The media attention may spark a flurry of symbolic political behavior on the part of public officials, but little more.

DISCUSSION

This chapter has shown that the news media can, and often do, influence public policy agendas. Policymakers find media content useful because they often have no better indicator of public opinion.

Public opinion polls were becoming more and more common in the early 1990s, however, and to the extent that policymakers have access to polling data about relevant issues, the direct influence of the news media's self-generated content may diminish. However, many news organizations sponsor and prominently report the results of polls. Through their reporting of polls, the news media may remain policymakers' principal source of information about the state of public opinion.

Much of this chapter has talked about the media-policy relationship as if it were a rather simple, linear, and unidirectional process. The reality, however, is complex and multidimensional.

The creation of media content and policymaking influence each other. Molotch and colleagues label this an ecological approach, writing that "media and policy are part of a single ecology in which systemic transfers of cultural materials cumulate and dissipate, often imperceptibly, throughout a media-policy web (Molotch, Protess, & Gordon, 1987, p. 28).

Cook's participant observation of interactions between the media and congressional policymakers resulted in a similar conclusion. "Making laws and making news are not contradictory. Nor are they synonymous. Instead, they are different but complementary parts of the same process" (Cook, 1989, p. 9).

Given the available knowledge about the role played by the news media in the policy-making process in the United States, it is rather surprising that serious descriptions of the policy process continue to ignore the news media (e.g., Waste, 1989). It is clear that policy-making cannot be fully understood without an understanding of the role played by the media.

It is also clear that the nature of democracy in a political system with the media acting as broker between citizens and policymakers is different from the nature of democracy in which citizens interact directly with policymakers. The complexity of modern life is such that it may be impossible to increase contact between citizens and policymakers; the media may be here to stay as the link between the governed and the government, even in relatively small communities.

If so, then the challenge for those who would prefer a more democratic society may be to democratize the news media by making them more accountable to the people. Although a discussion of the topic is far beyond the scope of this chapter, experiments with a variety of ways of holding the media accountable—including press councils, ethics codes, and news ombudsmen—have been undertaken in North America in the past 25 years. The success of these experiments has been mixed, but they suggest the possibility of news organizations being more responsive to citizens' interests and needs, which in turn could lead to greater democratization of policymaking.

7

Marching to the Police and Court Beats: The Media-Source Relationship in Framing Criminal Justice Policy

Jack C. Doppelt

INTRODUCTION

News is often described as "a product of transactions between journalists and their sources" (Ericson, Baranek, & Chan, 1989, p. 377). Because it is a finite commodity limited by time, space, budget, and organizational constraints, news is necessarily not everything that happens but a depiction of what happens from the perspective of a society's participants and observers.[1]

The metaphor of a net, in contrast to a blanket, has been used to convey the media's limits in reporting on a societal landscape so vast that important events naturally fall through its holes (Tuchman, 1978, p. 21). The catch on a given day is dependent upon the media's ability to capture events efficiently and in a manner suitable for presentation as news. The selection process is not random.

It has been argued that the overriding need for efficiency dictates that news organizations consult an optimal number of sources, based pri-

---

1. This chapter derives from a larger study of the criminal justice system in Cook County, Illinois. The author wishes to acknowledge the indispensable contributions of Peter M. Manikas, John P. Heinz, Mindy S. Trossman, Peter Birkeland, and Lisa Anne Gurr in that project.

marily on their access to information and their willingness to cooperate in the informational transaction (Gans, 1979, p. 128). That dual criterion virtually guarantees that reporters will seek out elites and government officials since the latter have an interest in attracting media attention and are centrally located within society's power structure.

As Walter Lippmann wrote, "The established leaders of any organization have great natural advantages. They are believed to have better sources of information. The books and papers are in their offices. They took part in the important conferences. They met the important people. They have responsibility. It is, therefore, easier for them to secure attention and to speak in a convincing tone. But also they have a very good deal of control over the access to the facts" (1922/1943, p. 247). What results is a "presumption of hierarchy" in the search for authoritative sources (Sigal, 1986, p. 20), which in turn allows the news organizations to underscore their own authority by displaying legitimated leaders in society (Ericson, Baranek, & Chan, 1989, p. 5).

The characterization of news as a construction of source-based reality means that how reporters gather news and the types of sources they use are important to study because they determine not only what information is presented to the public and what image of society is presented (Soloski, 1989b, p. 864), but also what is reflected back to the policymaking elite. As part of an evolving ecology, reporters and their sources can be viewed as two of the three prongs in a chamber of reverberating effects among the media, policymakers, and the public. This multidirectional process often results in "agenda-building," a term used to connote the collective process of interacting and often reciprocal influences between the media and policymakers that helps create a climate that determines the likely composition of the public agenda (Lang & Lang, 1983).

In the criminal justice arena as in any other arena, the media's effect on both public opinion and policy comes from the capacity of reporters to play an interactive role in the larger ecology (Doppelt & Manikas, 1990, p. 134; Molotch, Protess, & Gordon, 1987, p. 46). Despite the integral role of sources in the newsmaking process and countless attempts to analyze the source-media relationship, surprisingly little attention has been focused on the source-media network in the criminal justice system (See Drechsel, 1983; Pritchard, 1986; Ericson, Baranek & Chan, 1989; Doppelt, 1991).

The relationship between the media and the actors within the criminal justice system is magnified in importance because the public gets information about the courts more frequently from broadcast news and newspapers than from schools, libraries, or any direct contact with the court system (Bennack, 1983, p. 21). Glimpses of the criminal justice system, through news accounts of crime and criminal trials, are provided on a daily basis (Shaw, 1984). One recent study in Cook County, Illinois, found that during May 1987, the *Chicago Tribune* and the *Chicago Sun-Times* ran an average of more than five legal stories per day in each paper, and reporting on criminal cases outnumbered the coverage of civil matters by a ratio of nearly three to one in both papers (Doppelt, 1991).

From the perspective of criminal justice policy, both the perception and the reality of an attentive public give the media the potential for inordinate influence in policy formation and ad hoc decision-making. Elites and government officials may make decisions in reaction to media coverage or in anticipation or fear of media attention. They may also be influenced more directly through their relationships with members of the media. After all, reporters and the media collectively, like elites and interest groups, may influence policy and frame public debate through direct professional contact (Laumann & Knoke, 1987, p. 8). In this capacity, the news media have been regarded as part of the "central circle" of elites who negotiate conflict among the major actors in a policy arena (Moore, 1979, p. 690; Heinz, Laumann, Salisbury, & Nelson, 1990, p. 357).

RESEARCH DESIGN

To analyze whether the relationship between the media and principal actors within the criminal justice system helps to frame policy and decisional choices, we designed a model that would explore the network of media contacts with actors in the system and the substance of those contacts. The media-source analysis was done as part of a larger study into the criminal justice system in Cook County, Illinois (Manikas, Heinz, Trossman, & Doppelt, 1990). Of the 211 criminal justice actors we interviewed in person between March 25, 1988, and March 14, 1989, 197 were potential news sources, 152 (72 percent of the sample) were government officials, and 45 (21 percent) were private interest group leaders. All were at or near the top of their particular organizational hierarchy. The remaining 14 (7 percent) were reporters, whose responses were analyzed primarily as a counterpoint to safeguard against self-serving answers from the others.

To explore their relationships with the media, each of the 197 nonmedia respondents was given a list of reporters affiliated with 16 media organizations. The respondents were instructed to add to the list of 16 if their degree of contact with other media was more than negligible. The 16 media organizations selected were those that covered criminal justice matters on a regular basis. We selected three metropolitan dailies (*Chicago Tribune, Chicago Sun-Times,* and *Chicago Daily Defender*), three legal specialty publications (*Chicago Daily Law Bulletin, Chicago*

Lawyer, and *National Law Journal*), one local wire service (City News), five radio stations (WBBM-AM, WMAQ-AM, WLS-AM, WGN-AM, and WBEZ-FM) and four television stations (CBS's WBBM-TV, NBC's WMAQ-TV, ABC's WLS-TV, and an independent station, WGN-TV).

The respondents were asked to identify the reporters with whom they had communicated over the past year and to note whether the frequency of their contacts was daily, weekly, monthly, every few months, once or twice a year, or never. The respondents were also asked whether they were generally in contact with the news media during the course of their work, with which two reporters they were in most frequent contact, what the substance of those communications was, whether it was generally adversarial or cooperative, whether they thought the reporters had a good understanding of how their organizations worked, and whether news accounts had led to any recent changes in their organizations' operations.

They were also asked seven questions relating to journalistic conventions, such as pretrial publication of prejudicial information, access to jurors after trial, and the identification of juveniles, street gangs, and the race of individuals accused of crime. Finally, a series of personal background and social value questions was asked of the 197 nonmedia respondents and the 14 media respondents to enable us to gauge roughly whether there were marked differences in gender, ethnicity, education, religion, political preference, or ideological orientation between the media and sources within the criminal justice system.

We used a statistical technique, known as smallest space analysis, to document the patterns of contacts among the respondents. The technique allowed us to represent the contacts as points in Euclidean space (see Figure 7.1). The proximity of these points on a three-dimensional graph reflects the degree of overlap in the sets of respondents who contact others within the system. To the extent that certain reporters or media organizations were contacted by the same respondents, they would tend to be located in the same region of the space; those reporters who shared few sources would be far apart. Individuals or organizations who are contacted frequently by diverse respondents would tend to be located near the center of the space. Studies have shown that actors who are connected to others in such a way that they "reach" most of the other actors are in a better position to mediate and influence activities in the system as a whole than are actors who are more peripherally connected (Laumann & Pappi, 1976, p. 20; Heinz et al., 1990).

One might speculate that the media, who rely on sources, would have a high frequency of contacts within the criminal justice system. A number of additional hypotheses might also be plausible. Would the media be clustered together because reporters covering the criminal justice system tend to use the same sources? Or would reporters cluster with different sectors within the criminal justice system, depending on what beats they covered or what personal, social, or ideological orientations they shared with particular sources? Would the media occupy the center of the space, indicating that their contacts were diverse and perhaps that their communications role was central to the system's operation?

EXTENT OF SOURCE-MEDIA CONTACT

Four out of five actors in the criminal justice system claimed to be in contact with the news media during the course of their work. For purposes of analysis, we divided the 152 government officials into seven functional subcategories: prosecution, law enforcement/investigations, court administration and the judiciary, defense, corrections, legislation and administration, and social services. The high frequency of contact was spread across most subcategories of sources but with some noteworthy gradations. As Table 7.1 indicates, more than 80 percent of the prosecutors, public defenders, public interest group leaders, lawmakers, and administrative heads had at least some contact with the media. They were followed by judges, court administrators, and law enforcement personnel. Only 56 percent of the corrections officials and 45 percent of the social service administrators surveyed said their responsibilities put them in contact with reporters.

Of the 18 actors who specified why they had no contact with the media, six valued their roles in the criminal justice system as not newsworthy, six said all media queries were directed to their agencies' public relations officer, three said only the agency head was to have contact with the media, two said their agency contact was limited to news releases and press conferences, and one said he needed approval before talking to reporters.

Though almost 80 percent of the respondents indicated that they had some contact with the media, we probed to determine whether the contact was extensive. We found that none of the 16 media organizations was in contact with a majority of the respondents. Table 7.2 shows that actors in the criminal justice system were in contact more with the daily newspapers than with the other media organizations. Even then, less than 40 percent of the potential sources were in contact with reporters at the *Chicago Tribune* or *Chicago Sun-Times*. Twenty-four percent of the respondents were in contact with reporters from the City News Bureau, the city's only wire service, and 21 percent were in contact with reporters from the *Chicago Daily Defender*, the daily newspaper that serves the black community. Between 14 and 19 percent of the respondents were in contact with television reporters, between 7 and 22 percent with radio reporters, and between 3 and 19 percent with reporters from the legal specialty publications. Clearly, the contact

Table 7.1
Respondents' Contact with the Media

Type of Respondents	Number of Respondents	Percent in Contact with News Media
Private interest group leaders	45	87
All government officials	143	76
Prosecutors	22	91
Law enforcement	38	76
Judges/Court administrators	28	79
Public defenders	17	88
Corrections officials	16	56
Lawmakers/Agency heads	11	82
Social service administrators	11	45
Total (Group leaders + officials)	188	79

Table 7.2

Respondents' Contact with Particular News Organizations

News Media Organization	Number of Contacts Respondents Had	Percent of Respondents in Contact with Media
Metropolitan Dailies		
Chicago Tribune	77	39
Chicago Sun-Times	73	37
Chicago Daily Defender	41	21
Television Stations		
WBBM-TV (CBS)	38	19
WMAQ-TV (NBC)	38	19
WLS-TV (ABC)	33	17
WGN-TV (Independent)	27	14
Radio Stations		
WBBM-AM	44	22
WMAQ-AM	22	11
WLS-AM	21	11
WGN-AM	33	17
WBEZ-FM (National Public Radio)	13	7
Legal Specialty Publications		
Chicago Daily Law Bulletin	38	19
Chicago Lawyer	12	6
National Law Journal	5	3
Local Wire Service--City News Bureau	47	24

between the media and actors in the criminal justice system was less extensive than one might have concluded simply by measuring whether the system's actors were in contact with the media.

When we broke down the contacts by subcategories of actors, it became apparent that some of the media's contacts were disproportionately greater with law enforcement and less with judges, public defenders, and social service administrators. This was the case at a statistically significant level with the *Chicago Daily Defender*, the *Chicago Tribune*, the City News Bureau, WLS-TV, WBBM-AM, and WGN-AM.

NATURE OF SOURCE-MEDIA CONTACT

Studies that examine the media-source relationship often conclude by debunking the conventional notion that reporting is an adversarial enterprise serving as a check on government, the powerful, and the privileged (Soloski, 1989b; Ericson, Baranek, & Chan, 1989; Tuchman, 1978; Gans, 1979). It has been suggested that there is an "elective affinity" at work in the ideas and interests journalists and their sources share (Weber, 1946, p. 280). As one reporter has said, "I write for my news sources because I have to deal with them" (Soloski, 1989b, p. 869).

We found that the relationship between criminal justice actors and the reporters they dealt with regularly was cooperative rather than adversarial. Only 4 percent of the relationships with reporters were described as adversarial; 87 percent were regarded as cooperative and 9 percent as neither. Of the 11 respondents who considered the relationship adversarial, only one felt the adversarial nature of the relationship was salutary. The others attributed the adversarial relationship to failings in the media, specifically bias, sensationalism, incompetence, or isolation from the community.

There was less of a consensus among respondents about whether the reporters they dealt with most frequently understood the role of the respondents' offices or organizations in the criminal justice system. In 78 percent of the reported media-source relationships, reporters were considered sufficiently competent; prosecutors, interest group leaders, judges, and law enforcement authorities tended to be more impressed than public defenders, lawmakers, administrative officials, social service administrators, or corrections officials. The media criticisms mentioned most often were the reporters' biases, lack of knowledge, lack of interest in how the system works, inexperience, and the sensationalistic bent of media coverage.

What did reporters discuss with their sources? Of the 293 matters that were discussed as part of the media-source relationship, 55 percent were policy oriented, 35 percent were breaking news, and 10 percent were non-news. Among the most common policy-related issues discussed were budget and personnel matters, juvenile issues (gang activity, Juvenile Court, and diversion alternatives), pending legislation, prison and jail overcrowding, crime and crime prevention, police misconduct, race relations and discrimination, crimes against women, drugs, and mental health. The breaking news discussions related primarily to investigations, arrests, indictments, litigation, and prison altercations and escapes. Included in the non-news interactions were community outreach efforts (panels, community appearances, and public service announcements), interviews for feature stories (profiles and human interest pieces), political discussions, exchanges in which the reporters provided the information, social conversations, gossip, and complaints about media coverage.

The same broad range of issues emerged when we focused on the reporters' perspective. The reporters were far more likely to discuss breaking news stories, such as high profile criminal cases, with gov-

ernment officials than with interest group leaders. As might be expected, reporters' discussions with interest group leaders focused more
on issues central to the interest groups' agendas, such as organized
crime with the Chicago Crime Commission, prisons with the John Howard Association, civil liberties with the ACLU, and bench and bar issues
with bar association leaders. The phrase "round up the usual suspects"
was used by a few of the reporters surveyed to indicate their tendency
to contact the same interest groups whenever they needed an informed,
reliable, yet predictable voice on a particular criminal justice issue.

Though the government officials and interest group leaders reported
overwhelmingly a cooperative relationship with the media, the reporters surveyed noted points of contention with their most frequently
contacted sources. Disagreements were more likely to arise in the interactions with government officials (45 percent of the contacts) than
with interest group leaders (21 percent). The most common point of
contention with government officials was over access to information
and sources. Also mentioned were issues arising from the media-source
relationship itself (such as confidentiality, the visual imperatives of
television, and complaints about media coverage) and ideological differences (regarding the death penalty, drugs, civil liberties, plea bar-
gaining, and releases on bond). Only one reporter stated that lack of
access was a point of contention with an interest group leader. Disagreements with interest group leaders, though infrequent, were more
likely to be ideological, such as differences over legalized gambling,
civil liberties, capital punishment, and attitudes toward criminals and
domestic violence.

SOURCE-MEDIA DIFFERENCES

Differences between the media and sources in the criminal justice
system might exist independent of their interactions. Personal, professional, political, or ideological differences might emerge in news coverage, through editorial perspective or story selection, despite a
cooperative veneer during the media-source relationship. The relationship between a reporter and a police official, for example, need not be
adversarial for the news coverage to reflect a sensitivity for civil liberties. The interactions between reporters and social service administrators might be frictionless, yet the news coverage might effectively
ignore their community-based progams. If reporters' backgrounds and
beliefs were similar to those prevalent in only certain sectors of the
criminal justice system and they tended to cluster with the sectors
whose views they shared to the exclusion of others, then the public
might be exposed to a distorted construction of reality.

Conventional stereotypes suggest that reporters are more liberal than many of the actors in the criminal justice system. However, as Table 7.3 indicates, we found that in the criminal justice network in Cook County, reporters tended to be no more liberal on economic and civil libertarian issues than were government officials, and were less liberal than interest group leaders. Although reporters were younger, more independent politically (none was Republican), and more likely to be born outside Cook County than either the government officials or the interest group leaders, such demographic characteristics did not nec- essarily translate into more liberal beliefs. Reporters were considerably more likely than other criminal justice actors to believe that consumers would be better protected through the free market than through gov- ernment regulation, for example. They were also less liberal on the question of whether the Constitution should be strictly construed, but more liberal in opposing punishment of feminists who removed their clothing in public to dramatize their protest against sexual exploitation.

When we divided the government officials into subcategories, we found no statistically significant differences among the groups. On eco- nomic matters, lawmakers, administrative heads, social service admin- istrators, and law enforcement officials were the more conservative, corrections officials were more liberal, and reporters were in between. On civil liberties issues, lawmakers, administrative heads, public de- fenders, and judges were the more conservative, while reporters and the other government officials were more moderate. In summary, we found no evidence that ideological beliefs were driving the media- source relationship or prompting reporters to seek out only those sources whose social values they shared.

We also examined whether professional attitudes might link reporters with particular sectors within the criminal justice system. Professional differences, for example, might encourage reporters to seek out certain sources and avoid others.

As Table 7.4 indicates, when asked "media-sensitive" questions about the criminal justice system, reporters expressed attitudes highly different from the government officials and interest group leaders on three of the seven questions. All or nearly all the reporters surveyed felt that the media should publish such potentially prejudicial pretrial information as confessions and prior criminal records; only about one- third of the other criminal justice actors felt the information should be published.

Though the other four questions yielded less difference of opinion, they still demonstrate an attitudinal difference between reporters and other criminal justice actors. Those differences, however, do not nec- essarily reflect a propublication orientation by reporters. The accepted journalism convention is for the media to suppress the race of criminal defendants and the names and race of juvenile defendants. The re-

Table 7.3
Economic Liberalism and Civil Libertarian Scores

	Government (N = 150)	Private Groups (N = 41)	News Media (N = 14)	Total Sample (N = 205)
Economic Liberalism Mean Score	3.43	3.92	3.49	3.53
Civil Libertarian Mean Score	3.23	3.63	3.43	3.32
Summary Liberalism Mean Score	3.35	3.80	3.43	3.45

Note: The questions used to examine social values were identical to those used in a national probability sample administered by the Opinion Research Corporation in 1960 and reported by the University of Michigan's Survey Research Center (Robinson, Rush, & Head, 1968) and replicated in a survey of Chicago lawyers in 1975 (Heinz & Laumann, 1982).

Table 7.4
Responses to "Media-Sensitive" Questions about the Criminal Justice System (percent responding "yes")

Media-Sensitive Questions	Reporters (N = 14)	Government Officials and Private Group Leaders (N = 197)
Should the media publish information before trial about an accused's confession?*	100%	28%
Should the media publish a defendant's prior criminal record before trial?*	92%	36%
Should the media publish before trial evidence likely to be inadmissible?*	90%	30%
Should the media interview jurors after trial?	86%	69%
Should the media identify juveniles accused of crime?**	8%	21%
Should the media publish the names of street gangs?**	53%	64%
Should the media identify the race of defendants accused of crime?**	8%	32%

* Confessions, prior criminal records, and information that is likely to be inadmissible at trial have been isolated as the more nettlesome areas in the fair trial-free press debate since the Reardon Commission studied the controversy 25 years ago (American Bar Association Advisory Committee on Fair Trial and Free Press, 1966).
** The accepted journalism convention is *not* to make such identifications.

porters surveyed overwhelmingly favored those self-censoring practices, yet the other criminal justice actors were more willing to have the information published. One in five said the media should identify juveniles accused of crime, and one in three said the media should identify the race of criminal defendants. Despite the journalism convention that suppresses the names of street gangs, a majority of reporters and an even stronger majority of government officials and interest group leaders felt that street gangs should be identified by name.

When we examined the government officials by subcategories, we found, surprisingly, that public defenders were the most likely group other than reporters to favor pretrial publication of an accused's confession (nearly half did). Public defenders and prosecutors were the most likely government officials to favor pretrial publication of a defendant's prior criminal record and information likely to be inadmissible at trial. And public defenders, along with corrections officials, were the most likely to favor the identification of juveniles accused of crime. These findings, coupled with the similarities in the liberalism scores of public defenders, prosecutors, and reporters, make it even more puzzling that the defense bar is so inordinately dissatisfied with media coverage of the criminal justice system (Doppelt, 1991).

MEDIA IMPACT ON POLICY

Media coverage influences not only the public's perception of the criminal justice system but also the policy agendas of the actors in the system. Of the 152 government officials we surveyed, 46 (or 30 percent) said news coverage had led to recent changes in their agencies' operations. The agencies that reported such changes, however, were not necessarily those that had the closest relationships with the news media. Despite the limited relationship between the media and the social service sector, for instance, one-half of the social service administrators said media coverage led to recent changes. The cited changes included firings, internal investigations, and the privatization of services.

About one-third of the judges and court administrators, law enforcement officials, corrections officials, lawmakers, and administrative heads said news coverage led to substantive changes. Judges mentioned personnel changes on the bench, increases in resources, and higher bonds as a result of media attention. Court administrators and corrections officials cited technological improvements, personnel changes, and budgetary increases. The two groups that reported the least change prompted by media coverage were public defenders (17 percent) and prosecutors (8 percent). In fact, one prosecutor noted that the media-inspired change was detrimental and required the imposition of protective orders to prevent further media attention.

As a check against the possibility that the nonmedia respondents would understate the media's influence on policy or practices, we asked the same questions of our media respondents. Their perspective on the media's impact on policy did not differ significantly from what the nonmedia respondents reported. Five of the 14 reporters (36 percent) believed that their work had led to substantial change by a criminal justice agency. They mentioned legislative and personnel changes, budgetary increases, investigative measures, and judicial decision-making. Most of the media-inspired changes resulted from in-depth stories focusing on systemic problems rather than from breaking news stories or editorial advocacy.

SOURCE-MEDIA NETWORK

To help gauge how central the media-source relationship was to criminal justice policy formation, we plotted the patterns of contacts among the actors in the system. Figure 7.1 reflects the degree of overlap among the respondents who contacted each of the organizations at least as often as "every few months." Therefore, in computing this solution, we included only the 56 actors having a minimum of 30 contacts among our 211 respondents. (Eleven of the 14 media respondents we surveyed are included.)

Organizations that were contacted by large numbers of diverse respondents, for example, tend to be located near the center of the space. Organizations whose contacts tended to be with the same respondents locate in the same general region of the space; organizations that share few of the same contacts are far apart.

Figure 7.1 depicts a general pattern in which most of the news organizations are located on the right side of the space, almost all of them quite tightly grouped. Their proximity to one another demonstrates that reporters covering the criminal justice system tended to be in contact with the same sources.

Who were those sources? The analysis shows that the media organizations share the right side of the space principally with law enforcement and prosecutorial agencies; specifically, the FBI, the U.S. attorney's office, the Chicago corporation counsel's office, the Illinois attorney general's office, the Cook County medical examiner's office, the Illinois State Police, the Chicago Police Department, and the suburban police. The media's most frequent sources in the criminal justice system, therefore, were those who were also in most frequent contact with law enforcement and the prosecution.

Two exceptions are worth noting. The Cook County state's attorney's office and the Cook County sheriff's office are located just outside the cluster of prosecutorial offices, law enforcement agencies, and media organizations, to the left of the center of the space. It is likely that their affiliations with other sectors of the criminal justice system pull them toward other clusters, but this is not to say that their relationships with the media were more tenuous than those of the other prosecutorial and law enforcement agencies.

Lawmakers and administrative agencies, such as the Cook County Board of Commissioners, the mayor's office, the governor's office, and the Illinois secretary of state's office, are also located in the same general area on the space as the media. Only two interest groups—the Chicago Crime Commission and the ACLU—are located in the same general area. Both deal extensively with law enforcement matters. Clearly outside the network of media contacts are those respondents whose pri-

Figure 7.1
Smallest Space Analysis of Media-Source Relationships

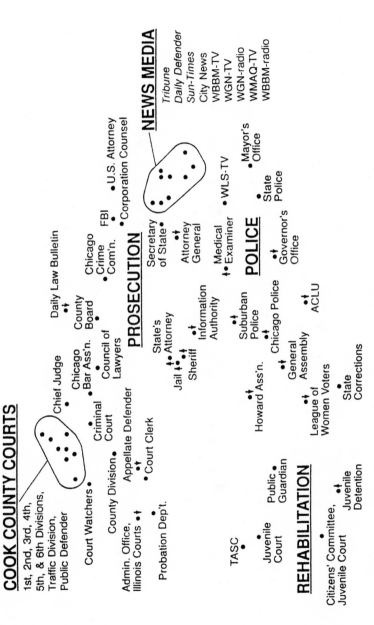

Note: This is a three-dimensional smallest space solution. The third dimension of the space is represented by arrows next to some of the points. Points with an arrow pointing up are located substantially above the plane of the page; points with an arrow pointing down are located substantially below it. Points without an arrow are located relatively close to the middle of the third dimension of the space.

mary affiliations are with the courts, the defense, corrections, and social service agencies.

CONCLUSION

A number of conclusions emerge from our analyses. Contrary to what one might have expected, reporters were not located in the center of the space. Reporters' contacts were not as diverse as one might have thought. In addition, because the media's circle of contacts was circumscribed largely by law enforcement and the prosecution, and to a lesser extent by lawmakers and administrative agencies, news coverage was more likely to reflect the perspective of those actors. We found no evidence, however, that the connection between the media and those located nearby derived from personal, professional, political, or ideological similarities. The media-source relationship appeared to be cooperative rather than adversarial across all sectors.

We found that reporters were no more liberal than other actors in the system and that no discernible pattern emerged that linked reporters and particular sources along ideological lines. The liberalism rating of reporters was most similar to those of prosecutors, public defenders, and social service administrators. Yet in the smallest space analysis, the media clustered with prosecutors but not with the other two groups. The most liberal groups—corrections officials and private interest group leaders—did not cluster with the media.

One pattern in the smallest space graph may provide a clue into the clustering of media with law enforcement and the prosecution. Figure 7.1 depicts a system proceeding counterclockwise that approximates the flow of a criminal case, from investigation and arrest (law enforcement in the lower right), through charge (prosecution located right of center), through the courts (judges and public defender in the upper left), and around to sentencing and rehabilitative alternatives such as prison, probation, and treatment programs (corrections and social service providers in the lower left).

The media are found clustered at the inception, literally beating the clock to report on breaking news at the earliest access point. Because much of the interaction between reporters and sources in the criminal justice system derives from breaking crime news, it is understandable that reporters will seek out not those whose ideologies or politics they share, but those most likely to have information and most willing to share it as soon as it is available. In that regard, judges, juvenile court officials, social service providers, corrections officials, and public defenders lack one and maybe both prerequisites.

Information about breaking crime stories comes to the attention of these actors later in the flow of a case than information comes to law enforcement and prosecutors. And in varying degrees, they are often less willing to share information with reporters. Judges are constrained from commenting on pending cases or controversies, juvenile court officials face statutory limitations on confidentiality, social service providers must often consider client confidentiality, corrections officials have security considerations that limit access, and public defenders not only confront issues of client confidentiality and access if their clients are in jail, but often perceive that no news is the best news for their accused clients. Moreover, public defenders in Cook County, as in most jurisdictions, do not get assigned to a case until the first appearance in court. They are not involved in a case at the investigation and charging stages.

A potential danger in such patterns of media contact is that news coverage of the criminal justice system will construct the reality of those with whom the media interact most frequently. This may be particularly relevant in a system in which source interactions are relatively sparse. As noted earlier, none of the 16 media organizations was in contact with a majority of the criminal justice actors. One possible consequence is that even when policy issues arise independent of breaking crime news, reporters seek out those whose acquaintance they have made and whose views and opinions will be predictable and forthcoming. The confined media-source network becomes self-perpetuating.

One factor appears to mitigate against serious policy consequences resulting from a media-source network that favors interactions with law enforcement and the prosecution. We found no indication from the actors in the system that substantive change brought on by media coverage corresponded with the media's place within the criminal justice network. Most noticeably, prosecutors, who are clearly part of the media network, reported almost no changes resulting from media coverage. Public defenders, who are clearly not part of that network, also reported few changes resulting from media coverage. Yet other sectors of the criminal justice system, those in close proximity to the media and those not, reported a greater media impact on their agency's operations.

It is conceivable that the closer the relationship with the media, the more likely media coverage will prompt change, through sheer exposure. That might have been the case with law enforcement officials who said they restructured police beats and responded to news reports of graffiti. It is conceivable, however, that the closer the relationship, the less likely the media will be to unearth problems needing change. That might be the case with prosecutors whose interactions with reporters arise most often in breaking news settings where efficient cooperation is more likely than scrutiny or criticism. It is also possible that those sectors in the criminal justice system remote to the media, such as social service agencies, might be more apt to change their operations as a hypersensitive reaction to media attention when it is directed their way. Further inquiry will be needed to determine how the media's place within the criminal justice network affects the agendas and operations of the other actors in the system.

8

Reporting on the Public Mind

Leonard Tipton

INTRODUCTION

In the last edition of his public opinion textbook, political scientist Bernard Hennessy made a rather offhanded and wry comment about mass media's linking role between policymakers and the public. "Political actors," he wrote, "tend to believe that the mass media have insight into the 'public mind' (an illusion carefully nurtured by the press)" (1985, p. 249).

Other political scientists have made similar comments that would substantiate at least the first part of that statement. For instance, policymakers' belief in media's effect on public concerns formed the basis for Bernard Cohen's original formulation of what came to be the media agenda-setting hypothesis. Cohen (1963) had noted that policymakers often were forced to divert their attention from pressing policy problems to respond to issues being covered by media, because they perceived that media issues were those that constituents would soon be posing as concerns to their elected representatives. Wolfgang Donsback, then president of the International Association for Public Opinion Research, argued the point this way: "Pollsters have taken away the several hundred years old monopoly of journalists to assess what the public thinks." (1989, p. 14).

There is, however, little hard evidence to substantiate Hennessy's parenthetical comment about journalism's carefully nurturing such an illusion. On the contrary, one of the premises of this chapter is that journalists have never really understood or accepted the role they are presumed to play as a source of information about "the public mind." That term was deliberately chosen for this chapter to represent something different from "public opinion." It is intended to evoke associations with the "minding" concept of symbolic interactionism: that meanings and actions are rooted simultaneously not only in what we think but also in what we think others think.

Perhaps a reference to the model presented in the introductory chapter of this volume will make that point clearer. Journalists do accept that they serve as a link from policymakers to public. That is a function widely recognized in the journalistic profession as "public affairs reporting." However, being a link to policymakers about public thought or providing a kind of feedback loop to the public itself about collective thought are not functions that are as clearly identified or as widely recognized among journalists. Phrases like "serving as the public's representative" are not entirely foreign to the vocabulary of journalism. But a "tap into the public mind" is foreign vocabulary, although journalists might recognize Minogue's explanation:

In talking of a "public mind" I am talking of an informed sensibility in which a very large part of the citizen body participates, a part much larger than any elite, yet obviously not the whole of the electorate. The borderlines are inevitably vague, and a significant one separates those educated people who are intensely responsive to the currents of opinion in the serious newspapers from the considerable majority of people for whom politics, most of the time, is little more than background noise. (1989, p. 475)

Even if journalists recognize that description of their audience, it is questionable whether their traditions and literature recognize a need to monitor and describe a "public mind." Certainly, the past few years have seen a dramatic increase in journalism's use of public opinion polls. However, the point to be argued in this chapter is that, perhaps because the trend is so recent, there is a kind of "cultural lag." A responsibility to report on public opinion has not been incorporated into journalism's institutionalized values. Journalists may be doing that kind of reporting, but their reasons for doing so are markedly different from expectations that underlie public opinion theory.

That creates a somewhat crucial gap between what political theorists, policymakers, and perhaps the public as well want to use journalism for and what the journalists see themselves as providing. The point to be argued in the next section of this chapter is that both classical and contemporary views of public opinion assume that media do provide that "tap into the public mind." In the absense of reporting that does it specifically, political actors are forced to appropriate some forms of media content as "surrogate measures" of public opinion in ways the journalists never intended (Pritchard & Berkowitz, 1989).

Such surrogate measures include the amount of attention devoted to a given issue, as well as coverage of various events like campaigns and assemblies or protests and demonstrations. Other kinds of surrogates more obviously tap public voices directly, most notably letters to the editor, straw polls, and formal systematic polling. The latter part of this chapter reviews some of that content.

While the chapter itself is not so organized, an alternative way of thinking about the various kinds of media content of interest is in terms of the model presented in the introductory chapter. Content represented by the link from public to media would include polling, both formal and informal, and letters to the editor. The link between special interest groups and media would include protests and demonstrations, pseudoevents such as news conferences, and reaction quotes. The policymaker-to-media link constitutes the staple of journalistic content, public affairs reporting. A useful heuristic provided by that model-based view of media content is that it focuses attention on the two-way aspects of the links. One should keep in mind not only the content that flows from media to the model's other components—particularly content that tells one component about the others—but also the nature of the media connections to each component in the first place. In other words, how accurate and complete is the information that flows through those links, and what gets screened out of the final presentation?

POLITICAL THEORY PERSPECTIVES

Most political histories concerned with the term "public opinion" and its various linguistic alternatives tie the concept's origins to the development of democracy. While there is scholarly argument over whether such terms meant the same thing to the "classicists" as they do now (Hennessy, 1985; Noelle-Neumann, 1989), there is little dispute over the importance attached to newspapers as a source of evidence. In his overview of the history of public opinion theory, Chisman (1976) makes the point that classical methodologies were similar to those of modern scholars: the classicists utilized a "strong empirical component," albeit "empirical political science in the crudest sense" and "based on some fairly primitive research techniques" (p. 21). A key technique for the classicists, Chisman notes, was reading newspapers, with special attention to public assemblies, demonstrations, and riots. It should be noted that such accounts during this period, particularly in the American press, had a very different approach from that of mod-

ern reporting. Most accounts were political commentary. Little direct
observational reporting took place, on the commonsense grounds that
people already knew the facts about events occurring in their own
community.

As Leo Bogart (1985) noted in the introduction to the Transaction
Edition of *Polls and the Awareness of Public Opinion*, the columns of
the press and the transcripts of public debates might arguably have
been valid indicators of what the public at large thought about important issues during the eighteenth century. "This may well have been
true when a reader could select a newspaper to suit his prejudices from
a highly varied assortment," he wrote, "but it would be a bold historian
who would equate the views of the press and those of the public today"
(p. x).

Nevertheless, modern public opinion theorists do make key assumptions about media accounts being exactly such indicators. This is particularly true in what Nimmo (1988) calls contemporary "pretheories"
that offer a perspective in public opinion that is receiving wide acceptance, "albeit frequently under diverse, sometimes contradictory, labels" (p. 2). These perspectives include three that are discussed much
more extensively in other chapters of this volume: the spiral of silence,
pluralistic ignorance, and the third-person effect. They are discussed
briefly here to emphasize two points about these perspectives. First,
they explicitly incorporate perceptions of the range and strength of the
opinions of "others" as a key component in the public opinion process.
Second, they make crucial assumptions about the importance of media
content as a source of information about the distribution of opinion in
the public at large.

The spiral of silence claims individual fear of isolation as the underlying explanatory factor in an assumed need on the part of individuals to constantly monitor the climate of opinion in their political
environment. Noelle-Neumann's stance on the role of media has shifted
and evolved over the years. But her recent work strongly emphasizes
the need for incorporation of media content analysis in testing her ideas.
Of particular importance is the "intensity of and slant in the way a
topic is treated in trend-setting media" (1989, p. 20).

Pluralistic ignorance posits a conservative bias as an underlying
mechanism. Note that "conservative" is used here in its traditional
sense of resistance to change. In that sense, for example, a "prochoice"
position on abortion would be the conservative position, to the extent
that it reflects current legal status. Individuals assume that because a
status quo policy exists, a majority of citizens must support it. This
leads to states of public opinion in which an emerging new majority
mistakenly perceives itself to be in a minority, and a minority clinging
to an older tradition perceives itself to be in the majority. Media ac-

counts are suggested as a major source of information and legitimation of the status quo.

Third-person effect proposes a special case of mediated communication as the critical variable. Individuals do not think they are influenced by media messages, but they think others are. By extension, the perspective suggests that media reports influence the perception of opinion distribution, if not the actual distribution itself.

These contemporary theories, like their predecessors, build on assumptions regarding media content and its presumed effects. In many respects, however, political observers and actors may be influenced by the characteristics of the journalists themselves, and the peculiar niche they occupy in the political process, more than the actual content they produce. In an early attempt to link newspaper content with systematic public opinion appraisal, Robinson (1932) keyed on just such characteristics: "If anyone is able to gauge preelection sentiment accurately, it should be the skilled newspaperman. He is a trained observer of public opinion; he is close to the politicians who are endeavoring to manipulate public beliefs; he has the opportunity to gather information from all quarters; and, in addition, he has the newspaperman's intuition, which comes through long association with political affairs" (p. 14). More recent observers have added other factors that put journalists in the position to know more than they report. They have access not only to other polls and information sources (Lemert, 1986) but also to their company's own proprietary research (Bogart, 1989).

JOURNALISTIC PERSPECTIVES

Even granting that journalism is in a better position to tap the public mood more objectively than other social institutions, how widely journalists share their insights is still problematic. An examination of journalism texts and traditions suggests that describing public opinion is not one of journalism's high priorities.

Several major research projects have asked U.S. journalists themselves to respond to questions about how they perceive media functions. That line of inquiry began with Johnstone, Slawski, and Bowman (1976) and has been followed up by Weaver and Wilhoit (1986) and most recently by Cunningham and Henry of the American Society of Newspaper Editors (1989). The ASNE list of "things . . . that newspapers do or try to do today" is typical, as well as being the most recent. Journalists identified this rank order of important functions:

1. Provide analysis and interpretation of complex events.
2. Investigate claims and statements made by the government.

3. Get information to the public quickly.
4. Discuss national policy while it is still being developed.
5. Stay away from stories where factual content cannot be verified.
6. Provide entertainment and relaxation.
7. Concentrate on news that is of interest to the widest possible public.
8. Be an adversary of public officials by being constantly skeptical of their actions.
9. Be an adversary of businesses by being constantly skeptical of their actions.
10. Cover "chicken dinner" news.

Looking at that list in terms of this text's earlier model, what is notable is that the journalists regard their most important functions as those represented by the lines from policymakers and special interest groups to the public, and not vice versa. To be sure, identification of functions is constrained by what things researchers and textbook writers choose to include, and omission does not necessarily mean absence. Certainly it is more difficult to argue the absence of something than it is to find evidence of its presence. But the point remains that journalistic discussion of functions does not routinely include items that play well to political theorists' expectations about reporting on the public mind.

One reason is that journalists are not trained to think in those terms. When journalism reporting texts do offer up an explicit list of functions, it is apt to be a terse variant of the items above. Newsome and Wolert (1985) present a typical list: media functions are to inform, to provide a forum for advertising, to provide a forum for ideas, to educate, and to serve as a watchdog of government.

The texts are much more likely to stress traditionally accepted news values in lieu of functions. Mencher's widely used reporting text (1991) covers the typical litany of news values: impact (consequence or importance of the event), timeliness, prominence (notably well-known personalities), proximity (or "localness"), conflict, and oddity. In fairness, the more modern texts and revised editions, including Mencher, have begun to include a section on public opinion polling. Advanced reporting texts, like that of Keir, McCombs, and Shaw (1991), discuss not only how media should report polls, but how they should conduct their own, as well. Those developments will be discussed in a later section of this chapter.

The point to be repeated here is that much of the media content that serves policymakers and others as surrogate measures of public opinion was not produced with that purpose in mind.

The metaphor of media agenda-setting is a case in point. Without getting into the debate over whether media shape or reflect political reality, it is widely accepted that the extent of news coverage of an issue is directly correlated with public concern. Yet that relationship is largely irrelevant to journalistic decisions to cover or not cover issues. For journalists, the widespread acceptance of traditional news values means that certain events must be covered. To use another metaphor, the journalist has no degrees of freedom in terms of whether or not to cover them, and thus no real way to exercise agenda-setting powers. To use such coverage as the surrogate measure means one is tapping not public opinion, but merely public awareness of events that journalists, applying their own institutionalized values, have defined as newsworthy.

Other kinds of events, particularly those in which the public itself is actively involved, represent more valid surrogate measures. The obvious example is elections. Others that have been studied in terms of their validity or representativeness include protests and demonstrations (Burstein, 1979) and even jury trials (Krauss, 1988–89).

There is almost no evidence, however, about what journalists themselves think of the validity of such surrogate measures. Nine such possibilities, somewhat arbitrarily chosen, were included in a questionnaire that this chapter's author sent to editors of Kentucky newspapers in 1984. The editors were asked, "How valid do you think each of the following is in assessing public opinion?"

The editors selected elections—particularly referenda and presidential elections—as the most valid. State and local elections formed a second tier, about equal with formal polling. Public hearings, letters to the editor, and statements from community leaders were viewed as more problematic. Claims of political candidates were soundly rejected.

In most of these areas, however, the policymakers are not dependent upon the media content exclusively. Most such things are directly observable by the policymakers themselves. Of more interest in the context of this chapter are those that are under immediate media control and not directly observable by others. These include letters to the editor, straw polls, and formal media polling. In each case, policymakers may have similar alternatives—that is, they get their own letters from constituents and have their own polling results. But nonetheless the three are among the few media content areas that journalists have developed themselves as tools, however imprecise, for systematic public input.

Letters to the Editor

Conventional wisdom, backed up by some empirical research, takes the view that letters to the editor do not represent any valid gauge of the "real" state of public opinion. Such a conclusion may be too hasty for two reasons. First, the conclusion is generally based on the atypical characteristics of the letter writers themselves, rather than the distribution of opinions being expressed. Second, letters to the editor as a widespread forum are a relatively recent development in American journalism and have expanded greatly in the past few years. As they continue to evolve, that conventional wisdom may have to be reviewed.

Letters to the editor in their modern form—as a systematic, institutionalized forum with its own section and graphic display—began to develop in U.S. newspapers only in the 1930s (Pasternack, 1988). A major expansion occurred in the 1980s and shows all signs of continuing to grow (Terrell, 1989).

There is little doubt that historically, letter writers are atypical of the general public, though they do reflect traditional demographic differences between the newspaper reading and nonreading public. Writers generally are older, better educated, more conservative, and more involved politically. However, studies that have tracked the opinions expressed in letters to the editor with other measures of public opinion have found a surprisingly close match. This would seem to be the case in particularly prominent issues (Hill, 1981). Grey and Brown (1970) also argued that while opinions in letters may not be entirely unrepresentative, the reason may be that editors deliberately attempt a balanced selection in what they publish. They noted, "What causes hesitancy in making firmer conclusions about letters to the editor is less the problem of known characteristics of the letter-writers than the substantially unknown activities of editorial gatekeepers" (p. 455).

With the expansion of the letters forum in the 1980s, there is some evidence that a higher percentage of submitted letters are being published and more newspapers are formally specifying criteria for acceptance (Terrell, 1989). Reasons for rejection are less codified. The typical list includes length, libel, taste, harsh or too personal content, or evidence of an organized letter-writing campaign (in connection with candidate endorsements, for instance). Some newspaper policy statements still quaintly include "no poetry" as a criterion.

Much more research is needed before drawing any firm conclusions about letters to the editor as surrogate measures of public opinion, especially given their growth in popularity and scope. It is more than likely, however, that media gatekeepers will be much less interested in them as a gauge for the "real" state of the public mind than will public opinion theorists or political actors. Terrell's Presstime summary of recent developments in letters to the editor notes that the journalistic interest stems from their demonstrable popularity with readers and their obvious public relations value. The motivating interest is not that different from newspaper involvement in straw polls.

Nonsystematic Media Polling

In contemporary terminology, the term "straw poll" is used pejoratively and is often equated with media man-in-the-street reporting. Interestingly enough, the term did not always have such negative connotations. One of the earliest scholarly attempts to link newspaper content with systematic public opinion appraisal was Robinson's *Straw Votes* (1932). Robinson called a straw vote any attempt to apply the principle of statistical sampling, particularly by newspapers, to the measurement of political sentiment. Far from being condemnatory, Robinson was elated by the attempt. Like most other students of the history of polling, Robinson devotes a great deal of attention to the celebrated *Literary Digest* poll, which began in 1916 and folded in disgrace after its disastrous predictions in the 1936 presidential election.

Robinson's history is interesting because it foreshadows several developments that accompanied the resurgence of media polling in the 1970s and 1980s. One similarity was the early reliance on a consortium or joint venture approach to polling. Historical examples include the *New York Herald's* collaboration with the *Cincinnati Enquirer*, the *Chicago Record-Herald*, and the *St. Louis Republic*. The modern version of such consortia include *Washington Post*–ABC, the *New York Times*–CBS, and other such pairings at both the state and national level.

Another similarity is that the early newspaper straw polls were using the best available techniques. Some may appear primitive now, and a more serious modern complaint might be that some of those techniques live on through tradition, even though their sponsors admittedly know better now.

Like modern pollsters, newspapers experimented with a variety of techniques, many of which they have maintained through the years for reasons of tradition more than for any belief in their validity. While no systematic tally exists, various formats were widely used and reappear again and again in modern variants.

Clip or coupon polls appear typically on the editorial page, but sometimes on the front page. The paper runs a box with a question phrased in the style of public opinion survey questions (do you favor or oppose?). The tally of results, most often percentages without any indication of the base number, is presented at a later time, along with the next clip question.

A more recent variation is the call-in. Typically, newspapers or broadcast stations arrange to staff phones during an evening to take comments and quotes on some topic, following several days of promotion. A summary of results and, more interestingly, excerpts from comments is run in a subsequent story.

The man-in-the-street interviews have long been a staple feature of newspapers as well as broadcasting. The more modern variant as popularized by *USA Today* has become known as the "photo poll." These include both pictures and quotes from a half-dozen or so "average citizens," selected to represent both the pro and con position on some issue.

These schemes are not intrinsically bad as long as no grandiose claims are made about their representativeness or generalizability. They are mentioned primarily because they do represent some of the few ongoing and institutionalized efforts on the part of media to let the public speak for themselves in their own voices. The point to note, however, is that they are done more for promotional and public relations purposes than to monitor and report on public opinion. Even more "scientific" efforts may often have self-promotion as a goal. One reason for the apparent obsession with preelection polls is that such results are more apt to be picked up by other media, with a published reference to the "*Daily Herald*" poll. The next sections of this chapter discuss trends in media polls and surveys in terms of their history and current status, as well as the academic research and criticism of them.

Formal Media Polling

Given the controversy surrounding journalism's appropriation of public polling, it is somewhat ironic to note that the initial reaction among journalists to the development of modern survey techniques was one of open hostility. Felgenhauer (1972) summarized some of the reasons for that reaction: anti-intellectualism on the part of reporters, a personal bent toward humanities over mathematics, an equating of polling techniques with journalists' traditional adversaries, such as politicians and marketers. Another reason for the hostility was the notorious failure of polling to predict the 1936 and 1948 presidential elections.

One of the first systematic efforts to gauge journalistic reaction to polling was an attempt in part to assess whether the 1952 polls had "successfully vindicated themselves after their failures in 1948" (Price, 1953). Price concluded that in the main few editors were interested in technicalities: "In short—and this statement is obvious—public opinion polls for a newspaper are a method and not a substantive end" (p. 297). His sample's distrust of the major polls then in operation— Gallup primarily, but also state polls in Texas and California (Crespi, 1980)—led him to speculate that "the commercial-type election poll has outlived its usefulness." But he did detect a keen interest in "the state-wide or regional polls supported directly by daily newspaper research bureaus" that were then being developed primarily in the Midwest. The *Minneapolis Star and Tribune* and the *Des Moines Register and Tribune* were singled out as leaders in this movement.

Numerous events in the late 1960s and early 1970s converged into what Ismach (1984) termed a "conjunction of forces" to fuel the phenomenal growth in media polling that has occurred in the past decade and a half. One event seldom mentioned in studies of media polling was a series of congressional hearings on legislation that would have banned the reporting of polls in federal elections. Testimony from academics, politicians, and journalists expressed a sense of frustration with shoddy, inaccurate, and even faked polls that surfaced during elections. While the proposed legislation was never enacted, its mere threat prodded various associations of polling organizations to step up actions to police their industry. It also crystallized among journalists a sense that conducting their own polls was, to use A. Cantril's (1991) phrase, "the only way they could get information they trusted" (p. 67).

Arguably the seminal event was the 1973 publication of Philip Meyer's landmark text, *Precision Journalism*. Armed with a journalist's clear and understandable perspective on the research techniques and statistics involved, news organizations took to polling with a vengeance. A number of academic researchers followed in their stead with attempts to assess both the quantity and quality of media efforts.

Such academic surveys generally documented the trends Price had spotted earlier. A survey done in 1978 (Rippey, 1980) found about a third of U.S. newspapers conducting their own polls, with most of them starting such operations in the 1970s. Rippey's data suggested that papers that had already started polling operations would continue; those that had not probably would not. A replication in 1986 (Demers, 1987) concluded that newspaper polling had leveled out. Both the incidence and the pattern of future plans had remained constant. The replication did identify two new patterns: a trend away from relying on staff expertise toward utilizing outside organizations to help with design, fieldwork, and analysis; and a trend not necessarily away from social issues polling, but at least toward more election campaign or horse-race polling.

Academic research on the quality of media polling has concentrated mostly on the extent to which media accounts include methodological information: population, sample size, sponsor, dates, question wording, interviewing method, and sampling error (Miller & Hurd, 1982; Salwen, 1985). Generally, reports of in-house surveys and election polls contain more methodological detail than do commercial and nonelection polls. Perhaps the most serious lack is failure to report exact question wording. On the other hand, there is a trend toward greater inclusion of sampling error, despite controversy about whether either the journalists or the readers really understand that concept (Demers, 1988).

Cantril (1991) summed up some of the limitations on this work on reporting standards:

Regrettably, more recent data are not comprehensive enough to bring these trends up to date. Nor are we able to infer from these data much about the quality of the newspaper articles other than that some items were included. For example, we have no idea how carefully the story leads were written or how considered were the generalizations drawn from the findings. We do know that the television networks seldom provide the wording of questions in poll stories, even though sample size and sampling error generally are reported. As to local television, we have no systematic information regarding how polls are reported. (p. 168)

Criticisms of Media Polling

Much has been written about the pros and cons of media polling. One of the most sweeping airings of the arguments was done in a special edition of Public Opinion Quarterly, edited by Gollin (1980). More recently, the critical ground has been plowed in volumes by Crespi (1989) and Cantril (1991). The bulk of the criticism centers around only one aspect of the entire enterprise, election polls. Reduced to its essentials, the thrust of this complaint is that media polling distorts the election process by making news rather than merely reporting it. The common rebuttal is that any political reporting, not just poll stories, has that impact. More broadly, the criticisms can be boiled down to two distinct themes: (1) that media polling interferes with good journalism and (2) that media polling interferes with good polling.

Given the premise of this chapter that journalism has not explicitly recognized reporting on the public mind as one of its primary responsibilities, it is not surprising that many journalists would reject the whole notion of media-initiated polls. Almost any polling consultant could probably tell tales of the hostility and contempt they face from some quarters of the newsroom. That hostility stems not only from journalists' views that polling is irrelevant, but also from their idea that it gets in the way of their job as they have defined it. A media outlet's decision to commit to sponsoring a poll takes away resources that could be used elsewhere. Even a relatively small-scale effort requires considerable financial investment if it is to be done adequately. The cost of that one poll might very well pay the salary of an additional courthouse reporter for a year.

At a deeper level, the argument against media polling is that the method itself is intrinsically inadequate for thorough reporting. Polls must of necessity reduce complex issues to simple favor/oppose alternatives. Stories based on those results often cannot adequately background the issues and alternatives in all their subtlety and complexity and at the same time simplify the analysis and provide all the essential methodological background. The problem becomes especially acute when, as is most generally the case, the poll itself becomes the "event" being reported and the presentation must conform to what Crespi (1989) termed a straitjacket hard-news format (p. 110). Cantril (1991) adds other kinds of ways that polling may interfere with practices of good journalism, notably that it could foster a "pack" mentality and stifle the journalist's own news judgment.

It is difficult to separate criticism of media polling from criticisms of polling in general. But there is a second strain in the discussion of media polling that suggests that, whether or not it leads to bad journalism, it does lead to bad polling. Gollin phrased it this way:

In its narrowest sense, the assertion is made that a news organization that conducts its own polls creates the appearance of a conflict of interest, one that can lead to a restriction on the reporting of polls conducted by others. In its broadest sense, however, this critique sees press polls as reflecting or contributing to a serious misapprehension of the nature of public opinion—polling's crucial legitimating concept—and its ideal or actual relationship to representative democratic institutions and policy processes." (1980, p. 454)

Crespi (1980) makes the interesting argument that traditional journalistic news values lead even nonmedia polling enterprises away from the legitimate questions about the real state of public opinion and into topics that are merely newsworthy. For instance, prominence as a news value leads to too many questions about political figures and not enough about political issues. Timeliness leads to too many questions about immediate events at the expense of long-term trends, or even worse, firehouse polls that permit no time for callbacks and thus bias the sample.

Many of the aspects of the conflict of media polls with private, commercial, or nonprofit public polls can be dismissed as sour grapes. Not many journalists will worry overly much about the complaint that media polls weaken the financial stability of other polling organizations or that the widely divergent results of numerous media polls cause clients to discredit results from the private organizations. But to the extent that media polls do make the legitimate efforts of polling to assess public opinion seem haphazard, ill-conceived, and not credible, journalists have more cause for concern.

CONCLUSIONS

Perhaps the most convenient way to sum up is in terms of the model introduced in the first chapter. Because of its own traditions and self-defined functions, journalism has developed an extensive set of checks and balances regarding information that flows through the links from policymakers and special interest groups. Journalism assumes an adversarial stance with these groups and filters their views through its own well-developed goals of accuracy and objectivity. Similar checks and balances about information from the public, rather than to the public, have yet to be institutionalized.

That observation has consequences both for the way media fulfill and expand their role in reporting on the public mind and for the way political theorists incorporate media content into their theories.

In regard to the former, journalists can no longer afford to distance themselves from content that purports, either directly or indirectly, to reveal the public mind. Such content must be subjected to the same rigorous standards, qualifications, and skepticism reporters bring to bear on other kinds of stories. Otherwise, that content may yield systematic distortions in ways that the newly emerging theories of public opinion have begun to articulate. Traditional news values like oddity foster a spiral of silence or a third-person effect, to the extent that the most often-heard voices are those that express opinions in loud or odd ways. Prominence as a news value readily leads to patterns of pluralistic ignorance, to the extent that reporters rely most often on the same well-known sources representing the status quo.

At the same time, theorists must pay much more attention than they have in the past to media traditions and functions. Too often the academic research glosses over subtleties and latencies of media content, offering up instead naive, superficial, and even contradictory assessments of its presumed impact. Formulations that recognize the constraints under which that content was produced could lead to more valid interpretations of what it means.

9

The Spiral of Silence: Linking Individual and Society Through Communication

Charles T. Salmon and Chi-Yung Moh

Communication is at the very heart of the fundamental tension between individual liberties and societal boundaries. This tension is readily apparent in totalitarian regimes in which the interests of the individual are clearly subordinate to those of the state. However, as the title of a book by two Harvard Medical School professors, *Drug Control in a Free Society* (Bakalar & Grinspoon, 1984), illustrates, the tension is apparent in democracies as well, where it exists as something of a paradox: It represents conflict between societal limitations on individual freedom in a society dedicated to preserving individual freedoms.

We witness the manifestations of this tension in everyday life. It appears in conflicts between individuals who wish to smoke tobacco and a society that has defined those individuals as "social pariahs" and threatened them with loss of employment and condemnation by their peers (Levin, 1987); individuals who wish to make statements deemed offensive to persons of different gender or race and a society that has defined those individuals as engaging in unacceptable conduct;[1] and individuals who wish to induce major structural change in democratic institutions and a society that has marginalized those individuals as radicals or anarchists and hence not worthy of serious attention (e.g., see Gitlin, 1980).

Perhaps the most elaborate articulation of the role of communication in the dynamic between individual and society is that provided by

Elisabeth Noelle-Neumann, a noted German pollster and political scientist and a 1990 recipient of the Helen Dinerman Award from the World Association for Public Opinion Research for her work in public opinion research. Her model of the "spiral of silence" is predicated on the notion that society is a potentially intimidating environment for the individual, a setting in which intense social pressure can be brought to bear on the person who dares to test the boundaries of the crowd. It is a model steeped in European tradition, grand in scope and thick in political and social philosophy. One of the model's most important features is that the concept of communication—in mass and interpersonal forms—is considered central to the linking of the social and individual levels of analysis. This characteristic alone makes the model a rarity in communication studies, for the two modes of communication typically have been treated either as mutually exclusive or as antagonistic explanations for social processes (Chaffee, 1982; Reardon & Rogers, 1988; Pingree, Wiemann & Hawkins, 1988).

In the present paper, we focus on the use of communication to describe the individual's relationship to society. We first describe and explicate the model in Noelle-Neumann's terms, drawing on her various works (1973, 1974, 1977, 1979, 1980, 1984, 1985, 1991) and organizing the model into three major groupings: mass media and mass communication, the individual and interpersonal communication, and static and dynamic implications of these communication processes for public opinion. Next, we explore the ideological underpinnings of the model, with particular attention to her conceptualization of the mass media's role in the public opinion process. In so doing, we offer some avenues of exploration in heretofore unarticulated directions.

THE SPIRAL OF SILENCE: AN OVERVIEW

Noelle-Neumann (1991) has noted that the 1965 elections in the Federal Republic of Germany provided the impetus for her model. In that year, she found that although the two competing political parties, the Christian Democrats and the Social Democrats, had equivalent levels of support over a six-month period, expectations of who would win were far more dynamic, changing by some 18 percentage points over the same time period. It was this phenomenon of a changing electoral "mood" or political "climate" that served as the point of departure in her research program on the role of the mass media in influencing climates of opinion and, ultimately, personal expression.

For theoretical explanation, Noelle-Neumann turned to the writings of the German sociologist Ferdinand Tonnies, who is perhaps best known for his notions of gemeinschaft and gesellschaft in his discussions of traditional and modern societies, respectively. To Tonnies

(1922), public opinion represented a social force, an informal mechanism of social control: "Public opinion always claims to be authoritative. It demands consent or at least compels silence, or abstention from contradiction" (p. 138). Noelle-Neumann also traced allusions to this notion of public opinion as social control to the writings of such disparate political philosophers and scholars as John Locke, James Bryce, James Madison, Floyd Allport, Alexis de Tocqueville, as well as others.[2] Many of the constituent elements of the model were thus not newly conceived, but were instead similar to ideas expressed by Noelle-Neumann's predecessors and contemporaries. Hers is a comprehensive assemblage of ideas that have been available in the public domain in one form or another for centuries, but which have not previously been linked in this particular manner.

Mass Media and Mass Communication

Noelle-Neumann ascribes a particular importance to the mass media's position in contemporary society. The media are, in her words, "ubiquitous" and "consonant." Indeed, it is difficult to conceive of a day without exposure to mass media in one form or another, ranging from listening to a morning radio program, through reading a newspaper or magazine and observing posters or flyers, to reading or viewing television or a film in the evening. The inescapability of the media is potentially problematic, she argues, because media content tends to be remarkably consonant. That is, there is uncanny similarity of news and other media content that belies the liberal democratic ideal of "diversity." The combination of a ubiquitous and consonant media system results in a largely monolithic "climate" that envelops most individuals in society, providing in the process a largely homogeneous depiction of social reality.

In large measure, our view of social reality is distorted because of the underlying ideology of the progenitors of media content. Journalists, Noelle-Neumann argues, tend to be more liberal than the rest of society (1973, 1980). In part, this liberalness is largely a function of shared journalistic norms and values that serve to reinforce the role of journalist as critic, as a foil to government and the powerful. Reflecting this underlying liberal orientation, she continues, media content tends to be liberal, as well. The product is a media environment, forged by liberal newsmakers, enveloping the individual in society and exposing him or her to a predominantly liberal depiction of society and the social good. One of the most important functions of the media, to Noelle-Neumann, is their role as the predominant source of cues regarding majority culture. Immersed in a ubiquitous and consonant media en-

vironment, individuals rely heavily on the media as a source of information about social roles, customs, and practices.

Noelle-Neumann claims that this immersion in and dependency on
the media environment induces powerful effects on individuals and
that these effects occur as the result of an endless repetition of rein-
forcing messages and images. As a result, she argues, media effects
cannot be studied validly under sterile, artificial laboratory conditions
because such studies will necessarily underestimate the impact of a
prolonged diet of monolithic media output emanating from a variety
of media sources (1973).

The Individual in a Social Setting

The second major strain of thought in the spiral-of-silence model
deals with the linkage between micro and microsocial levels of analysis.
Drawing on the small-group conformity research of Solomon Asch and
others (1970), Noelle-Neumann contends that individuals have a virtually innate fear of social isolation. To be alone, apart from, or at odds
with the crowd is more than most individuals can endure. To wear an
unpopular fashion or to express an idea that many consider old-
fashioned or, even worse, socially unacceptable is to risk incurring the
wrath of others, a prospect that most find too unattractive to risk. As
a result of this concern, individuals must constantly monitor the environment, searching for cues regarding which sentiments, ideas,
knowledge, or fashions are shared by many or only by a few. Because
of this fear, individuals draw on their "quasi-statistical organ" (in her
later work, a quasi-statistical "sense," perhaps implying a shift from a
biological to a social explanation; compare Noelle-Neumann, 1974 and
1991) to gauge the nuances of culture and its dynamism. As stated
above, the mass media are seen as providing the bulk of the cues that
serve to structure options for an individual's behavior.

An unstated assumption of this model, like most models of public
opinion, is that individuals have opinions that they can and wish to
articulate (a seemingly basic assumption that itself is contested; see
Pierre Bordieu, 1979). Assuming that this is the case, the individual is
often confronted with a situation in which he or she must articulate
that opinion in some social context; that is, the private sentiment must
become public. In this sense, Noelle-Neumann's use of the term "public" in "public opinion" is as an adjective rather than a noun; it refers
to an opinion that can be expressed "publicly" without fear of censure
rather than the more typically American usage (as a noun) in which it
refers to a group of individuals (Salmon & Kline, 1985).

Implications for Public Opinion

Static Version. Given the above presuppositions, there are two distinct implications for public opinion, one static and the other a dynamic process. In the case of the static outcome, if the individual perceives that his or her personal convictions are shared by the majority, he or she will be willing to express an opinion in public. On the other hand, if the individual perceives that his or her opinion represents a minority viewpoint, he or she will be reluctant to express the notion publicly. There are thought to be two general exceptions to this outcome. First, if an individual perceives himself or herself to be in the minority but believes that his or her opinion is gaining ground—that it is viable and hence will be shared by the majority at some future point—the individual will be willing to express the opinion in public. Secondly, a few individuals who are apparently immune to social censure appear perennially willing to express unpopular opinions. These individuals, labeled "hardcores," are thought to represent a relatively small (Noelle-Neumann estimates about 15 percent) segment of the population.[3]

Dynamic Version. Unlike the static version, which can be tested with cross-sectional data, the dynamic version incorporates the element of time into the model and must be tested using longitudinal data. If relatively few persons are willing to express an unpopular viewpoint, according to this version, it will slowly slip from the public consciousness because it will have no vocal proponents. Over time, the majority faction will become increasingly confident and its view, increasingly pervasive. The disproportionate frequencies of expression will eventually result in a "silencing" of the proponents of the minority viewpoint, and their sentiment will follow the paths of other unpopular, obsolete, or dated notions. Policymakers, who themselves monitor the information environment to gauge trends in opinion climates either out of a sense of obligation to constituents or as a matter of political survival, observe that one opinion is frequently expressed and another is not. This social perception becomes translated into policy, as only expressed opinion influences social change; silence is thought to have no impact. It is for this reason that Noelle-Neumann has counseled supporters of the Christian Democrats to speak up in their everyday lives—to create and reinforce the impression that they are not afraid of expressing their views, thereby presumably implying to others that their viewpoint is "winning."

As should be evident from the above discussion, the spiral-of-silence model is an involved agglomeration of presuppositions, hypotheses, and conclusions—some warranted, some unwarranted by the available empirical data. Tests of the model usually have employed survey research,[4] occasional content analyses,[5] and cross-sectional as well as longitudinal designs. A disproportionately large amount of research on the model has been conducted in Germany (the Federal Republic of Germany prior to reunification), though a substantial number of replications, tests, and challenges have been conducted in such diverse settings as the United States (Taylor, 1982; Glynn & McLeod, 1982; Glynn & McLeod, 1984; Andreasen & Thompson, 1985; Bergen, 1986; Neuwirth, 1988; Salmon & Rucinski, 1988; Mutz, 1989; Sun, Salmon & Rucinski, 1989; Salmon & Oshagan, 1990; Salmon & Neuwirth, 1990; Stevenson & Gonzenbach, 1990; Rimmer & Howard, 1990; Lasorsa, 1991), Mexico (Neuwirth & Sanchez-Ilundian, 1984), the Phillipines (Gonzalez, 1988), Taiwan (Sun, 1991), South Korea (Lee, 1987), multiple nations in Asia (Tokinoya, 1989), and Great Britain (Webb & Wybrow, 1986).

One of the more curious aspects of the sociology of this model's diffusion and evolution in the academic arena is that the ratio of critiques to empirical tests approaches unity. This suggests at least one of the following: (1) that the model is difficult to test; (2) conversely, that the model is easy to criticize; or (3) that the model provokes an intense emotional response in readers, who feel obligated to comment. In any case, readers are encouraged to turn to any of several standard critiques (Katz, 1982; Glynn & McLeod, 1985; Merten, 1985; Salmon & Kline, 1985), countercritiques (Donsbach & Stevenson, 1984; Noelle-Neumann, 1985; Donsbach, 1988), and assorted commentary and prescriptions (McLeod, 1985; Rusciano, 1989; Kennamer, 1990; Price & Allen, 1990; Csikszentmihalyi, 1991; Moscovici, 1991; Noelle-Neumann, 1991) for detailed assessments of the model's internal logic and the validity of its presuppositions and conclusions.

It perhaps suffices to say that the entire spiral-of-silence model itself has never been subjected to a complete test, even by Noelle-Neumann herself, probably because it would be far too time-consuming (perhaps spanning several decades) and expensive to undertake. Instead, researchers have reduced the model into discrete, manageable fragments and tested hypotheses within those fragments. With few exceptions, researchers outside of Germany generally have not found much in the way of consistent empirical support for several of the model's pivotal assumptions and claims. They have found what might be characterized as a "modest" degree of reluctance, rather than a consuming fear, about publicly expressing a minority opinion on most issues. Indeed, it is very often the case that a plurality of those holding (or believing that they hold) the minority position are still willing to speak out, far more than the few hardcores that the model would predict. Further, other factors such as personal involvement, level of knowledge, nature of the issue, and mode of opinion expression have been found to be more important predictors of opinion expression than minority status. The above assessment is not necessarily a condemnation of the model; in fairness, lack of much empirical support to date may indeed reflect problems with the model itself, but it may also reflect (1) efforts at replications that are not faithful to Noelle-Neumann's (1985, 1991) criteria for satisfactory tests of her model; or (2) difficulties in testing the model in nations other than the one in which it was developed (or some combination of these factors).

IDEOLOGICAL FOUNDATIONS AND ANOMALIES

Despite a flurry of research attempts to empirically replicate or refute the model, virtually no attention has been paid to its implicit ideological assumptions and the degree to which these assumptions are compatible or incompatible with other conceptualizations of public opinion prevalent in the United States. Further, very little attention has been paid to the mass communication component of the model, as critics have instead focused on microsocial-level issues concerning conformity, personal fear, and opinion expression.

To claim that the model implies an ideology is not, in and of itself, an indictment; indeed, ideology is inherent in any type of communication, whether the dissemination of news to audience members or the advancement of a theory to scholarly colleagues. In the words of Raymond Boudon (1989), all human actors are "situated" in specific cultures at specific points in time, and their views necessarily depend upon their vantage point in the social milieu. Even (especially?) social scientists who "objectively" conduct empirical research are of a particular social class, view society and its operations in certain ways, ponder some questions and not others, and explain the world according to patterns of expectation and what, to them, "makes sense."

Of course, what makes sense to one social scientist is problematic to someone else who has been socialized in a different culture and taught to ask different questions and interpret patterns of behavior in different ways. In this manner, ideology extends beyond being merely one's worldview by framing struggles over which meanings are defined as "natural" or "common sensical" (Lannamann, 1991). It is rare indeed that the underlying assumptions or the apparent "common sense" of logical positivistic models are questioned; as Todd Gitlin (1978) observes,

Abstracted empiricism is not only concretely founded on the prevailing political and commercial culture, it is also, for the most part, justified by an ideological position. Such a position may be more or less conscious and, if conscious, more or less public. It is generally considered bad taste [among members of the scientific group] to assert that ideology matters in this setting, unless it is radical (p. 240).

It appears likely that at least a portion of the inspiration of the spiral-of-silence model can be traced to far before the 1965 elections, to the events of the 1940s and the rise of Fascism in Nazi Germany and the concomitant rise of wartime jingoism in the United States.[6] German and American societies at that time provided extreme examples of societies controlled by relatively monolithic media systems orchestrated by skillful propagandists who were capable of instilling fear into the hearts and minds of those "traitors" or "subversives" who would think of dissenting.

As a journalist for *Deutsche Allgemeine Zeitung* and *Das Reich* in Germany during the war, Noelle-Neumann was in a position to see firsthand the potency of social climates in inducing conformity. Her vivid descriptions of an individual's fear in ambiguous settings with strangers—especially if we consider that those strangers might be in positions of power to physically or emotionally punish the individual for his or her opinion expression—must certainly strike a chord in readers socialized in totalitarian states. Implicit in her thinking is that the individual is largely impotent, certainly not powerful enough to effect changes in public policy. The individual is viewed as malleable and manipulable, the object rather than the source of political influence. Further, the basis of opinion expression is seen as emotion or fear rather than detached rationality. It is no coincidence that a model particularly suited to explain the events of this era of psychological warfare adopts as its base a conceptualization of public opinion that emphasizes social control, obsessive monitoring of the changing environment, and fear, and that employs methodologies designed to assess what individuals can say in public without reprisal.

In interesting contrast, the pioneers of the American system of public opinion research were strongly influenced by the events of the 1930s and 1940s as well, but in an entirely different manner. George Gallup and Saul Forbes Rae (1940), two such pioneers, asked in 1940, "In the face of the rise of Fascism and Communism, is democracy doomed?" Like other American social scientists and industrialists, Gallup and Rae were genuinely concerned that the events of Germany might be replicated in the United States because of the burgeoning power of interest groups to create the "impression" of a spreading social movement. They viewed this power as undesirable to their vision of democracy, one firmly rooted in the ideology of James Bryce (1888) and predicated on the cherished myth that each individual in democracy *ought to have* the same power, the same ability to influence public policy ("one person, one vote").

To be intimidated by social pressure and not participate in a public opinion situation, to Gallup and Rae, was to fail to discharge one's civic duty, to foster the conditions for a totalitarian takeover. To the extent that public opinion should constitute a social force, they believed it should be an upward force from the individual to ruling elites rather than a downward force from media institutions to the individual. Gallup and Rae therefore positioned their "product" of public opinion polling as the savior of democracy, a mechanism for empowering individuals who were not themselves organized into groups in order to counterbalance the actual power of mobilized interest groups. Rather than acknowledging that social forces might influence individuals' opinions and reflecting this acknowledgment in their methodology (as Noelle-Neumann did), Gallup and Rae's prescription instead reflected their ideal of democracy: individual autonomy and simulated political participation (see Herbst, 1991, for a discussion of polling and participation). To this day, American public opinion polling is predicated upon the democratically inspired ideal of individualism, that is, that an individual is interested, knowledgeable, and rational (i.e., not motivated by fear) regarding a social issue, and that polling provides a mechanism for an individual's participation in the political system by formally channeling his or her preferences to responsive legislators (Hennessy, 1985).[7]

There are two important implications of this analysis of the two approaches to public opinion research. First, both are inherently ideological, though the ideological foundations are rarely considered or questioned. American public opinion researchers legitimize the product of the polling industry as a neutral, value-free "science" and tout it as a valid indicator of public sentiment without considering why it is as it is. Only by viewing it in the context of alternatives do we see that it is the result of a particular system of values and an endorsement of a specific role for individuals in society. The same is true, of course, for the spiral of silence. The notion of public opinion as a form of social control is certainly legitimate, but it implies the adoption of a specific worldview and acceptance of certain assumptions about the power (or lack thereof) of individuals in society. Differences in ideology and vantage points during the 20th century led to the development of different methodologies: Noelle-Neumann ultimately developed a model of public opinion research that could be used to *explain* the events she had witnessed; Gallup and Rae endorsed a model to *prevent* the events she had witnessed.

Although the two approaches to public opinion research are quite different in some respects, both are grounded in the ideology of individualism; both models are individual-centric models in the sense that explanations for social phenomena are explained in terms of individual perceptions and behavior. In Gallup and Rae's method of polling, society is treated as a mere aggregation of unattached individuals, and, in a related fashion, public opinion as a mere aggregation of individuals' opinions. In the spiral-of-silence model, public opinion is seen as possessing a necessary social dimension—the opinion climate forged by external forces—but the individual is still the focal point. Researchers measure the individual's opinion, and measure the climate of opinion by again asking individuals their perceptions of what others think. And yet, it would have been quite natural for the model to have reflected an ideology of holism rather than individualism had Noelle-Neumann pursued some interesting results reported in 1974. In the course of her analysis, she reported that individuals who were of higher education, from urban areas, and younger tended to be the most likely to express their opinions in general. This finding, which was dismissed at the time, is potentially very important, for it offers an entirely different explanation of the public opinion process. It suggests that social structural factors strongly influence public expression of opinions, and that it is the opinions of the higher socioeconomic status groups that are likely to dominate in social discourse. Had this interpretation, which is related to the notion of hegemony, been scrutinized at the time, Noelle-Neumann might have turned not to the writings of Tonnies and discussions of conformity, but to Marx and arguments of class, structure, and economic determinism.

IMPLICATIONS

The question remaining is whether any model influenced by a specific context under somewhat unique circumstances at a particular point in time can inform us about social phenomena in our situation in contemporary society. The answer is "certainly," with the caveat that all models differ in the degree to which they are importable and hence generalizable, both culturally as well as temporally. Mirroring our earlier organization of the model into two broad areas—mass media and mass communication and the individual in a social setting—we can make several observations about the model's relevance to contemporary life.

Clearly, a monolithic media climate is more readily achieved in political systems in which there is either little political diversity or heavy centralized control. In totalitarian regimes, the government has the power to formally mandate consistency of information, thereby closely approximating the conditions Noelle-Neumann describes. This is not to say that consonance is not a characteristic of democratic systems; indeed, at a certain institutional level it is very much so. For example, schools, businesses (including media organizations), government, and other institutions in the United States are consonant in their recognition of the legitimacy of such notions as private property, capitalism, or the pursuit of personal fulfillment. These fundamental tenets of the U.S.

political system are just a few of the many unacknowledged and undisputed (and hence, consonant) filters through which both the mundane and extraordinary events of life are routinely depicted (Herman & Chomsky, 1988). This level of consonance is veiled; consonance that is more visible, more apparent, tends to be situation-specific, and its nature is very often the opposite of what Noelle-Neumann has predicted.

Situational Aspects

First, consonance is more achievable under situations of severe system strain, as when a nation perceives that it is facing a crisis. Under such conditions, individual and social groups tend to pull together, often tolerating greater infringement upon personal freedoms, and accepting more restricted sets of policy options (Coser, 1956). The federal government has long capitalized on this basic principle of conflict theory and used it to gain the cooperation of the mass media in forging climates of opinion supportive of governmental policy. Recently, the government, in cooperation with the mass media, created a virtually monolithic climate of opinion during "Operation Desert Storm" that delegitimized and virtually silenced critics of that military incursion. Only a few individuals were given the opportunity to explain their objections to the conflict; most were instead automatically branded "unpatriotic" for attempting to prevent the loss of life of American men and women. Similarly, the federal government declared a "War on Drugs"— perhaps in part as a diversionary tactic to deflect attention from other shortcomings of the administration—and again, effectively mobilized media support to fashion a virtually monolithic climate of opinion, one that silenced arguments for the legalization of marijuana and other drugs defined as illegal by authorities. In both cases, the government's ability to "sell" the wars to the media and to society, in general, facilitated the squelching of dissent.

A second factor likely to affect the degree of consonance possible is the degree of pluralism in a social system (Tichenor, Donohue, & Olien, 1980). That is, in smaller, less pluralistic, less differentiated social systems, the media tend to be quite supportive of the power structure; in a homogeneous setting, there is, by definition, relatively little difference of opinion and there are relatively few distinct centers of power. On the other hand, in larger, more heterogeneous systems, the media may be more critical of a given powerful group; they must be responsive to the divergent interests of multiple power groups—several of which may be in conflict over some issue—that represent the greater degree of diversity. In addition, more pluralistic systems contain more pluralistic media outlets—the "alternative press," for example, tends to be more of an urban than a rural phenomenon. The existence of these conduits for alternative opinion legitimizes sentiments to a greater extent in larger than in smaller communities. In these settings, individuals are somewhat more likely to be exposed to arguments about structural—rather than individual—causes of social problems, but only if proponents of those arguments possess social power and legitimacy. This further implies that media consonance is likely to be more closely approximated in less rather than more pluralistic communities, and that opinion climates should exert greater influence in the former than in the latter (Salmon & Oshagan, 1990).[8]

The Nature of Consonance

If consonance can be achieved, a question remains as to its nature. Noelle-Neumann is politically conservative, having served as a consultant to the Christian Democrats and to Chancellor Helmut Kohl. Her charges of leftist media bias are reminiscent of those by conservative American media critics, such as Edith Efron (1971) in her book The News Twisters and Accuracy in Media (Irvine, 1984) in its book, Media Mischief and Misdeeds. We would argue that Noelle-Neumann's right-wing criticism of the leftist media is one of the conceptually weakest and most delimiting aspects of her treatise. If, for the moment, we divorce her charges of leftist media bias from other components of the model, we see many ideas compatible with the work of critical theorists from the Left. For example, Edward Herman and Noam Chomsky (1988) have developed their "propaganda" model of mass communication, in which the ideas of control and similarity of media content are viewed as necessary conditions for propaganda. And yet, their model is also predicated on the notion that the mass media constitute a powerful conservative force by virtue of the industry's economic structure and excessive reliance on establishment (government and industry) sources. Similarly, Todd Gitlin (1980) has proposed a model of powerful media influence in his description of how the media publicized and simultaneously delegitimized the Students for a Democratic Society during the Vietnam era. Gitlin describes the media as pervasive (ubiquitous) and argues that media effects occur over time through repetition, notions that echo the sentiments of Noelle-Neumann. And yet, like Herman and Chomsky, Gitlin conceptualizes the media as a defender of the status quo; a powerful agency inducing powerful effects, but powerful effects of system maintenance rather than change.

In general, there is far more evidence to suggest that the "mainstream" news media overwhelmingly act as guardians of the status quo than as agencies of meaningful change because of their political and economic location in society (Paletz, Reicher, & McIntyre, 1971; Gitlin, 1980;

Tichenor et al., 1980; Bennett, 1988; Paletz & Entman, 1984; Herman & Chomsky, 1988; Bagdikian, 1990). To the extent that media content is liberal at all, it is so in a narrow context; that is, the media generally accept the power structure's definition of the agenda of "legitimate" concerns for a given polity, their frames for defining certain social conditions as "worthy" of remedial action, and the options that are considered "viable." Media may adopt an oppositional stance within the structure that they routinely accept and legitimize, but this criticism pales in comparison to what they are not criticizing by failing to question or challenge the power structure's definition of the situation.

Attempting to demonstrate, therefore, that the media favor one of two legitimized political parties is to ignore the much greater bias of the media against groups that endorse significant proposals for change. The media routinely *report* about Democrats and Republicans—perhaps mildly favoring one over the other in the process—but *warn* society about, and simultaneously delegitimize, the actions of groups of the Left as well as the Right, such as Students for a Democratic Society or the American Association for the Advancement of White People. Extrapolating from the writings of the Sherif school of social psychology (e.g., Sherif & Hovland, 1961), we may say that the media fashion a societal-level "latitude of acceptance" around the status quo. They legitimize and consider viable those opinions—liberal as well as conservative—that accept the premise of the status quo and propose minor modifications within that structure, and dismiss as "extreme" or "radical" those opinions that do not accept the premise of the status quo and that instead call for major structural reform (Shoemaker, 1984).

The frequently observed quiescence (a type of "silence") on the part of journalists can be thought of as largely the result of institutional and organizational pressures exerted on their practices (Tuchman, 1978; Hirsch, 1977). Journalists in capitalist systems work in, and are subject to the conventions of, media organizations (often conglomerates), which are businesses operating with a profit motive. Like any worker staffing an assembly line in a corporation, journalists have a degree of autonomy, but only within the latitude created and allowed by the organization; their work is subject to managerial control, not the least of which includes assignment to "beats" (legitimized sources of news) and to specific stories. As a result, their news product will often fail to mirror their personal biases and will instead reflect the ideologies of management and the corporations.

One such ideology, that of individualism, is both congruent with the social-class backgrounds of most media managers (i.e., middle and upper) and with prevailing definitions of news. The term "personalized bias" has been used to describe the media's consistent preferences for individual explanations for social phenomena (Rucinski, 1992). It represents a type of consonance at a more abstract level than that of whether the media adopt a liberal stance on an issue. News decontextualizes; it focuses on individual actors while ignoring most structural or situational explanations for such social problems as drug use, poverty, or child abuse (Best, 1989). Comparing American to Soviet news, James Carey (1986) observes that in Soviet journalism, "stories are framed in terms of larger collective forces... rather than individual motives.... But for us, individuals act. Individuals make history"(pp. 182–183). In general, the efficacy of the individual, as well as his or her ability to overcome obstacles and succeed in the manner of Horatio Alger, is an American cultural value. That is certainly one of the traits that made Clarence Thomas an attractive Supreme Court candidate to the Republican party: He believed that an individual could triumph over the structural barriers of poverty and race.

Focusing on individual-level explanations of social problems accentuates the media's role in supporting the status quo. The ideology of individualism tends to divert scrutiny and criticism from government and the existing social structure to the individual (Paletz, Pearson & Willia, 1977; Bennett, 1988). This ideology underlies beliefs that individuals who are poor are so because they are lazy, not because society sustains structural discrimination; that individuals who use drugs do so because they are "weak" or "criminals," not because government fails to eradicate festering social conditions that promote drug use. A classic example of this is provided in the construction of the social problem of drunk driving (Schneider, 1985). The dominant frame used by policymakers and the media has been that individual drivers—inebriated ones, at that—are the cause of the problem. By constructing the problem in this manner, claims-makers simultaneously have implied individual-centric solutions: laws to punish the individual drunk driver, inculcation of social norms to make society disdain the individual drunk driver, and educational programs to change the behaviors of the individual drunk driver. If, alternatively, the problem were to be constructed in an entirely different manner—as a problem of unsafe automobiles (industry), of political decisions that have promoted personal rather than mass transportation (legislative branch of government), or of roads not designed to maximize protection of drivers (governmental agencies and departments of transportation)—then other, different solutions would simultaneously be implied.

Similarly, the media's coverage of the Iran-Contra scandal, Watergate, and the savings and loan fiasco point fingers at individual villains rather than at structure. Upon reading media accounts of these topics, a person gets the impression that these scandals are not the product of a fundamentally troubled political system in need of major overhaul, but instead the work of unscrupulous individuals. The Passion play is repeated continually: The guilty individuals are punished, the structure is able to remain intact, and attention is diverted to a new social problem. The power to define the problem therefore is the power to ascribe blame, the power to divert blame, and the power to define the locus of social change—the individual or the system (Salmon, 1989).

CONCLUSION

In general, the spiral-of-silence model can make some important contributions to our understanding of public opinion phenomena. The model may overstate the degree of "silencing" that is likely to occur in many public opinion situations, and it may underestimate the media's role in maintaining the status quo. As is the case for all depictions of social reality, this one is rooted in a particular worldview, a particular ideology. But the essence of the model—that individuals' perceptions of their environment do have some bearing on their communication and behavior, and that the mass media play an important role in influencing these perceptions—is incontestable. Further, the many ways in which the media portray a consonant ideology—particularly that of individualism—are subtle and veiled. By consistently structuring problems in certain ways and by accepting the inevitability of existing political and social institutions, the media contribute to the delimiting of human potential by failing to seek and legitimize alternatives for meaningful change. It is up to future generations of researchers to further elaborate on these ideas, to further our understanding of the intricacies among media influence, social pressures, and individual freedoms.

NOTES

1. Incidents involving Jimmy "the Greek" Snyder and Al Campanis, the former a CBS sports commentator and the latter vice-president of the Los Angeles Dodgers baseball team, provided perhaps the most dramatic examples of the power that can be exerted on individuals who express opinions that are racially offensive. Both were fired from their jobs after making statements about black athletes. Similarly, individuals who smoke cigarettes have been threatened with loss of employment if they continue their habit. Although Noelle-Neumann has not explored the use of economic sanctions against individuals whose opinion expression violates social norms, it is an interesting avenue to pursue because it forces us to take into account different value systems of different societies. Hence in a culture in which social integration is highly valued, "fear of isolation" may be the most powerful sanction; in contrast, in a culture in which money and materialism are highly valued, a financial penalty may be the most powerful sanction, and hence the most effective for inducing conformity.

2. To her list, we can add the writings of W. Phillips Davison (1958), who described a very similar notion in his description of the public opinion process:

"Therefore, [people] are likely to speak or act in one way if they anticipate approbation and to remain silent or act in another way if they anticipate hostility or indifference.... People who do not share the opinions expressed by the crowd's leaders are likely to remain silent, fearing the disapproval of those around them. This very silence isolates others who may be opposed, since they conclude that, with the exception of themselves, all those present share the same attitude" (p. 101). In addition, Jacques Ellul (1965) and Paul Lazarsfeld and Robert Merton (1948/1960) express a number of similar ideas in their work, especially the idea that for propaganda to be effective, it must monopolize an environment and be reinforced throughout the institutional fabric of society.

3. The notion of "hardcores" is one of the most intriguing elements of her model. These individuals represent a means for social change that is antithetical to the process described by Noelle-Neumann—persons who constitute a minority faction, gain support over time, and dominate public policy agendas rather than getting silenced. Research on minority influence (Moscovici, 1976, 1980) would certainly be relevant to this phenomenon. Studies conducted in the United States indicate that some hardcores are issue-specific; that is, a hardcore on the issue of abortion might not necessarily be willing to be a hardcore on the issue of drug legalization. On the other hand, some individuals consistently appear to relish the role of "devil's advocate" or the idea of arguing a seemingly untenable position regardless of the topic. This suggests that "hardcore" may in fact not be a unidimensional concept.

4. Survey research has been used almost exclusively for tests of the spiral of silence—as it has for virtually all public opinion research since the 1930s. However, there is growing sentiment that it is particularly inappropriate for studying this phenomenon for two reasons: first, even a survey with a good response rate—80 to 85 percent or so—misses a fairly substantial segment of the population through terminations and refusals. If these individuals who refuse to be interviewed do so because they are reluctant to express what they believe to be an unpopular opinion, then the survey is missing the very people who are exemplifying the silencing phenomenon. Secondly, the survey interview is itself a communication setting in which a person is forced to express an opinion to a stranger—the very situation that Noelle-Neumann claims is likely to elicit the silencing effect. No doubt this effect can be mitigated through assurances of anonymity and interviewer professionalism, but it still remains something of a contradiction between theory and methodology. See Kennamer (1990) for an alternative.

5. Noelle-Neumann (1973, 1980) has occasionally used content analysis in her research, but only in a limited fashion. In one case, for example, she combines three months worth of content analytic data with twenty years of polling data and makes claims about causal linkages. See Salmon and Kline (1985) for a review.

6. Leo Bogart (1991, p. 49) makes precisely this point. He claims that, while a journalist in the 1940s, Noelle-Neumann wrote about how American Jews "monopolized" the American media system, and concludes that her model represents "more of a footnote to the history of Nazism than to the study of public opinion." In response, Noelle-Neumann (1992) describes how she personally endured social sanctions as an adolescent for not joining the Hitler

Youth and later for writing articles of which the German Ministry of Propaganda did not approve. At the very least, the dialogue between Bogart and Noelle-Neumann provides unusually rich insight into potential implicit and explicit influences of historical context on the development of social theory.

7. These assumptions have been criticized for their obvious shortcomings. See Blumer (1948) and Ginsberg (1986) for critiques.

8. We can also extend this argument beyond the level of community to nation; that is, some nations are more pluralistic than others, some nations have political cultures that are more consensual than others. We would therefore expect the magnitude of the influence of opinion climates to vary greatly according to such macrosocial characteristics.

10

Policymakers and the Third-Person Effect

Dominic L. Lasorsa

INTRODUCTION

Just before the February 1987 airing of the controversial TV mini-series *Amerika*, well-known political scientist George Kennan wrote a letter to the *New York Times* in which he said the program contained false suggestions, namely, that the dangers of a bloodless Soviet takeover of the United States with the help of the United Nations were quite real. While noting that he himself considered such messages "outrageous," he added that "it is useless to suppose that 12 solid hours of such suggestions will not leave their marks" on TV viewers. He made it clear that if he had been in charge of programming at ABC, *Amerika* would not have been beamed into American living rooms (Kennan, 1987).

Professor emeritus at Princeton's Institute for Advanced Study and a former U.S. ambassador to the Soviet Union, Kennan has been regarded generally as one of the world's most insightful political experts. When Kennan speaks, the *New York Times* often prints his words. One of the basic premises of this chapter, however, is that Kennan's fears about the effects of this dramatic TV presentation on its audience may not have been justified and that, furthermore, it may have been precisely his political expertise that led him to worry unjustifiably about its effects.

In trying to understand the role of political communication in the process of policymaking and in attempting to develop models of the relationships among policymakers, their constituents, the mass media, and their audiences, scholars have been guided recently by a promising new theoretical approach about how these players relate to one another. It is known as "the third-person effect."

This chapter deals with this social-psychological condition, with special emphasis upon its role in public policymaking. First, the term is defined and its short history described. Next, empirical evidence for the existence of the third-person effect is considered, followed by a discussion of the scope of the effect. That leads to consideration of possible causes of the effect, as well as contingent conditions that might strengthen or weaken it. The chapter ends with a discussion of how the third-person effect is especially relevant to policymakers and the policymaking process, that is, it considers how policymakers' assumptions about the effects of media content on others affect their approaches toward regulating media.

WHAT IS THE THIRD-PERSON EFFECT?

The twentieth century saw the introduction of important new mass communication technologies, such as radio and television, and the effective use of these media by national leaders, advertisers, and others who attempted to mobilize mass publics through these media. In such a context it is no wonder that the notion of the mass media as having powerful, direct, and uniform effects on their audiences has for many years remained a popular one. Yet, almost from the beginning, empirical research on the effects of mass communication seemed to provide little support for the idea. These findings of limited media effects were summarized neatly in Klapper's (1960) *The Effects of Mass Communication*, in which he noted that mass communication "ordinarily does not serve as a necessary and sufficient cause of audience effects, but rather functions among and through a nexus of mediating factors and influences," including selective perception, exposure, attention, and retention; group dynamics; and opinion leadership. More recent research has confirmed the indirect, subtle, and contingent nature of many, if not most, mass media effects on audiences.

Despite these findings of limited effects, however, mass media messages sometimes do have direct and powerful effects on their audiences. Often, these effects result from changes in persons' cognitions, not their attitudes. Orson Welles, for instance, showed that quite spectacularly when "The War of the Worlds" radio broadcast caused such a panic in 1938 (H. Cantril, 1947). Among others who have demonstrated direct and powerful effects of mass media messages on their audiences have been Hovland, Janis, and Kelley (1953), Ball-Rokeach, Rokeach, and Grube (1984), and McCombs and Shaw (1972).

However, some mass media messages might have rather different effects—unintended ones on unintended audiences. For example, a message might lead to action not because of its direct impact on those presumed to be its target audience but because others (third persons) believe it will have such an impact on that audience and *they* act on that belief, regardless of whether or not the message has direct effects on the presumed target audience at all. W. Phillips Davison published this idea in 1983 and labeled it the third-person effect. He theorized that the effect is driven by a general human tendency to see mass media messages as having a greater effect on others than on oneself (Davison, 1983).

Davison gave the example of a black military unit on Iwo Jima in World War II. The Japanese dropped propaganda leaflets on the island telling the unit not to fight a "white man's war." Though there was no evidence that the message affected the fighting spirit of the unit, it was withdrawn from combat the next day. Davison also recounted a study of journalists' impressions of the effect of newspaper editorials: They essentially expected editorials to affect "ordinary readers" but not "people like you and me" (Davison, 1957).

A more recent example stems from the *Amerika* broadcast mentioned earlier. As its airing approached and as bits of its plot trickled and then cascaded into the news, this major TV production grew more and more controversial. Despite rising expectations of blockbuster ratings, just before the show aired one of the program's primary sponsors pulled its multi-million-dollar advertising campaign, apparently worried that the juxtapositioning of the program's controversial message with its own "Pride in America" advertising campaign might cause viewers to turn away from its products. In retrospect, the program's message turned out to be no more memorable than the name of the sponsors whose ads did run (Lasorsa, 1989).

Even the *threat* of a mass media message that is not subsequently delivered could have this kind of indirect effect. For example, a candidate for the U.S. presidency is told by a national news medium of a message about him that it intends to publish. Believing that the message will ruin his campaign, the candidate gives up the race. Meanwhile, polls indicate that the message may not have affected voters as the ex-candidate thought it would. The effect may be indirect yet profound (Mutz, 1989).

Anecdotes such as these have led social scientists to wonder about the existence and extent of this so-called third-person effect. In the next section, the empirical literature providing evidence for the effect is examined.

EVIDENCE FOR THE THIRD-PERSON EFFECT

Since the third-person effect was identified by Davison in 1983, empirical evidence for it has been mounting steadily. In his original article on the third-person effect, Davison himself reported the results of four small and admittedly crude experiments in which enough confirmation for an effect was found to suggest more rigorous investigations of it. It was a few years, however, before the first publications of empirical studies began to emerge. One of the first was a report in 1988 of an experiment in which the third-person effect was found in the context of libel juries (Cohen, Mutz, Price, & Gunther, 1988). These Stanford University researchers found that readers exposed to defamatory newspaper articles estimated that others would be significantly more affected by the message than they themselves were. Juries in recent years have awarded remarkably large amounts to persons who have claimed to have had their reputations seriously damaged as the results of news reports, and, often, these inordinately large awards have been lowered subsequently by the courts. Perhaps the third-person effect is responsible at least in part for this phenomenon.

Concurrent with the publication of the libel study came a report of a cross-sectional survey study of peoples' perceptions of the existence of "public opinion" and, of particular relevance here, their perceptions of how much "public opinion" influences people (Glynn & Ostman, 1988). In terms of peoples' perceptions of the impact of public opinion, these Cornell researchers found no general tendency across the population of a third-person effect. In other words, the mean levels of perceived influence of public opinion on self and on others were almost identical. As the researchers pointed out, however, a third-person effect was found in a subset of the population, which, they said, "suggests that these two groups (those who perceive a third-person effect and those who do not) might be very different from each other in the way they view public opinion and public opinion processes" (p. 306). This difference in susceptibility to the third-person effect is a topic we will examine in greater detail below.

In early 1989, Diana Mutz, one of the Stanford University researchers, published the results of her dissertation, a cross-sectional survey study, in which she found strong evidence of a third-person effect among students, staff, and faculty at Stanford on a controversial issue there at that time—university divestment of financial interests in South Africa (Mutz, 1989). As hypothesized by the third-person effect, perceptions of the influence of media reports on others were consistently greater than perceptions of influence on self. Groups of both students and faculty/staff demonstrated the third-person gap, and the gap was found in regard to media coverage of both local happenings (campus South African protests) and more distant ones (rioting in South Africa).

Also in 1989, two studies were published that shed light on a question raised by Davison at the end of his seminal 1983 paper: If a third-person gap does indeed exist, is it because people tend to overestimate media influence on others or because they underestimate media influence on themselves? In April 1989 Richard Perloff of Cleveland State University published a report of two experiments in which a third-person effect was found among viewers of television news broadcasts (Perloff, 1989). In one of these experiments, however, the real effects of the message were assessed, and it was found that news coverage did not significantly influence subjects' attitudes. In other words, while subjects tended to perceive a gap between the influence of the message on others and on themselves (the third-person effect), they also tended to overestimate the effect on others rather than underestimate the effect on themselves.

In the summer of 1989, a second study corroborated Perloff's findings. Using a panel design, in which the same persons were questioned both before and after the reception of a mass media message, a third-person effect was again found among a subset of the population. Furthermore, the message—the seven-part TV miniseries Amerika—was found to have affected peoples' real attitudes very little. Again, respondents in this study tended to overestimate the effects of the message on others rather than underestimate the effect on themselves (Lasorsa, 1989).

Two other third-person effect studies have made recent contributions to the empirical literature. In a cross-sectional telephone survey study, a general tendency toward a third-person effect was found, with nearly nine in ten respondents exhibiting the gap (Tiedge, Silverblatt, Havice, & Rosenfeld, 1991). This conflicts somewhat with the lack of a general third-person effect found by Glynn and Ostman, but recall that the latter looked for a gap only in terms of peoples' perceptions of the effects of "public opinion." Tiedge and his colleagues looked for a gap in specific messages, such as the buying behavior believed to be driven by such advertising gimmicks as "Buy Now While Supplies Last," which is based on the premise that people will expect others to heed such a message and that they themselves consequently should rush to buy. Perhaps most people do believe that they and others are equally affected by "public opinion" in general, but the third-person gap appears when people think about other more specific types of "media messages." This study also made a methodological contribution in its examination of question-order effects. It did not matter whether a person was asked first about perceptions of media effects on others and then asked about self or vice versa, a question that had been raised (but not answered) by other third-person effects studies.

In another recent study, Kim, Ahn, and Song (1991) addressed a question recently raised by Tichenor (1988): Is the third-person effect culturally bound and more characteristic of some social structures than others? Since all of the studies reported to this point were conducted in the United States, the question was worth considering. Kim and colleagues found a third-person effect among college students in Korea, suggesting that the third-person effect extends beyond the U.S. population.

EXTENT OF THE THIRD-PERSON EFFECT

Within a population, however, the third-person effect does not seem to apply to all persons in all situations. A number of studies of the third-person effect, including those of Cohen and colleagues, Glynn and Ostman, and Perloff, did not report the numbers of their subjects or respondents who exhibited the third-person effect. From other studies, however, it appears that the third-person gap may occur in roughly half the cases.

Davison found the effect in 48 percent of his experimental subjects, whereas 36 percent showed no such gap between perceived effects on self and others. Six percent demonstrated a "reverse third-person effect," perceiving greater effects on self than on others (9 percent had no answer or opinion).

In Mutz's study, 50 percent of the respondents demonstrated the third-person effect. In the case of a media report about distant happenings—South African rioting—41 percent of her respondents perceived equal effects of such coverage on both self and others, and 9 percent demonstrated the reverse third-person effect. In the case of a media report about local happenings—campus protests—50 percent of the respondents again demonstrated the third-person effect, 43 percent perceived equal effects, and 7 percent demonstrated the reverse third-person effect.

Kim and colleagues found that about 55 percent of their respondents perceived greater effects on self than on the "general public." About 35 percent perceived no gap between effects on self and others, and about 10 percent demonstrated the reverse third-person effect.

In Lasorsa's study, 31 percent of the respondents demonstrated the third-person effect, 51 percent expected equal effects on self and others, and 5 percent showed the reverse third-person effect. As he noted, however, question placement may have led to an underestimation of the third-person effect in his study since questions about perceived effects were asked back-to-back. That might encourage respondents to close the "third-person gap" by moving the answer to the second question (perception of effects on self) closer to that of the first (perception of effects on others).

Tiedge and colleagues found a discrepancy between perceived effects on self and others in almost nine out of ten respondents. That figure, however, includes both those demonstrating the third-person effect and those demonstrating the reverse third-person effect. Additionally, the figure may be inordinately high because of other methodological considerations. Respondents were asked to strongly agree, agree, disagree, or strongly disagree with each of three statements about media effects on others (additionally, there was a neutral position, essentially giving each respondent five response options on each question). Respondents then were asked to perform the same task for statements dealing with effects on self. A third-person effect was said to exist if there were any disagreements whatsoever. With so many degrees of freedom, the chance for a discrepancy was high. For example, even if for two of the messages I perceived no difference in effects on self and others but in the case of the third message I reported that I "strongly agree" with the statement about effects on others but only "agree" with the statement about effects on self, I would be considered to have demonstrated the third-person effect. Perhaps that explains why Tiedge and colleagues found the effect in a higher percentage of the population than did other researchers.

If one were to attempt to draw a general conclusion from the empirical literature, it might be that about half the population typically exhibits the third-person effect, that is, about 50 percent tends to perceive greater media effects on others than on themselves.

Conditions Affecting the Gap

Convinced that a third-person effect does indeed exist, some researchers have turned their attention to trying to uncover the causes of the effect and other contingent conditions that might intensify or weaken it. What makes some people in some situations perceive greater media effects on others than on themselves and what factors strengthen or weaken the effect?

If I believe that a mass media message affects others more than it affects me, I must have some reason, valid or not, for doing so. Specifically, I must consider myself different in some way from most of the rest of the message's audience. In probing for causes for the gap, therefore, researchers have looked for ways in which those who exhibit the third-person effect differ from those who do not.

In his article, Davison suggested that experts may be more inclined to see a third-person gap. Experts may reason that since they know more about an issue, they are less likely than nonexperts to be swayed by arguments for or against it. Others have taken Davison's suggestion and tested it.

Cohen and colleagues found that when subjects read a defamatory article, they perceived it to have a greater effect on others within their immediate community ("other Stanford students") than on themselves, but this perception of a gap between effects on self and others was even greater when the "others" represented a different community ("Californians"). The gap was at its widest when the "others" were the public "at large."

Kim and colleagues found essentially the same pattern. As respondents were asked about a message's effects on progressively more distant populations, the more they tended to expect the message to affect these others. Thus, for example, while 22 percent of college students at Kwangju University expected a newspaper story about a Kwangju protest to affect other Kwangju students more than themselves, 38 percent expected the story to have greater effects on the "citizens of Kwangju" city than on themselves, and 55 percent expected the story to affect themselves less than the "general public living outside Kwangju."

Perloff found that when the "others" were more psychologically distant from the subject, they perceived stronger media effects on these others. Subjects were exposed to a rather long TV news story about the Arab-Israeli conflict in which both Israeli and Palestinian aggressions were depicted. Subjects who were not particularly partisan expected the story to affect a neutral audience moderately. In contrast, partisans expected the message to affect neutrals—those not like themselves—to a significantly greater extent.

Mutz found that in both the stories she used, university faculty and staff exhibited a greater third-person effect than did students. As she noted, "The larger discrepancy among faculty and staff members suggests hat perceived expertise may play a role in producing this effect" (p. 12).

In his study of the effects of *Amerika*, Lasorsa found that to be the case. Those who perceived themselves to be political experts perceived the TV miniseries to have substantially greater effects on others than on themselves.

If a second general conclusion might be distilled from the empirical literature on the third-person effect, it is that the more unlike myself I think the "others" who receive a mass media message are, the more likely I am to widen the gap between perceived effects on myself and perceived effects on others. From what evidence exists so far, it appears that this like-unlike difference that drives the third-person effect may be social, psychological, geographical, cultural, or cognitive, but, regardless, it leads to a perception of knowing something that others may not.

Other Factors That Open or Close the Gap

Other factors also have been shown to increase or decrease the gap between perceived media effects on self and others. These are age, source credibility, and issue importance. Education also may be related to susceptibility to the third-person effect, but that evidence is less clear.

Glynn and Ostman examined the effects of demographic and media use variables on susceptibility to the third-person effect. The one strong predictor of a positive third-person gap was age. They found that older respondents tended to perceive greater media effects on others than on themselves. Tiedge and colleagues also found a significant relationship between age and the third-person effect. Their analyses led them to suggest that the effect of age is due primarily to older respondents' perceptions that the media have little effect on their own beliefs and behaviors. We might speculate that as people get older they tend to believe that their greater life experiences will blunt the effects of the mass media on themselves and that consequently they tend to expect others, lacking such life experiences, to be swayed more by media messages. To put it another way, perhaps aging leads to a type of perceived expertise, which leads to the third-person gap.

This line of reasoning might also lead one to suspect that there would be a relationship between education and the third-person effect: Those who are more highly educated will perceive themselves as experts and therefore perceive a third-person gap. The evidence, however, is not conclusive. Tiedge and colleagues did find that their more educated respondents tended to overestimate media effects on themselves. Lasorsa's findings also pointed to such a relationship between education and susceptibility to the third-person effect, but the correlation just missed being statistically significant. Kim and colleagues, however, found that education made no difference in susceptibility to the third-person effect, and Glynn and Ostman also found that education was unrelated to the third-person effect. With such mixed evidence, we might want at this time to reserve judgment on the effect of education on susceptibility to the third-person effect.

Another factor that does appear to influence the third-person gap is source credibility. Cohen and colleagues found that when the source of the mass media message was perceived to be biased against the subject's position, the subject tended to expect the message to have greater effects on others than on self. Kim and colleagues also found a greater third-person effect among those who considered the medium to be less credible. When a person perceives that a mass media message is biased against one's own side, the person may reason thusly: I know how biased this message is but others may not recognize its propagandistic nature and, therefore, they will "fall for" what I "see through."

Finally, Mutz found that the salience of the issue discussed in the message affected the third-person gap. Those in her study who thought that divestment from South African interests was a highly important issue were more likely to perceive greater effects on others than on themselves of messages dealing with that topic. Perhaps this, too, is related to perceived expertise. As Davison said in the 1983 article that propagated much of the research discussed here, "In a sense, we are all experts on those subjects that matter to us, in that we have information not available to other people. This information may not be of a factual or technical nature; it may have to do with our own experiences, likes, and dislikes. Other people, we reason, do not know what we know. Therefore, they are more likely to be influenced by the media" (p. 9).

The ultimate conclusion one might draw from the empirical literature is that the third-person effect is driven by a belief that others are unlike me in important ways that relate to their inability to evaluate "correctly" a mass medium message. I reason that others may not be as insightful, as experienced, as interested—as knowing, generally—as I am and, therefore, I believe they are more susceptible than I am to media influence. Ironically, however, it may be I who, in an indirect yet important way, am most susceptible to the influence of the message.

IMPLICATIONS FOR POLICYMAKERS

As this attempt to synthesize and make sense of the empirical literature shows, the notion of a gap in perception of mass media effects has only recently received much systematic study. The findings of what studies do exist, however, are at least as consistent as the findings in many other areas of mass communication theory. Certainly, there is still much work to be done. Questions remain about the scope of the third-person effect, about the types of individuals who may be most susceptible to it, about situations that may strengthen or weaken it, and about its possible effects both on the ways people interact with others in their personal lives and on the ways they make public policy.

The above findings about factors that influence susceptibility to the third-person effect may be of special interest to policymakers. Since policymakers are quite likely to consider themselves different from their constituents, especially in terms of political expertise, they may be especially susceptible to the perceptual gap of expecting mass media messages to affect others while having little effect on themselves. This social-psychological condition may be especially troublesome in cases where policymakers are responsible for the management of others whom they perceive to be different from themselves in important ways. If the third-person effect explains why the white officers who commanded the black troops on Iwo Jima were so quick to react to the Japanese propaganda, one must wonder if black officers would have reacted the same way.

The third-person phenomenon may also explain why some people are so willing to accept censorship of materials they do not believe will harm themselves. Censors often justify their positions by claiming to fulfill an important social function, namely, protecting others from the harmful effects of certain types of messages. Yet, in the course of their jobs these censors may expose themselves to the very same messages from which they are trying to shield others. The fact that censors believe they can be exposed without harmful effect to messages that supposedly harm others seems to be a classic case of a third-person effect.

RELEVANCE OF THE THIRD-PERSON EFFECT
TO THEORY

In this book, Kennamer introduces a simple model of the process by which public opinion may translate into public policy. As any good model does, this one identifies important components in a system (object, event, process) and shows how they are connected. Kennamer identifies four sets of principal actors in the public-opinion-to-policymaking process: policymakers, special-interest groups, publics, and the news media. In his model, the news media play a central role, essentially serving as convenient bridges that the other components may use to reach each other.

It is worth noting, however, that the news media themselves, and other mass media, may act not merely as conduits but on occasion may attempt to reach the other system components with their own messages or may attempt to modify the messages they convey for other components to suit their own needs. Also, the media themselves sometimes become the *object* of policymaking ventures, cases where policy is made to (de)control or otherwise affect media organizations and operations. However, regardless of how active the news media themselves are in the public-opinion-to-policy process (admittedly a big question), and regardless of whether the media themselves are the target of policymaking activity (another big question), the conduit role alone may make the news media crucial to the success of the other components of the system. That alone makes it worthy of study. Indeed, one of the major values of a model is that it allows us to simplify complicated matters in just such a way as has been done here.

A model, however, goes only so far. Even if it identifies the important components in a system and shows how they are connected, that is but a first step in understanding how the system works. For the model to be useful, its components need to be defined carefully, connections need to be clearly delineated, and these differentiations among components and connections must be both clear (a matter of conceptualization) and worth making (a matter of theory).

The third-person effect may help guide us here—it may even help direct us to a theory of public opinion and policymaking—but it is important to note that the third-person effect is not a theory. If it is anything, it is a social condition. That, however, is not to belittle its relevance to our understanding of important political processes.

First, the third-person effect may help us in the area of conceptualization. For example, it may help us decide that the components of the system we are studying are or are not clearly enough defined and differentiated. If one's goal is to understand how public opinion translates into political decision-making then it may be found, for instance, that when we consider how the third-person effect works on different types of persons, the distinction we might make between "policymaker" or "special interest groups" is not as clear as we at first thought. We might wonder, for instance, whether in some cases special interest groups *are* policymakers, or vice versa. Our recognition of the third-person effect may help us explicate and develop our concepts.

Secondly, our understanding of the third-person effect may help us in the area of theory. For example, because the third-person phenomenon describes a person's perception of media effects, it may help explain how public opinion influences policymaking, how special interest groups influence policymaking, and how they use the news media to reach each other. Thus, we might wonder if those who believe the news media affect others more than they affect themselves may take a different approach to the regulation of the media than do those who believe the news media affect everyone equally. We might find, for instance, that those who exhibit a third-person effect might be less willing to entertain the notion of the media as important platforms for the free and open negotiation of ideas, the principle underlying the libertarian theory of the press. Such a person might instead be inclined to support a "social responsibility" approach to media regulation, or even an authoritarian one. The point to be made here is that the third-person effect may guide us to interesting concepts and distinctions worth making but, at the same time, that a theory is required to allow us to understand why these concepts are interesting and why these distinctions are worth making.

Jurors in libel cases, media company executives, programming consultants, government commissioners, and other policymakers who regulate the mass media all make assumptions about the effects of media content. It may well be that these assumptions themselves have more serious societal effects than the media content itself. In a society that endeavors to run on the notion that all ideas are subject to scrutiny and that truth emerges from a battle with falsehood in a free and open marketplace of ideas, those responsible for regulating the mass media might do well to bear in mind the potential, and perhaps destructive, power of the third-person effect.

References

Abbott, E. A., & Brassfield, L. T. (1989). Comparing decisions on releases by TV and newspaper gatekeepers. *Journalism Quarterly, 66,* 853–856.

The age of indifference: A study of young Americans and how they view the news. (1990, June 28). Washington, DC: Times Mirror Center for the People and the Press.

Alexander, J. (1982). The mass news media in systematic, historical, and comparative perspective. In E. Katz & T. Szecsko (Eds.), *Mass media and social change* (pp. 17–51). Beverly Hills, CA: Sage.

Allport, F. (1937). Toward a science of public opinion. *Public Opinion Quarterly, 1,* 7–23.

Altheide, D. L. (1976). *Creating reality: How TV news distorts events.* Beverly Hills, CA: Sage.

Altheide, D. L. (1991). The impact of television news formats on social policy. *Journal of Broadcasting and Electronic Media, 35,* 3–21.

Althusser, L. (1971). Ideology and ideological state apparatuses. In L. Althusser (Ed.), *Lenin and philosophy, and other essays* (pp. 127–186). London: New Left Books.

American Bar Association Advisory Committee on Fair Trial and Free Press (1966). *Standards relating to fair trial and free press* (Reardon Report). Chicago: American Bar Association.

The American media: Who reads, who watches, who cares. (1990, July 15). Washington, DC: Times Mirror Center for the People and the Press.

Andreasen, M. S., & Thompson, M. E. (1985, August). *The silence effect: Fear of isolation or association.* Paper presented at the annual meeting of the

Association for Education in Journalism and Mass Communication, Memphis, TN.

Aronoff, C. (1975). Credibility of public relations for journalists. *Public Relations Review, 1*, 45–56.

Asch, S. E. (1970). Effects of group pressure upon the modification and distortion of judgments. In J. H. Campbell & H. Hepler (Eds.), *Dimensions in communication: Readings* (pp. 170–183). Belmont, CA: Wadsworth.

Atwater, T., & Fico, F. (1986). Source reliance and use in reporting state government: A study of print and broadcast practices. *Newspaper Research Journal, 8*, 53–61.

Bachrach, P., & Baratz, M. (1970). *Power and poverty: Theory and practice.* New York: Oxford University Press.

Bagdikian, B. H. (1990). *The media monopoly* (3rd ed.). Boston: Beacon Press.

Bakalar, J. B., & Grinspoon, L. (1984). *Drug control in a free society.* New York: Cambridge University Press.

Ball-Rokeach, S. J., Rokeach, M., & Grube, J. W. (1984). *The great American values test: Influencing behavior and belief through television.* New York: Free Press.

Bantz, C. R. (1985). News organizations: Conflict as a crafted cultural norm. *Communication, 8*, 225–244.

Bantz, C. R., McCorkle, S., & Baade, R. C. (1980). The news factory. *Communication Research, 7*, 45–68.

Baxter, B. L. (1981). The news release: An idea whose time has gone? *Public Relations Review, 7*, 27–31.

Bennack, F. A., Jr. (1983, October). *A Hearst report* presented at the national conference of metropolitan courts, San Antonio, TX.

Bennett, S. E. (1988). Know-nothings revisited: The meaning of political ignorance today. *Social Science Quarterly, 69*, 476–490.

Bennett, S. E. (1989). Trends in Americans' political information. *American Politics Quarterly, 17*, 422–435.

Bennett, S. E. (1990, September). *The dimensions of Americans' political information.* Paper presented at the meeting of the American Political Science Association, San Francisco.

Bennett, T. (1982). Theories of the media, theories of society. In M. Gurevitch, T. Bennett, J. Curran, & J. Woollacott (Eds.), *Culture, society and the media* (pp. 30–55). London: Methuen.

Bennett, W. L. (1980). *Public opinion in American politics.* New York: Harcourt Brace Jovanovich.

Bennett, W. L. (1988). *News: The politics of illusion* (2d ed.). New York: Longman.

Benson, L. (1967–68). An approach to the scientific study of past public opinion. *Public Opinion Quarterly, 31*, 522–567.

Berelson, B., Lazarsfeld, P., & McPhee, W. (1954). *Voting.* Chicago: University of Chicago Press.

Bergen, L. (1986, May). *Testing the spiral of silence with opinions on abortion.* Paper presented at the annual meeting of the International Communication Association, Chicago, IL.

Berk, R. A., Brackman, H., & Lesser, S. (1977). *A measure of justice: An em-*

pirical study of changes in the California penal code. New York: Academic Press.

Berkowitz, D. (1987). TV news sources and news channels: A study in agenda-building. Journalism Quarterly, 64, 508–513.

Berkowitz, D. (1990a). Refining the gatekeeping metaphor for local television. Journal of Broadcasting and Electronic Media, 34, 55–68.

Berkowitz, D. (1990b, August). Routine newswork and the what-a-story: A case study of organizational adaptation. Paper presented at the annual meeting of the Association for Education in Journalism and Mass Communication, Minneapolis, MN.

Berkowitz, D. (1991). Assessing forces in the selection of local television news. Journal of Broadcasting and Electronic Media, 35, 245–251.

Berkowitz, D., & Adams, D. B. (1990). Agenda-building and information-subsidy in local television news. Journalism Quarterly, 67, 723–731.

Berkowitz, D., & Beach, D. W. (1991, August). News sources and news context: The effect of routine news, conflict, and proximity. Paper presented at the annual meeting of the Association for Education in Journalism and Mass Communication, Boston.

Best, J. (1989). Dark figures and child victims: Statistical claims about missing children. In J. Best (Ed.), Images of issues: Typifying contemporary social problems (pp. 21–37). Hawthorne, NY: Aldine de Gruyter.

Biddle, B. U., & Thomas, E. J. (1966). Role theory: Concepts and research. New York: Wiley.

Bishop, G. F. (1990). Issue involvement and response effects. Public Opinion Quarterly, 54, 209–218.

Bishop, G. F., Oldendick, R. W., & Tuchfarber, A. J. (1983). Effects of filter questions in public opinion surveys. Public Opinion Quarterly, 47, 528–546.

Bishop, G. F., Oldendick, R. W., Tuchfarber, A. J., & Bennett, S. E. (1980). Pseudo-opinions on public affairs. Public Opinion Quarterly, 44, 198–209.

Blumer, H. (1946). The mass, the public, and public opinion. In A. M. Lee (Ed.), New outline of the principles of sociology (pp. 185–193). New York: Barnes and Noble.

Blumer, H. (1948). Public opinion and public opinion polling. American Sociological Review, 13, 542–552.

Blumler, J. G., & Gurevitch, M. (1981). Politicians and the press: An essay on role relationships. In D. Nimmo & K. Sanders (Eds.), Handbook of political communication (pp. 467–493). Beverly Hills, CA: Sage.

Bogart, L. (1985). Polls and the awareness of public opinion. New Brunswick, NJ: Transaction Books.

Bogart, L. (1989). Press and public. Hillsdale, NJ: Lawrence Erlbaum.

Bogart, L. (1991, August). The pollster and the Nazis. Commentary, 92, 47–49.

Bordieu, P. (1979). Public opinion does not exist. In A. Mattelart & S. Siegelaub (Eds.), Communication and class struggle: An anthology in 2 volumes (Vol. 1) (M. Axtmann, Trans.). New York: International General (Original published in 1973.)

Boudon, R. (1989). *The analysis of ideology*. (M. Slater, Trans.). Chicago: University of Chicago Press.

Boyte, H. C. (1980). *The backyard revolution: Understanding the new citizen movement*. Philadelphia: Temple University Press.

Breed, W. (1955). Social control in the news room: A functional analysis. *Social Forces, 33*, 326–355.

Breed, W. (1958). Mass communication and sociocultural integration. *Social Forces, 37*, 109–116.

Brooks, J. E. (1985). Democratic frustration in the Anglo-American polities: A quantification of inconsistency between mass public opinion and public policy. *Western Political Quarterly, 38*, 250–261.

Brooks, J. E. (1987). The opinion-policy nexus in France: Do institutions and ideology make a difference? *Journal of Politics, 49*, 465–480.

Brooks, J. E. (1990). The opinion-policy nexus in Germany. *Public Opinion Quarterly. 54*, 508–529.

Brown, J. D., Bybee, C. R., Weardon, S. T., & Straughan, D. M. (1987). Invisible power: Newspaper news sources and the limits of diversity. *Journalism Quarterly, 64*, 45–54.

Bryce, J. (1888). *The American commonwealth* (Vol. 2). London: Macmillan.

Buckalew, J. K. (1970). News elements and selection by television news editors. *Journal of Broadcasting, 14*, 47–54.

Burstein, P. (1979). Public opinion, demonstrations, and the passage of anti-discrimination legislation. *Public Opinion Quarterly, 43*, 157–172.

Campbell, A., Converse, P. E., Miller, W. E., & Stokes, D. E. (1960). *The American voter*. New York: Wiley.

Cantril, A. H. (1991). *The opinion connection*. Washington, DC: CQ Press.

Cantril, H. (1947). *The invasion from Mars*. Princeton, NJ: Princeton University Press.

Carey, J. W. (1986). The dark continent of American journalism. In R. K. Manoff & M. Schudson (Eds.), *Reading the news* (pp. 146–196). New York: Pantheon.

Chaffee, S. (1982). Mass media and interpersonal channels: Competitive, convergent or complementary? In G. Gumpertz & R. Cathcart (Eds.), *Inter/media: Interpersonal communication in a media world* (pp. 57–77). New York: Oxford University Press.

Chisman, F. P. (1976). *Attitude psychology and the study of public opinion*. University Park: Pennsylvania State University Press.

Cobb, R. W., & Elder, C. D. (1981). Communication and public policy. In D. Nimmo and K. Sanders (Eds.), *Handbook of political communication* (pp. 391–416). Beverly Hills, CA: Sage.

Cobb, R. W., & Elder, C. D. (1983). *Participation in American politics: The dynamics of agenda-building* (2nd ed.). Baltimore, MD: Johns Hopkins University Press.

Cohen, B. C. (1963). *The press and foreign policy*. Princeton, NJ: Princeton University Press.

Cohen, B. C. (1973). *The public's impact on foreign policy*. Boston: Little, Brown.

Cohen, J., Mutz, D., Price, V., & Gunther, A. (1988). Perceived impact of defamation: An experiment on third-person effects. *Public Opinion Quarterly, 52,* 161–173.

Cohen, S. & Young, J. (1981). *The manufacture of news* (Rev. ed.). Beverly Hills, CA: Sage.

Cohen, Y. (1986). *Media diplomacy.* London: Frank Cass.

Constituents most influential with congressmen, says university study (1981, July 27). *Broadcasting,* p. 101.

Converse, P. E. (1962). Information flow and the stability of partisan attitudes. *Public Opinion Quarterly, 26,* 578–599.

Converse, P. E. (1964). The nature of belief systems in mass publics. In D. Apter (Ed.), *Ideology and discontent* (pp. 206–261). New York: Free Press.

Converse, P. E. (1990). Popular representation and the distribution of information. In J. A. Ferejohn & J. H. Kuklinski (Eds.), *Information and democratic processes* (pp. 369–388). Urbana: University of Illinois Press.

Cook, F. L., Tyler, T. L., Goetz, E. G., Gordon, M. T., Protess, D., Leff, D. R., & Molotch, H. L. (1983). Media and agenda setting: Effects on the public, interest group leaders, policy makers, and policy. *Public Opinion Quarterly, 47,* 16–35.

Cook, T. E. (1989). *Making laws and making news: Media strategies in the U.S. House of Representatives.* Washington, DC: Brookings Institution.

Coser, L. (1956). *The functions of social conflict.* New York: Free Press.

Coughlin, R. M. (1980). *Ideology, public opinion, and welfare policy: Attitudes toward taxes and spending in industrialized societies.* Berkeley, CA: Institute of International Studies, University of California.

Crespi, I. (1980). Polls as journalism. *Public Opinion Quarterly, 44,* 462–477.

Crespi, I. (1989). *Public opinion, polls, and democracy.* Boulder, CO: Westview Press.

Csikszentmihalyi, M. (1991). Reflections on the "spiral of silence." In J. A. Anderson (Ed.), *Communication Yearbook 14* (pp. 288–297). Newbury Park, CA: Sage.

Cundy, D. T. (1973, June). *Can representatives represent?* Unpublished doctoral preliminary examinations paper, Department of Political Science, University of Oregon.

Cunningham, L. G., & Henry, B. A. (1989). *The changing face of the newsroom.* Washington, DC: American Society of Newspaper Editors.

Cutlip, S. M. (1988). Public relations in the government. In R. E. Hiebert (Ed.), *Precision public relations* (pp. 30–57). New York: Longman.

Danielian, L. H. (1986, November). *Special interest groups and mass media access: Group goals, resources, and attitudes toward the media.* Paper presented at the Midwest Association for Public Opinion Research, Chicago.

Danielian, L. H. (1988, May). *From "bouncing bosoms" to the ERA: L.A. Times coverage of L.A. NOW mass media activities, 1970 to 1983.* Paper presented at the meeting of the International Communication Association, New Orleans.

Danielian, L. H. (1989). *Network news coverage of interest groups: Implications for mass media and democracy.* Unpublished doctoral dissertation, University of Texas at Austin.

Danielian, L. H., & Reese, S. D. (1989). A closer look at intermedia influences on agenda-setting: The cocaine issue of 1986. In P. Shoemaker (Ed.), *Communication campaigns about drugs* (pp. 47–66). Hillsdale, NJ: Lawrence Erlbaum.

Davison, W. P. (1957). The mass media in West German political life. In H. Speier & W. P. Davison (Eds.), *West German leadership and foreign policy* (pp. 242–281). Evanston, IL: Row Peterson.

Davison, W. P. (1958). The public opinion process. *Public Opinion Quarterly, 22*, 91–106.

Davison, W. P. (1983). The third-person effect in communication. *Public Opinion Quarterly, 65*, 299–306.

Delli Carpini, M. X. (1986). *Stability and change in American politics: The coming of age of the generation of the 1960s.* New York: New York University Press.

Delli Carpini, M. X., & Keeter, S. (1990, September). *The structure of political knowledge: Issues of conceptualization and measurement.* Paper presented at the meeting of the American Political Science Association, San Francisco.

Delli Carpini, M. X., & Keeter, S. (1991). Stability and change in the U.S. public's knowledge of politics. *Public Opinion Quarterly, 55*, 583–612.

Demers, D. P. (1987). Use of polls in reporting changes slightly since 1978. *Journalism Quarterly, 64*, 839–842.

Demers, D. P. (1988). Commentary: A qualitative analysis of newspaper polls. *Newspaper Research Journal, 9*(3), 105–114.

Dimmick, J. (1974). The gatekeeper: An uncertainty theory. *Journalism Monographs*, no. 37.

Dimmick, J., & Coit, P. (1982) Levels of analysis in mass media decision making: A taxonomy, research strategy and illustrative data analysis. *Communication Research, 9*, 3–32.

Dominick, J. R. (1990). *The dynamics of mass communication* (3rd ed.). New York: McGraw-Hill.

Donohue, G. A., Olien, C. N., & Tichenor, P. J. (1989). Structure and constraints on community newspaper gatekeepers. *Journalism Quarterly, 66*, 807–812.

Donohue, G. A., Olien, C. N., Tichenor, P. J., & Demers, D. P. (1990, August). *Community structure, news judgments and newspaper content.* Paper presented at the annual meeting of the Association for Education in Journalism and Mass Communication, Minneapolis, MN.

Donsbach, W. (1988). The challenge of the spiral-of-silence theory. *Communicare, 8*(1), 5–16.

Donsbach, W. (1989, April). Concluding remarks. *WAPOR Newsletter*, p. 14.

Donsbach, W., & Stevenson, R. L. (1984, May). *Challenges, problems and empirical evidence of the theory of the spiral of silence.* Paper presented at the annual meeting of the International Communication Association, San Francisco.

Doppelt, J. (1991). Strained relations: How judges and lawyers perceive the coverage of legal affairs. *Justice System Journal, 14*(3), 419–444.

Doppelt, J., & Manikas, P. (1990). Mass media and criminal justice decision making. In R. Surette (Ed.), *The media and criminal justice policy: Recent research and social effects* (pp. 129–142). Springfield, IL: Thomas.

Downs, A. (1957). *An economic theory of democracy.* New York: Harper's.

Drechsel, R. (1983). *News making in the trial courts.* New York: Longman.

Drechsel, R. (1987). Accountability, representation and the communication behavior of trial judges. *Western Political Quarterly, 40,* 685–702.

Dreyer, E. C., & Rosenbaum, W. A. (1966). *Political opinions and electoral behavior: Essays and studies.* Belmont, CA: Wadsworth.

Dye, T. R. (1984). *Understanding public policy* (6th ed.). Englewood Cliffs, NJ: Prentice-Hall.

Edelman, M. (1964). *The symbolic uses of politics.* Urbana: University of Illinois Press.

Efron, E. (1971). *The news twisters.* Los Angeles: Nash.

Eliasoph, N. (1988). Routines and the making of oppositional news. *Critical Studies in Mass Communication, 5,* 313–334.

Ellul, J. (1965). *Propaganda* (K. Kellen & J. Lerner, Trans.). New York: Knopf.

Emerson, R. M. (1983). Holistic effects in social control decision making. *Law and Society Review, 17,* 425–455.

Entman, R. (1989). *Democracy without citizens: Media and the decay of American politics.* New York: Oxford University Press.

Epstein, E. J. (1973). *News from nowhere.* New York: Vintage Books.

Erfle, S., McMillan, H., & Grofman, B. (1990). Regulation via threats: Politics, media coverage, and oil pricing decisions. *Public Opinion Quarterly, 54,* 48–63.

Ericson, R., Baranek, P., & Chan, J. (1989). *Negotiating control: A study of news sources.* Toronto: University of Toronto Press.

Erikson, R. S., & Luttbeg, N. R. (1973). *American public opinion: Its origins, content, and impact.* New York: Wiley.

Erikson, R. S., Luttbeg, N. R., & Tedin, K. L. (1988). *American public opinion: Its origins, content, and impact* (3rd ed.). New York: Macmillan.

Erskine, H. G. (1962). The polls: The informed public. *Public Opinion Quarterly, 26,* 669–677.

Erskine, H. G. (1963a). The polls: Textbook knowledge. *Public Opinion Quarterly, 27,* 133–141.

Erskine, H. G. (1963b). The polls: Exposure to domestic information. *Public Opinion Quarterly, 27,* 491–500.

Erskine, H. G. (1963c). The polls: Exposure to international information. *Public Opinion Quarterly, 27,* 658–662.

Ettema, J. S., & Kline, F. G. (1977). Deficits, differences, and ceilings: Contingent conditions for understanding the knowledge gap. *Communication Research, 4,* 179–202.

Felgenhauer, N. (1972). Precision journalism. In E. E. Dennis (Ed.), *The magic writing machine* (pp. 65–75). Eugene: University of Oregon Press.

Fiorina, M. P. (1981). *Retrospective voting in American national elections.* New Haven, CT: Yale University Press.

Fishman, M. (1980). *Manufacturing the news.* Austin: University of Texas Press.

Gallup, J., & Rae, S. (1940). *The pulse of democracy: The public-opinion poll and how it works.* Westport, CT: Greenwood Press (1968 reprint).

Gandy, O. H., Jr. (1982). *Beyond agenda-setting: Information subsidies and public policy*. Norwood, NJ: Ablex.

Gans, H. G. (1979). *Deciding what's news: A study of CBS Evening News, NBC Nightly News, Newsweek and Time*. New York: Vintage Books.

Gaunt, P. (1990). *Choosing the news: The profit factor in news selection*. New York: Greenwood Press.

Gaventa, J. (1980). *Power and powerlessness*. Chicago: University of Illinois Press.

Gaziano, C. (1978). Relationship between public opinion and Supreme Court decisions: Was Mr. Dooley right? *Communication Research, 5*, 131–149.

Gaziano, C. (1983). The knowledge gap: An analytic review of media effects. *Communication Research, 10*, 447–486.

Gaziano, C. (1984). Neighborhood newspapers, citizen groups, and public affairs knowledge gaps. *Journalism Quarterly, 61*, 556–566.

Gibson, J. L. (1980). Environmental constraints on the behavior of judges: A representational model of judicial decision-making. *Law and Society Review, 14*, 343–370.

Gilberg, S., Eyal, C., McCombs, M., & Nicholas, D. (1980). The State of the Union address and the press agenda. *Journalism Quarterly, 57*, 584–588.

Ginsberg, B. (1986). *The captive public: How mass opinion promotes state power*. New York: Basic Books.

Ginsberg, B., & Shefter, M. (1990). *Politics by other means: Institutional conflict and the declining significance of elections in America*. New York: Basic Books.

Gitlin, T. (1978). Media sociology: The dominant paradigm. *Theory and Society, 6*, 205–253.

Gitlin, T. (1980). *The whole world is watching: Mass media in the making and unmaking of the New Left*. Berkeley: University of California Press.

Glenn, N. (1972). The distribution of political knowledge in the United States. In D. Nimmo & C. Bonjean (Eds.), *Political attitudes and public opinion* (pp. 273–283). New York: McKay.

Glynn, C., & McLeod, J. M. (1982). Public opinion, communication processes, and voting decisions. In M. Burgoon (Ed.), *Communication yearbook 6* (pp. 759–774). Beverly Hills, CA: Sage.

Glynn, C., & McLeod, J. M. (1984). Public opinion du jour: An examination of the spiral of silence. *Public Opinion Quarterly, 48*, 731–740.

Glynn, C. J. & McLeod, L. M. (1985). Implications of the spiral of silence for communication and public opinion research. In K. R. Sanders, L. L. Kaid, & D. Nimmo (Eds.), *Public communication yearbook, 1984* (pp. 43–65). Carbondale: Southern Illinois University Press.

Glynn, C. J., & Ostman, R. E. (1988). Public opinion about public opinion. *Journalism Quarterly, 65*, 299–306.

Goldenberg, E. (1975). *Making the papers: The access of resource-poor groups to the metropolitan press*. Lexington, MA: Heath.

Gollin, A. E. (Ed.) (1980). Polls and the news media: A symposium. *Public Opinion Quarterly, 44*(4).

Gonzalez, H. (1988). Mass media and the spiral of silence: The Philippines from Marcos to Aquino. *Journal of Communication, 38*(4), 33–48.

Graber, D. A. (1984). *Mass media and American politics.* Washington, DC: CQ Press.

Grey, D. L., & Brown, T. R. (1970). Letters to the editor: Hazy reflections of public opinion. *Journalism Quarterly, 47,* 450–456, 471.

Hackett, R. A. (1985). Decline of a paradigm: Bias and objectivity in news media studies. In M. Gurevitch & M Levy (Eds.), *Mass communication review yearbook* (Vol. 5, pp. 251–274). Beverly Hills, CA: Sage.

Hagan, J. (1980). The legislation of crime and delinquency: A review of theory, method, and research. *Law and Society Review, 14,* 603–628.

Hall, S. (1979). Culture, the media and the "ideological effect." In J. Curran, M. Gurevitch, & J. Woollacott (Eds.), *Mass communication and society* (pp. 315–348). Beverly Hills, CA: Sage.

Heinz, A. M. (1985). The political context for the changing content of criminal law. In E. S. Fairchild & V. J. Webb (Eds.), *The politics of crime and criminal justice* (pp. 77–95). Beverly Hills, CA: Sage.

Heinz, J., & Laumann, E. (1982). *Chicago lawyers: The social structure of the bar.* Chicago: Russell Sage and the American Bar Association.

Heinz, J., Laumann, E., Salisbury, R., & Nelson, R. (1990). Inner circles or hollow cores? Elite networks in national policy systems. *Journal of Politics, 52,* 356–390.

Hennessy, B. (1985). *Public opinion* (5th ed.). Monterey, CA: Brooks/Cole.

Herbst, S. (1991). Classical democracy, polls, and public opinion: Theoretical frameworks for studying the development of public sentiment. *Communication Theory, 1,* 225–238.

Herman, E. S., & Chomsky, N. (1988). *Manufacturing consent: The political economy of the mass media.* New York: Pantheon Books.

Herring, P. (1967). *Group representation before Congress.* New York: Russell and Russell. (Original published in 1929.)

Hess, S. (1986). *The ultimate insiders: U.S. Senators in the national media.* Washington, DC: Brookings Institution.

Hilgartner, S., & Bosk, C. L. (1988). The rise and fall of social problems: A public arenas model. *American Journal of Sociology, 94,* 53–78.

Hill, D. B. (1981). Letter opinion on ERA: A test of the newspaper bias hypothesis. *Public Opinion Quarterly, 45,* 384–392.

Hirsch, P. M. (1977). Occupational, organizational, and institutional models in mass media research: Toward an integrated framework. In P. M. Hirsch, P. V. Miller, & F. G. Kline (Eds.), *Strategies for communication research* (pp. 13–42). Beverly Hills, CA: Sage.

Hirsh, M. (1976). The sins of Sears are not news in Chicago. *Columbia Journalism Review, 5,* 29–30.

Holusha, J. (1989, April 21). Exxon's public-relations problem. *New York Times,* pp. 25, 28.

Hovland, C. I., Janis, I. L., & Kelley, H. (1953). *Communication and persuasion.* New Haven, CT: Yale University Press.

Hungerford, S. E., & Lemert, J. B. (1973). Covering the environment: A new Afghanistanism? *Journalism Quarterly, 50,* 475–481, 508.

Hyman, H., & Sheatsley, P. (1947). Some reasons why information campaigns fail. *Public Opinion Quarterly, 11,* 412–423.

Inglehart, R. (1977). *The silent revolution*. Princeton, NJ: Princeton University Press.

Irvine, R. (1984). *Media mischief and misdeeds*. Chicago: Regnery Gateway.

Ismach, A. H. (1984). Polling as a news-gathering tool. *Polling and the democratic consensus (Annals of the American Academy of Political and Social Science, 472)*. Beverly Hills, CA: Sage.

Iyengar, S. (1990). Shortcuts to political knowledge: The role of selective attention and accessibility. In J. A. Ferejohn & J. H. Kuklinski (Eds.), *Information and democratic processes* (pp. 160–185). Urbana: University of Illinois Press.

Iyengar, S., & Kinder, D. R. (1987). *News that matters: Agenda-setting and priming in a television age*. Chicago: University of Chicago Press.

Jefferson, T. (1899). *Writings of Thomas Jefferson* (P. L. Ford, Ed., Vol. 10). New York: Putnam.

John, K. (1984, Nov. 19). Reagan mandate or no, the GOP is in high favor. *Washington Post National Weekly Edition*, p. 37.

Johnstone, J. W. C., Slawski, E. J., & Bowman, W. W. (1976). *The news people*. Urbana: University of Illinois Press.

Joslyn, R. A. (1990). Election campaigns as occasions for civic education. In D. L. Swanson and D. Nimmo (Eds.), *New directions in political communication* (pp. 86–122). Newbury Park, CA: Sage.

Kairys, D. (1982). Freedom of speech. In D. Kairys (Ed.), *The politics of law: A progressive critique* (pp. 140–171). New York: Pantheon Books.

Katz, E. (1982). Publicity and pluralistic ignorance: Notes on the "spiral of silence." In H. Baier, H. M. Kepplinger, & K. Reumann (Eds.), *Public opinion and social change: For Elisabeth Noelle-Neumann* (pp. 28–38). Opladen: Westdeutscher Verlag.

Katz, E. (1983). Publicity and pluralistic ignorance. Notes on "The spiral of silence." In E. Wartella, D. C. Whitney, and S. Windahl (Eds.), *Mass communication review yearbook* (Vol. 4, pp. 89–99). Beverly Hills, CA: Sage.

Keeter, S., & Zukin, C. (1983). *Uninformed choice: The failure of the new presidential nominating system*. New York: Praeger.

Keir, G., McCombs, M., & Shaw, D. L. (1991). *Advanced Reporting*. Prospect Heights, IL: Waveland Press.

Kennamer, J. D. (1990). Self-serving bias in perceiving the opinions of others. *Communication Research, 17*, 393–404.

Kennan, G. (1987, January 5). TV's misguided Cold-War games. *New York Times*, p. A16.

Kessel, J. (1988). *Presidential campaign politics*. Homewood, IL: Dorsey Press.

Key, V. O., Jr. (1958). *Politics, parties and pressure groups*. New York: Cromwell.

Key, V. O., Jr. (1961). *Public opinion and American democracy*. New York: Knopf.

Key, V. O., Jr. (1966). *The responsible electorate*. New York: Vintage Books.

Kim, Y., Ahn, J., & Song, J. (1991, May). *Perceived media influence on self and others on a controversial issue*. Paper presented at the meeting of the International Communication Association, Chicago.

Kingdon, J. W. (1984). *Agendas, alternatives, and public policies.* Boston: Little, Brown.

Klapper, J. T. (1960). *The effects of mass communication.* New York: Free Press.

Kopenhaver, L. L. (1985). Aligning values of practitioners and journalists. *Public Relations Review, 11,* 34–42.

Krauss, S. D. (1988–89). Representing the community: A look at the selection process in obscenity cases and capital sentencing. *Indiana Law Journal, 64,* 617–664.

Kriesberg, M. (1945). What congressmen and administrators think of the polls. *Public Opinion Quarterly, 9,* 333–337.

Kuklinski, J., Metlay, D., & Key, W. D. (1982). Citizen knowledge and choices on the complex issue of nuclear energy. *American Journal of Political Science, 26,* 615–642.

Lambeth, E. B. (1978). Perceived influence of the press on energy policy making. *Journalism Quarterly, 55,* 11–18, 72.

Lang, G. E., & Lang, K. (1981). Watergate: An exploration of the agenda-building process. In G. C. Wilhoit & H. De Bock (Eds.), *Mass Communication Review Yearbook* (Vol. 2, pp. 447–468). Beverly Hills, CA: Sage.

Lang, G. E., & Lang, K. (1983). *The battle for public opinion: The president, the press, and the polls during Watergate.* New York: Columbia University Press.

Lannamann, J. W. (1991). Interpersonal communication research as ideological practice. *Communication Theory, 1*(3), 179–203.

Lasorsa, D. L. (1989). Real and perceived effects of *Amerika. Journalism Quarterly, 66,* 373–379, 529.

Lasorsa, D. L. (1991). Political outspokenness: Factors working against the spiral of silence. *Journalism Quarterly, 68,* 131–140.

Lasswell, H. (1948). The structure and function of communication in society. In L. Bryson (Ed.), *The communication of ideas* (pp. 37–51). New York: Institute for Religious and Social Studies.

Laumann, E., & Knoke, D. (1987). *The organizational state: Social choice in national policy domains.* Madison: University of Wisconsin Press.

Laumann, E., & Pappi, F. (1976). *Networks of collective action: Perspectives on community influence systems.* New York: Academic Press.

Lazarsfeld, P. F., Berelson, B., & Gaudet, H. (1944). *The people's choice.* New York: Columbia University Press.

Lazarsfeld, P. F., & Merton, R. K. (1960). Mass communication, popular taste, and organized social action. In W. Schramm (Ed.), *Mass communications* (pp. 492–512). Urbana: University of Illinois Press. (Original published in 1948.)

Lee, H. (1987). *A study of spiral of silence theory.* Unpublished master's thesis, University of Wisconsin-Madison.

Leff, D. R., Protess, D. L., & Brooks, S. C. (1986). Crusading journalism: Changing public attitudes and policy-making agendas. *Public Opinion Quarterly, 50,* 300–315.

Lemert, J. B. (1970, November). *Craft attitudes, the craft of journalism and Spiro Agnew.* Paper presented at the meeting of the Western Speech Association, Portland, OR.

Lemert, J. B. (1971, June). *Legislators' sources of public opinion information.* Unpublished manuscript, School of Journalism, University of Oregon.

Lemert, J. B. (1981). *Does mass communication change public opinion after all? A new approach to effects analysis.* Chicago: Nelson-Hall.

Lemert, J. B. (1986). Picking the winners: Politician vs. voter predictions of two controversial ballot measures. *Public Opinion Quarterly, 50,* 208–221.

Lemert, J. B. (1989). *Criticizing the media: Empirical approaches.* Newbury Park, CA: Sage.

Lemert, J. B., Elliot, W. R., Bernstein, J. M., Rosenberg, W. R., & Nestvold, K. J. (1991). *News verdicts, the debates, and presidential campaigns.* New York: Praeger.

Lemert, J. B., Mitzman, B. N., Seither, M. A., Cook, R. H., & O'Neil, R. M. (1977). Journalists and mobilizing information. *Journalism Quarterly, 54,* 721–726.

Levin, L. S. (1987). Every silver lining has a cloud: The limits of health promotion. *Social Policy, 18*(1), 57–60.

Lindblom, C. E. (1968). *The policy making process.* Englewood Cliffs, NJ: Prentice-Hall.

Linsky, M. (1986). *Impact: How the press affects federal policymaking.* New York: Norton.

Lippmann, W. (1925). *The phantom public.* New York: Harcourt, Brace.

Lippmann, W. (1943). *Public Opinion.* New York: Macmillan. (Original published in 1922.)

Locke, J. (1894). *An essay concerning human understanding.* Oxford: Clarendon. (Manuscript drafted in 1671, original published in 1690.)

Lovrich, N. P., & Pierce, J. C. (1984). Knowledge gap phenomena: Effect of situation-specific and transitional factors. *Communication Research, 11,* 415–434.

Lukes, S. (1974). *Power: A radical view.* London: Macmillan.

Luttbeg, N. R. (1974). Political linkage in a large society. In N. R. Luttbeg (Ed.), *Public opinion and public policy* (rev. ed., pp. 1–10). Homewood, IL: Dorsey Press.

Madison, J. (1961). The Federalist no. 49. In J. E. Cooke (Ed.), *The Federalist.* Middletown, CT: Wesleyan University Press (Original published in 1788.)

Manikas, P., Heinz, J., Trossman, M., & Doppelt, J. (1990). *Criminal justice policymaking: Boundaries and borderlands.* Evanston, IL: Center for Urban Affairs and Policy Research, Northwestern University.

Margolis, M., & Mauser, G. A. (Eds.) (1989). *Manipulating public opinion: Essays on public opinion as a dependent variable.* Pacific Grove, CA: Brooks/Cole.

Marshall, T. R. (1989). *Public opinion and the Supreme Court.* Boston: Unwin Hyman.

May, Ernest R. (1964). An American tradition in foreign policy: The role of public opinion. In W. H. Nelson (Ed.), *Theory and practice in American politics.* Chicago: University of Chicago Press.

McCombs, M. E., & Becker, L. B. (1979). *Using mass communication theory.* Englewood Cliffs, NJ: Prentice-Hall.

McCombs, M. E., & Danielian, L. H. (in press). Issues in the news and the public agenda: The agenda-setting tradition. In T. Glasser & C. Salmon (Eds.), *Public opinion and the communication of consent*. New York: Guilford.

McCombs, M. E., & Gilbert, S. (1986). News influence on our pictures of the world. In J. Bryant & D. Zillman (Eds.), *Perspectives on media effects* (pp. 1–15). Hillsdale, NJ: Lawrence Erlbaum.

McCombs, M. E. & Shaw, D. L. (1972). The agenda-setting function of mass media. *Public Opinion Quarterly, 36*, 177–187.

McCombs, M. E., & Shaw, D. L. (1977). Agenda-setting and the political process. In D. L. Shaw & M. E. McCombs (Eds.), *The emergence of American political issues: The agenda-setting function of the press* (pp. 149–156). St. Paul, MN: West.

McGarrell, E. F. (1988). *Juvenile correctional reform: Two decades of policy and procedural change*. Albany: State University of New York Press.

McLeod, J. M., Sandstrom, K. L., Olien, C. N., Donohue, G. A., & Tichenor, P. J. (1990, August). *The impact of community structure and systemic change on editorial judgments*. Paper presented at the meeting of the Association for Education in Journalism and Mass Communication, Minneapolis, MN.

McLeod, J. M. (1985). An essay: Public opinion—Our social skin. *Journalism Quarterly, 62*, 649–653.

McLeod, J. M., Becker, L. B., & Byrnes, J. E. (1974). Another look at the agenda-setting function of the press. *Communication Research, 1*, 131–165.

McQuail, D. (1979). Influence and effects of mass media. In J. Curran, M. Gurevitch, & J. Woollacott (Eds.), *Mass communication and society* (pp. 70–94). Beverly Hills, CA: Sage.

McQuail, D. (1986). Diversity in political communications: Its sources, forms and future. In P. Golding, G. Murdock, & P. Schlesinger (Eds.), *Communicating politics: Mass communications and the political process* (pp. 133–149). New York: Holmes and Meier.

Mencher, M. (1991). *News reporting and writing* (5th ed.). Dubuque, IA: Brown.

Merten, K. (1985). Some silence in the spiral of silence. In K. Sanders, L. Kaid, & D. Nimmo (Eds.), *Political communication yearbook 1984* (pp. 31–42). Carbondale: Southern Illinois University Press.

Merton, R. K. (1968). *Social theory and social structure* (Enlarged ed.). New York: Macmillan.

Meyer, P. (1973). *Precision journalism*. Bloomington: Indiana University Press.

Meyer, P. (1985). *The newspaper survival book: An editor's guide to marketing research*. Bloomington: Indiana University Press.

Miliband, R. (1969). *The state of capitalist society*. London: Weidenfed and Nicolson.

Miller, M. M., & Hurd, R. (1982). Conformity to AAPOR standards in newspaper reporting of public opinion polls. *Public Opinion Quarterly, 46*, 243–249.

Miller, W. E., & Stokes, D. (1963). Constituency influence in Congress. *American Political Science Review, 57*, 45–56.

Minogue, K. (1989). Journalism and the public mind. *Government and Opposition, 24*(4), 473–488.

Molotch, H., & Lester, M. (1974). Accidents, scandals, and routines: Resources for insurgent methodology. In G. Tuchman (Ed.), *The TV establishment: Programming for power and profit* (pp. 53–65). Englewood Cliffs, NJ: Prentice-Hall.

Molotch, H., Protess, D. L., & Gordon, M. T. (1987). The media-policy connection: Ecologies of news. In D. L. Paletz (Ed.), *Political communication research: Approaches, studies, assessments* (pp. 26–48). Norwood, NJ: Ablex.

Moore, G. (1979). The structure of a national elite network. *American Sociological Review, 44,* 673.

Morin, R. (1991, April 8). Reagan may have fired a shot heard around the Capitol. *Washington Post National Weekly Edition,* p. 38.

Morris, M. B. (1973). The public definition of a social movement: Women's liberation. *Sociology and Social Research, 57,* 526–543.

Morton, L. (1986). How newspapers choose the releases they use. *Public Relations Review, 12,* 22–27.

Moscovici, S. (1976). *Social influence and social change.* London: Academic.

Moscovici, S. (1980). Toward a theory of conversion behavior. In L. Berkowitz (Ed.), *Advances in experimental social psychology* (Vol. 13, pp. 209–239). New York: Academic Press.

Moscovici, S. (1991). Silent majorities and loud minorities. In J. A. Anderson (Ed.), *Communication yearbook 14* (pp. 298–308). Newbury Park, CA: Sage.

Mutz, D. C. (1989). The influence of perceptions of media influence: Third person effects and the public expression of opinions. *International Journal of Public Opinion Research, 1,* 3–23.

Nachmias, D., & Henry, G. T. (1980). The utilization of evaluation research: Problems and prospects. In D. Nachmias (Ed.), *The practice of policy evaluation* (pp. 461–476). New York: St. Martin's Press.

Neuman, W. R. (1986). *The paradox of mass politics.* Cambridge, MA: Harvard University Press.

Neuwirth, K. (1988, November). *Noelle-Neumann and spirals of affect and behavioral intention.* Paper presented at the meeting of the Midwest Association for Public Opinion Research, Chicago.

Neuwirth, K., & Sanchez-Ilundian, C. (1984, November). *Family communication patterns and the spiral of silence.* Paper presented at the meeting of the Midwest Association for Public Opinion Research, Chicago.

Newsome, D., & Wolert, J. A. (1985). *Media writing.* Beaumont, CA: Wadsworth.

Nie, N., Verba, S., & Petrocik, J. (1976). *The changing American voter.* Cambridge, MA: Harvard University Press.

Nimmo, D. (1988). The mysteries of opinion formation and change: Positioning and related demystifications. *Political Behavior Annual, 2,* 1–19.

Nimmo, D., & Combs, J. E. (1983). *Mediated political realities.* New York: Longman.

Noelle-Neumann, E. (1973). Return to the concept of powerful mass media. *Studies of broadcasting, 9,* 67–112.

Noelle-Neumann, E. (1974). The spiral of silence: A theory of public opinion. *Journal of Communication, 24*(2), 43–51.

Noelle-Neumann, E. (1977). Turbulences in the climate of opinion: Methodological applications of the spiral of silence theory. *Public Opinion Quarterly, 41*, 143–158.

Noelle-Neumann, E. (1979). Public opinion and the classical tradition: A reevaluation. *Public Opinion Quarterly, 43*, 143–156.

Noelle-Neumann, E. (1980). The public opinion research correspondent. *Public Opinion Quarterly, 44*, 585–597.

Noelle-Neumann, E. (1984). *The spiral of silence: Public opinion—Our social skin.* Chicago: University of Chicago Press.

Noelle-Neumann, E. (1985). The spiral of silence: A response. In D. Nimmo, L. Kaid, & K. Sanders (Eds.), *Political communication yearbook 1984* (pp. 66–94). Carbondale: Southern Illinois University Press.

Noelle-Neumann, E. (1989). Advances in spiral of silence research. *KEIO Communication Review, 10*, 3–34.

Noelle-Neumann, E. (1991). The theory of public opinion: The concept of the spiral of silence. In J. A. Anderson (Ed.), *Communication yearbook 14* (pp. 256–287). Newbury Park, CA: Sage.

Noelle-Neumann, E. (1992). Letter to the editor in response to Leo Bogart's "The pollster and the Nazis" in the August 1991 issue of *Commentary, 93*(1), 9–15.

O'Gorman, H. (1975). Pluralistic ignorance and white estimates for white support for racial segregation. *Public Opinion Quarterly, 39*, 313–330.

Olson, M. (1965). *The logic of collective action.* Cambridge, MA: Harvard University Press.

Opinion Roundup (1985). *Public Opinion, 8* (April/May), 19–42.

Orren, G. R. (1986). Thinking about the press and government. In M. Linsky, *Impact: How the press affects federal policymaking* (pp. 1–20). New York: Norton.

Owen, D., & Stewart, M. (1987, November). *Explaining political knowledge: Problems of conceptualization and measurement.* Paper presented at the meeting of the Southern Political Science Association, Charlotte, NC.

Page, B. I., & Shapiro, R. Y. (1982). Changes in Americans' policy preference, 1935–1979. *Public Opinion Quarterly, 46*, 24–42.

Page, B. I., & Shapiro, R. Y. (1983). Effects of public opinion on policy. *American Political Science Review, 77*, 175–190.

Page, B. I., & Shapiro, R. Y. (1989). Educating and manipulating the public. In M. Margolis & G. A. Mauser (Eds.), *Manipulating public opinion: Essays on public opinion as a dependent variable* (pp. 294–320). Pacific Grove, CA: Brooks/Cole.

Page, B. I., & Shapiro, R. Y. (1991). *The rational public.* Chicago: University of Chicago Press.

Page, B. I., Shapiro, R. Y., & Dempsey, G. R. (1987). What moves public opinion. *American Political Science Review, 81*, 23–43.

Paletz, D. L., & Entman, R. M. (1984). Accepting the system. In D. Graber (Ed.), *Media power in politics* (pp. 81–88). Washington, DC: Congressional Quarterly Press.

Paletz, D. L., Pearson, R. E., & Willia, D. L. (1977). *Politics in public service advertising on television.* New York: Praeger.

Paletz, D. L., Reichert, P., & McIntyre, B. (1971). How the media support local government authority. *Public Opinion Quarterly, 35,* 80–95.

Pasternack, S. (1988, August). *The open forum: A study of letters to the editor and the people who write them.* Paper presented at the meeting of the Association for Education in Journalism and Mass Communication, Portland, OR.

Perloff, R. M. (1989). Ego-involvement and the third person effect of televised news coverage. *Communication Research, 16,* 236–262.

Phillips, K. (1990). *The politics of rich and poor: Wealth and the American electorate in the Reagan aftermath.* New York: Random House.

Pingree, S., Wiemann, J. M., & Hawkins, R. P. (1988). Editor introduction: Toward conceptual analysis. In R. P. Hawkins, J. M. Wiemann, & S. Pingree (Eds.), *Advancing communication science: Merging mass and interpersonal process* (pp. 7–18). Newbury Park: CA: Sage.

Portal, A. (1991, March 20). Mail ballot measure puzzles city voters. *Register-Guard,* Eugene, OR, p. 1C.

Price, V., & Allen, S. (1990). Opinion spirals, silent and otherwise: Applying small-group research to public opinion phenomena. *Communication Research, 17,* 369–392.

Price, W. (1953). What daily news executives think of public opinion polls. *Journalism Quarterly, 30,* 287–299.

Pritchard, D. (1986). Homicide and bargained justice: The agenda-setting effect of crime news on prosecutors. *Public Opinion Quarterly, 50,* 143–159.

Pritchard, D. (1991). *Holding the media accountable: Citizens, ethics, and the law.* Unpublished manuscript.

Pritchard, D., & Berkowitz, D. (1989, May). *The influence of the press and public opinion on political responses to crime in nine American cities from 1950 to 1980.* Paper presented at the annual meeting of the International Communication Association, San Francisco, CA.

Pritchard, D., & Berkowitz, D. (1991). How readers' letters may influence editors and news emphasis: A content analysis of 10 newspapers, 1948–1978. *Journalism Quarterly, 68,* 388–395.

Pritchard, D., Dilts, J. P., & Berkowitz, D. (1987). Prosecutors' use of external agendas in prosecuting pornography cases. *Journalism Quarterly, 64,* 392–398.

Protess, D. L., Cook, F. L., Curtin, T. R., Gordon, M. T., Leff, D. R., McCombs, M. E., & Miller, P. (1987). The impact of investigative journalism on public opinion and policymaking: Targeting toxic waste. *Public Opinion Quarterly, 51,* 166–185.

Protess, D. L., Leff, D. R., Brooks, S. C., & Gordon, M. T. (1985). Uncovering rape: The watchdog press and the limits of agenda-setting. *Public Opinion Quarterly, 49,* 19–37.

Reardon, K. K., & Rogers, E. M. (1988). Interpersonal versus mass media communication: A false dichotomy. *Human Communication Research, 15,* 284–303.

Reese, S. D. (1991). Setting the media's agenda: A power balance perspective. In J. A. Anderson (Ed.), *Communication yearbook 14* (pp. 309–340). Newbury Park, CA: Sage.

Reese, S. D., & Danielian, L. H. (1989). Intermedia influence and the drug issue: Converging on cocaine. In P. Shoemaker (Ed.), *Communication campaigns about drugs* (pp. 29–46). Hillsdale, NJ: Lawrence Erlbaum.

Rehnquist, W. (1986, April 17). *Judicial isolation. New York Times*, p. 12.

Rimmer, T., & Howard, M. (1990). Pluralistic ignorance and the spiral of silence: A test of the role of the mass media in the spiral of silence hypothesis. *Mass Communications Review, 17*(1, 2), 47–56.

Rippey, J. N. (1980). Use of polls as a reporting tool. *Journalism Quarterly, 57,* 642–646.

Robinson, C. E. (1932). *Straw Votes.* New York: Columbia University Press.

Robinson, J., Rush, J., & Head, K. (1968). *Measures of political attitudes.* Ann Arbor: University of Michigan Survey Research Center.

Rogers, E. M., & Dearing, J. W. (1988). Agenda-setting research: Where has it been, where is it going? In J. Anderson (Ed.), *Communication Yearbook 11* (pp. 555–593). Newbury Park, CA: Sage.

Rogers, E. M., Dearing, J. W., & Chang, S. (1991). AIDS in the 1980's: The agenda-setting process for a public issue. *Journalism Monographs,* no. 126.

Rucinski, D. (1992). Personalized bias in news: The potency of the particular. *Communication Research, 19,* 90–107.

Rusciano, R. L. (1989). *Isolation and paradox: Defining "the public" in modern political analysis.* New York: Greenwood Press.

Sabato, L. (1984). *PAC power.* New York: Norton.

Salmon, C. T. (1989). Campaigns for social "improvement": An overview of values, rationales, and impacts. In C. T. Salmon (Ed.), *Information campaigns: Balancing social values and social change* (pp. 19–53). Newbury Park, CA: Sage.

Salmon, C. T., & Kline, F. G. (1985). The spiral of silence ten years later: An examination and evaluation. In K. Sanders, L. Kaid, & D. Nimmo (Eds.), *Political communication yearbook 1984* (pp. 3–29).

Salmon, C. T., & Neuwirth, K. (1990). Perceptions of opinion "climates" and willingness to discuss the issue of abortion. *Journalism Quarterly, 67,* 567–577.

Salmon, C. T., & Oshagan, H. (1990). Community size, perceptions of majority opinion and opinion expression. *Public Relations Research Annual, 2,* 157–171.

Salmon, C. T., & Rucinski, D. (1988, May). *Fear of isolation from whom? Environmental cues and willingness to express opinions on controversial issues.* Paper presented at the annual meeting of the International Communication Association, New Orleans, LA.

Salwen, M. B. (1985). The reporting of public opinion polls during presidential years, 1968–1984. *Journalism Quarterly, 62,* 272–277.

Scammon, R. M., & Wattenberg, B. J. (1970). *The real majority.* New York: Coward-McCann.

Schattschneider, E. E. (1960). *The semi-sovereign people.* New York: Holt, Rinehart and Winston.

Scheingold, S. A., & Gressett, L. A. (1987). Policy, politics, and the criminal courts. *American Bar Foundation Research Journal,* 461–505.

Schlozman, K., & Tierney, J. T. (1986). *Organized interests and American democracy*. New York: Harper and Row.

Schneider, J. W. (1985). Social problems theory: The constructionist view. *Annual Review of Sociology, 11*, 209–229.

Schudson, M. (1978). *Discovering the news: A social history of American newspapers*. New York: Basic Books.

Schutz, A. (1962). *Collected papers* (Vol. 1), *The problem of social reality*. The Hague: Nijhoff.

Schwantes, D. L., & Lemert, J. B. (1978). Media access as a function of source-group identity. *Journalism Quarterly, 55*, 772–775.

Shaw, D. (1984). *Press watch: A provocative look at how newspapers report the news*. New York: Macmillan.

Shaw, D., & McCombs, M. (1977). *The emergence of American political issues: The agenda-setting function of the press*. St. Paul, MN: West.

Sherif, M., & Hovland, C. I. (1961). *Social judgment: Assimilation and contrast effects in communication and attitude change*. New Haven, CT: Yale University Press.

Shoemaker, P. J. (1982). The perceived legitimacy of deviant political groups. *Communication Research, 9*, 249–286.

Shoemaker, P. J. (1984). Media treatment of deviant political groups. *Journalism Quarterly, 61*, 66–75.

Shoemaker, P. J., Chang, T., & Brendlinger, N. (1987). Deviance as predictor of newsworthiness: Coverage of international events in the U.S. media. In M. McLaughlin (Ed.), *Communication yearbook 10* (pp. 348–365). Beverly Hills, CA: Sage.

Shoemaker, P. J., & Mayfield, E. K. (1987). Building a theory of news content. *Journalism Monographs, 103*.

Sigal, L. (1973). *Reporters and officials: The organization and politics of newsmaking*. Lexington, MA: Heath.

Sigal, L. (1986). Sources make the news. In R. Manoff & M. Schudson (Eds.), *Reading the news* (pp. 9–37). New York: Pantheon.

Sigelman, L., & Yanarella, E. (1986). Public information on public issues. *Social Science Quarterly, 67*, 402–410.

Smith, D. (1970). Dark areas of knowledge revisited: Current knowledge about Asian affairs. *Social Science Quarterly, 51*, 668–672.

Smith, E. R. (1989). *The unchanging American voter*. Berkeley: University of California Press.

Soloski, J. (1989a). News reporting and professionalism: Some constraints on the reporting of the news. *Media, Culture and Society, 11*, 207–228.

Soloski, J. (1989b). Sources and channels of local news. *Journalism Quarterly, 66*, 864–870.

Sood, R., Stockdale, G., & Rogers, M. (1987). How the news media operate in natural disasters. *Journal of Communication, 37*, 27–41.

Stevenson, R. L., & Gonzenbach, W. J. (1990, August). *Media use, political activity and the "climate of opinion."* Paper presented at the meeting of the Association for Education in Journalism and Mass Communication, Minneapolis, MN.

Stinchecombe, A. L. (1968). *Constructing social theories.* New York: Harcourt, Brace and World.

Strouse, J. C. (1975). *The mass media, public opinion, and public policy analysis: Linkage explorations.* Columbus, OH: Merrill.

Sun, H. (1991). *A test of the spiral of silence theory in Taiwan.* Unpublished doctoral dissertation. University of Wisconsin-Madison.

Sun, H., Salmon, C. T., & Rucinski, D. (1989, November). *Hardcores and other opinion publics.* Paper presented at the meeting of the Midwest Association for Public Opinion Research, Chicago.

Sutherland, E. H. (1951). The diffusion of sexual psychopath laws. *American Journal of Sociology, 56,* 142–148.

Swanson, A. H. (1960). Sexual psychopath statutes: Summary and analysis. *Journal of Criminal Law, Criminology and Police Science, 51,* 215–227.

Swanson, D. L. (1988). Feeling the elephant: Some observations on agenda-setting research. In J. A. Anderson (Ed.), *Communication yearbook 11* (pp. 603–619). Newbury Park, CA: Sage.

Taylor, D. G. (1982). Pluralistic ignorance and the spiral of silence: A formal analysis. *Public Opinion Quarterly, 46,* 311–335.

Terrell, P. M. (1989). Letters pages flourish as never before. *Presstime, 11*(4), 6–9.

Tichenor, P. J. (1988). Public opinion and construction of social reality. In J. A. Anderson (Ed.), *Communication yearbook 11* (pp. 547–554). Newbury Park, CA: Sage.

Tichenor, P. J., Donohue, G. A., & Olien, C. N. (1970). Mass media flow and differential growth in knowledge. *Public Opinion Quarterly, 34,* 159–170.

Tichenor, P. J., Donohue, G. A., & Olien, C. N. (1980). *Community conflict and the press.* Beverly Hills, CA: Sage.

Tiedge, J. T., Silverblatt, A., Havice, M. J., & Rosenfeld, R. (1991). The discrepancy between perceived first-person and perceived third-person mass media effects. *Journalism Quarterly, 68,* 141–154.

Tokinoya, H. (1989). Testing the spiral of silence theory in East Asia. *Keio Communication Review, 10,* 35–49.

Tonnies, F. (1922). *Kritik der öffentlicher Meinung.* Berlin: Springer.

Toqueville, A. de (1948). *Democracy in America* (H. Reeve, Trans.). New York: Knopf. (Original published in 1835–1840.)

Truman, D. B. (1958). *The governmental process.* New York: Knopf.

Tuchman, G. (1978). *Making news: A study in the construction of reality.* New York: Free Press.

Turk, J. V. (1986). Information subsidies and media content: A study of public relations influence on the news. *Journalism Monographs, 100.*

Turk, J. V. (1987, August). *Between president and press: White House public information and its influence on the news media.* Paper presented at the annual meeting of the Association for Education in Journalism and Mass Communication, San Antonio, TX.

Walker, J. (1977). Setting the agenda in the U.S. Senate: A theory of problem selection. *British Journal of Political Science, 7,* 423–445.

Waste, R. J. (1989). *The ecology of city policy-making.* New York: Oxford University Press.

Waxman, J. J. (1973). Local broadcast gatekeeping during natural disasters. *Journalism Quarterly, 50,* 751–758.

Weaver, D. (1991). Issue salience and public opinion: Are there consequences of agenda-setting? *International Journal of Public Opinion Research, 3,* 53–68.

Weaver, D. H., & Elliott, S. N. (1985). Who sets the agenda for the media? *Journalism Quarterly, 62,* 88–94.

Weaver, D. H., Graber, D. A., McCombs, M., & Eyal, C. H. (1981). *Media agenda-setting in a presidential election: Issues, images and interest.* New York: Praeger.

Weaver, D. H., & Wilhoit, G. C. (1980). News media coverage of U.S. senators in four Congresses, 1953–1974. *Journalism Monographs, 67.*

Weaver, D. H., & Wilhoit, G. C. (1986). *The American journalist: A portrait of U.S. news people and their work.* Bloomington: Indiana University Press.

Webb, N., & Wybrow, R. (1986). The spiral of silence: A British perspective. In I. Crewe & M. Harrop (Eds.), *Political communications: The general election campaign of 1983* (pp. 265–279). Cambridge: Cambridge University Press.

Weber, M. (1946). In H. Gerth & C. W. Mills (Eds.), *From Max Weber: Essays in sociology.* New York: Oxford University Press.

Weiss, C. (1974). What America's leaders read. *Public Opinion Quarterly, 38,* 1–22.

White, D. M. (1950). The gatekeeper: A case study in the selection of news. *Journalism Quarterly, 27,* 383–396.

Whitney, D. C. (1982). Mass communicator studies: Similarity, difference, and level of analysis. In J. S. Ettema & D. C. Whitney (Eds.), *Individuals in mass media organizations: Creativity and constraint* (pp. 241–254). Beverly Hills, CA: Sage.

Wilcox, D. L., Ault, P. H., & Agee, W. K. (1989). *Public relations: Strategies and tactics* (2nd ed.). New York: Harper and Row.

Wilhoit, G. C., & Weaver, D. (1980). *Newsroom guide to polls and surveys.* Washington, DC: American Newspaper Publishers Association.

Wilkins, L. C. (1976). *The missing linkage: Public opinion and the 1975 Oregon legislature.* Unpublished master's thesis, School of Journalism, University of Oregon.

Yankelovich, D. (1991). *Coming to public judgment: Making democracy work in a complex world.* Syracuse, NY: Syracuse University Press.

Zaller, J. (1986). Analysis of information items in the 1985 NES pilot study. Unpublished report to the National Election Study Board.

Ziegler, L. H., & Haltom, W. (1989). More bad news about news. *Public Opinion, 11,* 50–52.

Zimmerman, D. H. (1970). The practicalities of rule use. In J. D. Douglas (Ed.), *Understanding everyday life: Toward the reconstruction of sociological knowledge* (pp. 221–238). Chicago: Aldine.

Index

About the Contributors

DAN BERKOWITZ is an assistant professor in the School of Journalism and Mass Communication at the University of Iowa.

LUCIG DANIELIAN is an assistant professor in the Department of Communication at the State University of New York at Albany.

MICHAEL X. DELLI CARPINI is an assistant professor of political science at Barnard College, Columbia University.

JACK C. DOPPELT is an associate professor at Northwestern University's Medill School of Journalism and a member of the research faculty at Northwestern's Center for Urban Affairs and Policy Research.

SCOTT KEETER is an associate professor of political science and has been director of the Survey Research Laboratory at Virginia Commonwealth University.

J. DAVID KENNAMER is an associate professor in the School of Mass Communications and is a research associate in the Survey Research Laboratory at Virginia Commonwealth University.

DOMINIC L. LASORSA is an associate professor in the Department of Journalism at the University of Texas at Austin.

JAMES B. LEMERT is a professor in the School of Journalism at the University of Oregon.

CHI-YUNG MOH is a doctoral candidate in the School of Journalism and Mass Communication at the University of Wisconsin-Madison.

DAVID PRITCHARD is an associate professor of Mass Communication at the University of Wisconsin-Milwaukee. He previously taught in the School of Journalism at Indiana University.

CHARLES T. SALMON is an associate professor in the School of Journalism and Mass Communication at the University of Wisconsin-Madison.

LEONARD TIPTON is a professor in the College of Journalism and Communications at the University of Florida.